Lifestyle revolution

Manchester University Press

Lifestyle revolution

How taste changed class in late 20th-century Britain

Ben Highmore

Manchester University Press

Published by Manchester University Press
Oxford Road, Manchester M13 9PL

www.manchesteruniversitypress.co.uk

British Library Cataloguing-in-Publication Data
A catalogue record for this book is available from the British Library

ISBN 978 1 5261 0882 1 hardback

First published 2023

Typeset
by Cheshire Typesetting Ltd, Cuddington, Cheshire
Printed in Great Britain
by Bell & Bain Ltd, Glasgow

In memory of my mother, Angela Highmore,
15 August 1924–21 April 2020

Contents

List of figures *page* viii
Acknowledgements xi

Introduction 1
1 Taste and tastemakers 13
2 Instant good taste: the Habitat story 30
3 The good life 56
4 Colour supplement living 83
5 Welcome to the village 102
6 Through the plateglass window 123
7 Status striving and other myths we live by 146
8 But isn't that a class thing? 166
9 From the West Indian front room to *Root* 182
10 Adrian Mole, the future of taste, and me … 197

Notes 210
Index 226

Figures

Every effort has been made to obtain permission to reproduce copyright material, and the publisher will be pleased to be informed of any errors and omissions for correction in future editions.

1.1 *Good Housekeeping*, January 1968, p. 12. Advert for a Slumberdown duvet. *page* 25
2.1 Habitat, Fulham Road, London, May 1964. 31
2.2 Habitat, Fulham Road, London: first floor window display – Chesterfield sofa and bent-cane, fan-back chair. 32
2.3 Habitat, Fulham Road, London, 1964. Basement displays. 33
2.4 'The people behind habitat', photograph in the *Sunday Times*. 34
2.5 Dump display of the chicken brick. 38
2.6 Habitat in Glasgow. 40
2.7 That 'Can't wait to get it home feeling', Habitat catalogue, 1980. 42
2.8 1966 Broadsheet brochure by Juliet Glynn Smith and Caroline Conran. 43
2.9 The Habitat annual catalogue 1971, Winter/Autumn supplement. 45
2.10 From Habitat, Autumn and Christmas catalogue 1971. The foreground features Scoop seating and Magistretti tables. The background includes 'basic' range desk and drawers, with two hard plastic wall pockets on the back wall. The duvet on the bed would still have been a novelty in 1971. 46
2.11 Habitat catalogue, 1977–78, p. 80, 'with duvet, sheet and pillows in Kimono, a grey and cream check with more than a whisper of Oriental charm'. 48
2.12 Habitat catalogue, 1977–78, p. 96, 'Folding chair/cane seat. Tablecloth, tile print'. 49
2.13 Habitat catalogue, 1975, p. 45, 'A very professional draughtsman's table or drawing desk. Lay the top flat and use it as a table'. 50
3.1 Span Housing estate, Blackheath. © Google Maps. 57
3.2 'Farmhouse Style', *The House Book* (1974), p. 9. Courtesy of Octopus Publishing Group. 62

3.3 The Conrans' basement kitchen, *The House Book* (1974), p. 219. Courtesy of Octopus Publishing Group. 64

3.4 The Conrans' living room, *The House Book* (1974), p. 187. Courtesy of Octopus Publishing Group. 65

3.5 Len Deighton Cook Strip from the *Observer*, 15 July 1962, p. 23. © Len Deighton. Reproduced by permission of Peters, Fraser & Dunlop. 69

3.6 The first PizzaExpress, Wardour Street, Soho, London 1965 (pictured 2015). © Google Maps. 70

3.7 Biba 1964 gingham dress for *Daily Mirror*, modelled by Paulene Stone. © John French / Victoria & Albert Museum, London. 73

3.8 Shop manager Elanor Powell Biba in front of Biba, Kensington Church Street, 1967. 75

3.9 Poster for Biba cosmetics. Photo: Sarah Moon, model: Ingrid Boulting. 76

3.10 and 3.11 The Mirror Dinghy from the brochure, 1963. Photo: Eileen Ramsay, with permission from PPL Media Ltd. 80

4.1 *Observer* colour supplement, 7 June 1970. © Guardian News & Media Ltd 2022. 86

4.2 and 4.3 Mary Gilliatt's home photographed by Michael Boys for *Good Housekeeping*, January 1968. Courtesy of Hearst Magazines UK. 92

4.4 Michael Boys photograph for *Good Housekeeping*, March 1968, 'Make Mine Country Style', featuring Sumna storage units designed by Terence Conran. Courtesy of Hearst Magazines UK. 94

4.5 *Spare Rib*, issue 1, July 1972. © Angela Phillips. 98

4.6 *Nova*, January 1966. Courtesy of NOVA/Future Publishing. 100

5.1 Terraced houses in Islington, London, 1960s, pre-gentrification. 103

5.2 Dilapidated housing in Notting Hill Gate in the 1960s. © Alamy. 105

5.3 Notting Hill, boutique shops and restored facades. © Google Maps. 106

5.4 Learning gentrification at the Daily Mail Ideal Home Exhibition in 1968. Two houses from Countrycraft Terrace. British Pathé video. 108

5.5 Notting Hill in the 1960s. 114

5.6 Currys advert from 1977. © Currys Group Ltd. 117

5.7 'Trent', three-bedroom detached chalet house, Ideal Home Exhibition, 1976, p. 83. 120

5.8 Wiggins Construct Limited. Ideal Home Exhibition 1977, p. 42. 120

5.9 Barratt's 'Stavanger' house, Ideal Home Exhibition, 1976, p. 38. 121

5.10 Laing Homes Ltd. Ideal Home Exhibition, 1982, p. 65. 122

6.1 University of East Anglia, architect Denys Lasdun, opened in 1963. Photo: John Fielding, 2015. CC BY 2.0. 126

6.2 Ski yogurt in conical pot. © Alamy. 128

6.3 Stamp of the University of Essex and others. Part of a range of stamps representing university buildings released in 1971. 129
6.4 and 6.5 University of Sussex library. The library was designed by Sir Basil Spence and the London branch of the architectural firm Spence, Bonnington and Collins. Work began on the building in 1962 and it was opened in 1964. © University of Sussex Special Collections 130
6.6 *New Society*, first issue, 4 October 1962. 133
6.7 The Kirks as played by Antony Sher and Geraldine James, outside their 'legal squat'. *The History Man* (BBC, 1981). 138
6.8 The Kirks with their pine kitchen table and bentwood chairs preparing for a day of 'controlled casualness'. *The History Man* (BBC, 1981). 139
6.9 George Weber in his garden writing. © Posy Simmonds. 142
6.10 On holiday in the fictional Cornish village of Tresoddit. © Posy Simmonds. 144
6.11 Jocasta Wright's commentary on her father and stepmother's party preparations. © Posy Simmonds. 145
7.1 Axminster fitted carpet, *Good Housekeeping*, October 1967, p. 55. Courtesy of Heart Magazines UK. 152
7.2 Vincent Van Gogh, *Chair*, 1888, National Gallery. The Yorck Project, Wikimedia. 154
7.3 Stephen Pearson, *Wings of Love*, *c.* 1972. Reproduced by permission of Barry Pearson, Container Gallery. 155
7.4 Mike Leigh, *Abigail's Party* (BBC, 1977). From left to right: Angie (Janine Duvitski), Beverly (Alison Steadman), Laurence (Tim Stern), Sue (Harriet Reynolds), Tony (John Salthouse). 156
7.5 Furni-Kit, *Homes and Gardens*, February 1968, p. 132. 156
7.6 Terry and Bob, *Whatever Happened to the Likely Lads?* (BBC, 1973–74) in Terry Collier's working-class childhood home. 158
7.7 Thelma and Bob, *Whatever Happened to the Likely Lads?* (BBC, 1973–74) in Thelma and Bob's Barratt house with shelf dividers. 159
7.8 Fanny Cradock, 1972. Photo: David Edwards © BBC Archive. 162
7.9 Delia Smith, *Cookery Course*. © BBC Archive. 163
7.10 Keith Floyd, *Floyd on France*. © BBC Archive. 164
9.1 Michael McMillan, *The West Indian Front Room*. © Michael McMillan, photo: John Neligan. 191
9.2 Habitat catalogue 1975, featuring: Ny Chairs and chaise longue (top); Metro chairs (bottom). 195
10.1 Habitat closing down in Bristol, 2011. Photo © Ben Highmore. 198
10.2 Habitat catalogue, 1973, p. 26, 'the 10 second bed'. 205

Acknowledgements

This book would not have been possible without the generosity of the Leverhulme Trust, who in 2014 awarded me a Major Research Fellowship which allowed me time away from teaching to undertake the research for this book. The Leverhulme Trust is one of the few places that humanities scholars can go to get funding for projects that are driven primarily by curiosity, and I feel very lucky to have had their backing. Amelia Wakeford, Sue Thornham, Caroline Bassett, and Nick Till were all instrumental in the success of the funding application to the Trust, and Glenn Adamson, Tony Fry and Anne Massey kindly provided letters of support. Without such collegiality, research might not be impossible but it would be infinitely harder. I also want to thank the University of Sussex for research leave in Spring and Summer 2021, which gave me the time to complete the book. Particular thanks go to Claire Langhamer, Matthew Dimmock, and Carol Watts for making the grim reality of research audits manageable, sometimes even creative, and always wonderfully entertaining.

Between starting this project and finalising the manuscript I have tried out some of the ideas on a range of broadly sympathetic audiences at universities within the UK (Birmingham, Cambridge, University of West London, Leeds, Warwick, and Wolverhampton). Generous invitations from academics outside the UK have meant that I could discuss these very British themes in different national contexts: Japan, Denmark, Estonia, Lithuania, Sweden, and the United States. Writing this in 2022, all this travel seems so long ago, and it also seems like an excessive amount of carbon emissions. It will be interesting to see how we can remake international academic exchange in future years in more sustainable ways, while maintaining the warm conviviality that is best nourished by shared meals and can often be entirely lost in the virtual realm.

The writing of this book has benefited, in ways that are hard to quantify, from conversations with a large number of people including: Epp Annus, Jeremy Aynsley, Prudence Black, Charlotte Brunsdon, Stella Bruzzi, Gavin Butt, Romina Colombo, Karin Dannehl and Laura Ugolini from the Centre for the History of Retailing and Distribution (CHORD), Gail Day, Kjetil Fallan, Rita Felski, Fiona Fisher, Adrian Forty, Susan Fraiman, Hélène Frichot, Raiford Guins, Michelle Henning, Antoine Hennion, Joanne Hollows, Guy Julier,

Pat Kirkham, Sara Kristoffersson, Claire Langhamer, Grace Lees-Maffei, Anne Massey, Martin McMillan, Dave Morley, Stephen Muecke, Ceren Özpınar, Barbara Penner, Lucy Pickering, Louise Purbrick, Naaz Rashid, Pollyanna Ruiz, Alex Seago (who pointed me towards the importance of Len Deighton), Penny Sparke, Simon Stewart, Deborah Sugg Ryan, Carol Tulloch, Francisco Cruces Villalobos, Rob Waters (who suggested I look at *Root* magazine), and Janice Winship. I'm sure that there are many other names that should be on this list. Archivists at the Archive of Art and Design at the Victoria & Albert Museum were endlessly helpful: thank you. An early version of the arguments that drive this book was published as 'Feeling It: Habitat, Taste and the New Middle Class in 1970s Britain' in the journal *New Formations*. Thanks to Jeremy Gilbert and Jo Littler for feedback on that article.

At Manchester University Press I have to thank Emma Brennan for going above and beyond on this, and in helping me wrestle an unwieldy and overly academic manuscript into submission. In turning it into a book that is, I hope, readable I had to become much clearer about what I was saying. It is a lesson that the academy needs to learn and I'm still learning it. I also want to thank Thomas Dark and Alun Richards for their input too, and Rachel Evans for her excellent copyediting skills.

Closer to home, my friend and neighbour Tony Portus, who worked as a shop assistant and then as a store manager for Habitat in the 1970s was instrumental in giving me an idea of how the day-to-day running of Habitat stores was conducted. He also talked me through some of the catalogues from the 1970s. Much of this book has been written during a global 'confinement', so I want to thank my lovely household who have maintained an atmosphere of loving support, good food and good cheer: thank you Wendy, Molly, Zeb, Chloe, Spider, and Pablo – the last two are pets. My mother died in the first wave of the pandemic, and I dedicate this book to her. When we were clearing her house, we took an old Habitat chest of drawers that she probably bought in 1970 or 1971. It had lived in her 'box room' never quite managing to mingle with her other furniture – furniture that spoke of a previous world and a pre-Habitat sense of taste.

Introduction

In 1966, shortly before my fifth birthday, my family and I moved from the small satellite town of Musselburgh, just outside Edinburgh, to somewhere even smaller in Essex. We moved to a village that catered for people who worked elsewhere: primarily in towns and cities within Essex or else in London, a commutable forty-five-minute train journey away. The nearest town, Witham, two miles down the hill, was on the old Roman Road, midway between Chelmsford and Colchester. It was a town that massively expanded in the late 1950s and early 1960s due to the so-called 'slum clearances' of the East End of London and became known as an over-spill town. In the 1970s one of Witham's thriving industries was nuclear fall-out shelters for domestic use.

We moved into the first completed newly built house in one of the cul-de-sacs that were springing up in the village. This wasn't rural life; it was the 'good life'. Small modern detached houses: white weatherboard fronts mixed with red brick and picture windows. It looked like it belonged in an American suburb rather than in the English countryside. You imagined paperboys flinging rolled up newspapers from the comfort of their bikes onto front lawns as they sped along the wide concrete road. You can almost see the brochures: a young white family, two children (one of each, as they say) playing in the sunshine, mum waving through the open window, dad getting out of the car as he returns from work.

The reality was different, but not entirely. I was a paper boy and it often rained. We delivered our cargo in the dark and we were never allowed to leave papers on front lawns. We took them to the front door where they were often snatched from the other side of the letter box by what I assumed were rabid dogs. I became a paperboy because I was caught shoplifting toy 'Matchbox' cars (which was only the half of it), and this was how my dad and the newsagent felt I could make amends. Over the years the papers that I and my young comrades delivered grew heavier and heavier. Monthly 'leisure' magazines landed in people's hallways with a slap, sometimes with a thud. The worst day for paper deliveries was Sunday. Then your newspaper satchel strained under the weight and size of the Sunday papers. The 1960s was the decade when Sunday papers, particularly the broadsheets, started to expand to the point where it was hard to push them through some of the letter boxes. The *Sunday Times* was the first to introduce a colour magazine, in February 1962; the *Observer* and the *Telegraph* followed in September 1964 (though the *Telegraph*'s magazine came out on a Friday). These supplements combined social investigations, leisure features, lifestyle guidance, and lots of advertising. In my village the choice of Sunday newspapers were as likely to be the *Sunday Express*, the *Sunday Mail*, or the *News of the World*, as the *Sunday Times* or *Observer*, and yet the colour supplements were unavoidable: dog-eared copies graced every doctor's and dentist's waiting room; they were there at the hairdressers (but not the barbers!); and they were what you were given to cut up in art classes at school.

Our village was relentlessly white and seemed relentlessly affluent (but then you don't necessarily see the full spectrum of wealth and poverty as a child, nor the families that aren't invited round for neighbourly drinks at Christmas). There were lots of children about. For years, we played amongst scaffolding and breeze blocks as the cul-de-sac expanded. Employment never seemed to be a problem. Old industries existed alongside much newer ones. In Chelmsford, one of the big employers was the large Marconi electronics company, but the most obvious sign of industry was the massive gasworks – all gleaming metal, sodium lighting, and the aroma of something sulphurous – that greeted you as you entered the city and was already on the verge of extinction when we arrived. Natural gas would quickly make this 'town gas' factory redundant. Our neighbours worked as carpenters and plumbers, as secretaries and managers, and as technicians and dentists. No doubt in our village there were teachers and lawyers as well. I didn't pay that much attention to the lives of adults. What I did notice, though, were the drinks cabinets and the record players, the Parker Knoll recliners, and the new colour televisions that started appearing at the very end of the 1960s. We played outside, scoffed stolen sweets, and smoked cagey ciggies on the 'rec' (the recreation ground). I can still just about catch a whiff of a Players No. 6 if I think back to those times. What I was seeing in my own and my friends' homes was a form of 'colour supplement living'. Not in any straightforward sense: what was being promoted in the colour supplements didn't directly enter these houses. It was more that these supplements supplied the measure and compass for tasteful living. You might not quite measure up, but you could at least find approximations. A colour supplement could run a feature on Capri; your next holiday might be camping in France or a new 'all inclusive' hotel in Spain. Colour supplement cooking tips might show you how to make your own pasta; your next spaghetti Bolognaise might be made with dried pasta rather than coming directly from a tin manufactured by Heinz.

It was a good time for decorators, for kitchen installers, for furniture providers. It was a good time for hire-purchase agreements, and for renting televisions. Colours changed; patterns changed. For a while in about 1970 we had ochre yellow velvet curtains with dark brown hessian wallpaper. Turquoise flowered wallpaper made my sister's bedroom seem like it was an underwater stage set (welcome to aquaworld); my bedroom walls consisted of a migraine's worth of deep orange and yellow swirls. How long did these decorations last? I can't remember, but they lasted much longer than they remained up-to date. And where did the outlandish colour schemes come from? It was a decade or two before TV got obsessed with houses and with cooking, though interiors have always had a significant role in TV sitcoms and soap operas. In the 1960s and 1970s the images that had the greatest impact on the village where I lived were circulated primarily in print culture and on the high street. Today tastemaking has other vehicles: *Pinterest* and daytime TV.

The story I'm going to tell finds its evidence in colour supplements and magazines, in high-street shops and chain restaurants, in novels and sitcoms – the popular culture that featured this post-1950s suburban style. But rather than just charting the associated tastes of a 'colour supplement' lifestyle, I have a larger ambition as well. I want to talk about how British society and its class structure was changing, and to do this through what might seem to be the trivia of chairs and flooring, bedding and food. My claim is that much of what is recognisable today as mainstream domestic taste can be traced back to a period from the late 1950s, through the 1960s and 1970s. There is a line to be drawn from the birth of the colour supplements, from Habitat and PizzaExpress, to the pre-eminence of IKEA today, and to our obsession with the home as a place of personal expression and soaring expenses. The story this book tells is how a world of taste that in the mid-1960s would have been associated with bohemianism, trendiness, and middle-class lifestyles, became more and more prevalent, and less noticeable as a distinctive taste. Rather than being trivial and superficial I see a world of carpets and curtains, furniture, food, and fashion as directly linked to a politics and ethics of everyday life. Our tastes, the very stuff we fashion our lives from, is, for many of us, the most concrete expression of our attitudes and beliefs, our politics, and our passions – our feelings for life. These tastes can tell a story about how we think and feel about the family, about class, gender, and ethnicity, and about the environment. It might also offer some ideas about how we might create more sustainable and equitable lives in the future.

A soft revolution

Across the twentieth century, the UK underwent a soft revolution. This revolution was slow and uneven, and its outcomes often seemed vague and insubstantial. But it did have decisive consequences. Unlike the storming of the Winter Palace or the sacking of Rome, this was an incremental revolution, accumulating over the century. Gradually, a culture of deference was being replaced by more informal ways of living: less doffing of caps and tugging of forelocks, more wearing of jeans. Slowly, the sound of a population changed. On the airwaves the grating tones of 'received pronunciation' gave way to more regional accents and the dominance of estuary English. Social historians have described this and other phenomena as a form of cultural democratisation, or the rise of a more informal society. Aspects of this revolution can seem like superficial window dressing for a culture that maintains a monied elite in places of power, and a set of finely ranked institutions for perpetuating privilege.[1] That said, recognising that claims of social mobility are often inflated shouldn't stop us noticing some of the staggering changes that have taken place in the last hundred or so years. Take housing, for example. In the first decades of the twentieth century only 10 per cent of households were owner-occupied. By the end of the 1970s that figure was around 65 per cent, which is roughly where it has stayed ever since.

While the hard facts of house ownership give us a sense of quantifiable change across Britain, this book is more concerned with changes in feelings and moods. Investigating historical moods and feeling might be a ludicrously imprecise endeavour, but it is, I think, a necessary one. Our sense of our own past is animated by feelings: glee, trepidation, anxiety, optimism, expectation, and on and on. Feeling is the colour and ambience of our recollections. Without it the past can seem like a series of flavourless events. It would be odd indeed if such an exponential increase in property ownership didn't have wide ranging impacts on how the world felt to many people. What, for instance, happens to how social class is experienced when so many more people become part of a class of home owners? Did the experience of being working class alter when you became 'propertied', even if that meant being massively in debt to a building society?

Feelings aren't salvageable through statistics or surveys. Sociological interviews are nearly always oriented towards opinions and attitudes rather than feelings and mood. But if the feelings from the past are often hard to put your finger on, public feelings also surround us: newspapers and magazines trade in accounts of national mood and morale; dramas and stories constantly conjure up atmospheres and ambience; promotional culture in all its forms (from adverts to shopping centres) tell us how we would feel if only we bought this or that. Feelings and moods require either the luxury of description and elaboration or the emotional jolt of a joke, an anecdote, or an image. Our best diarists and memoirists turn this into an art form. Any hard-nosed economic or political historian, though, might claim that to treat memoirs and adverts as sources is to deal in unreliable evidence. So be it. Feelings are not facts in the way that unemployment figures are, but they are part of our rich and complex reality (and if you want to gauge the impact of unemployment then attending to feelings is going to be crucial). Unreliable they may be, but the evidence of feelings is testimony to our collective life. And they require their own story.

I focus on what has been called the golden age of affluence – the years 1955–74.[2] This period is seen to end with the 1973–74 oil crisis and the recession that it caused. But while the subsequent decades were syncopated with periods of boom and bust, the overall pattern since 1955 has been increased growth.[3] During these years, and especially from the 1960s and 1970s, consumerism became a leading factor of social life in Britain. One of my aims is to investigate what we mean by terms like 'consumer society' and 'lifestyle culture' – to put some flesh on the bones of those well-worn phrases. For me this means delving into the new shops and restaurants that were springing up in cities and towns across Britain. It means looking at magazines and novels, television programmes and films. It means seeing how the new tastes that were being developed were experienced. Any element of taste on its own might seem slight, but when taken together they present a new sensibility, a new world of feeling. As a sensibility it was a shift away from older tastes that were tied to styles of good manners, of knowing-your-place, and social formality. The new tastes that emerged celebrated spontaneity and informality and took their references from Scandinavia and the Mediterranean as much as they did from British culture or from America.

There are three claims that drive this book. The first is that from the mid-1950s, ideas about taste (what was 'in', what was 'good taste') became more important to larger numbers of people. The second is that during the same period, the way people experienced social class became more and more complex and contradictory. And thirdly, that as a population we became increasingly self-conscious about taste and class, partly through the mainstream popularisation of the social sciences. This book will, I hope, substantiate these claims. But before I start on the detail, I want to briefly explain how I'm using terms like taste and class, how I'm thinking about the relationship between the two, and how I'm imagining the role of the popularisation of the social sciences in all this.

Taste, at its most basic, is an activity concerned with choice and desire. The huge growth in the range of commodities that were becoming available to British consumers from the 1950s onwards, and the enormous amount of energy that was being spent on persuading people to like these new products, shows us the growing importance of taste in everyday life. Choices were increased; desire was amplified. At a general level I'm using taste to refer to this activity, and to the art of persuasion that goes with it (the activity of tastemaking). This persuasion has content. It shows us *how* this particular aftershave or that perfume will make us modern, attractive, and distinctive. It supplies an endless array of images of how life should and can be lived. We may be knowing consumers, deeply sceptical about the advertising puff that accompanies commodities, but the adverts for perfumes, furnishings, food, holidays, alcohol, wallpaper, and a myriad of other goods, make up a substantial part of how the world looks to us and how we are encouraged to participate in it. To live in a society where taste plays such an important role is to live within a world saturated by competing images of the good life.

Taste, though, exists at different levels and we can only really see its social importance if we look at it on two levels simultaneously. This sounds more complex than it is. Faced with a range of canned soups in a large supermarket, for instance, the modern shopper is faced with a number of choices, not just 'pea and ham' versus 'cream of mushroom', but whether to opt for the relatively cheap basic range or some of the fancier, more expensive brands. The way that the different ranges of soup are promoted might play on the supposed quality of the ingredients, the flavour of the soup (no supermarket offers 'game soup' in its basic range), and the images associated with the brand. The cheaper range might promote itself as good value, while the more expensive brand might want you to associate its flavour with an image of a lush, wild landscape. But what happens when we pull back a bit and look at this scene with more historical depth? Taste can also be seen to exist on another scale, across a population, to the point where we can say that this supermarket provides us with an image of a society that now values both choice and *convenience*. It is a society that isn't spending so many hours preparing soups at home and has opted, for the sake of an easier way of living, to regularly pick up soup up in a can. This is a level of generally shared taste that reveals changes in habits and behaviours over time. But it is taste, nevertheless. There are lots of tastes that emerge in Britain across the second half of the century that are pretty much ubiquitous now and reveal changes in value and behaviour: duvets, pasta, jeans, televisions, and so on. Sometimes these tastes began life as 'trendy', 'bohemian', 'cranky' even, before they become part of general taste. These are tastes that now don't belonging to specific groups, don't mark you out as distinctive – quite the opposite. Vegetarianism, for instance, used to mark someone out as a bit of a crank, and perhaps even a middle-class crank. Today it is, I hope, a more ubiquitous ethical taste. Today we could point to the smart phone as an example of a general taste across society: we are all, or so it seems, deeply attracted to them, we desire them for their convenience, for their power to help us live 'the good life' (though we probably all know that they are doing the opposite as well).

What makes taste so important for us is that it reveals that we are individuals with specific likes and dislikes, while it also connects us to others with similar tastes. And it ties us to a specific time in history. What makes it complicated is that these three layers of taste are often mixed together. But for simplicity's sake we can say that taste generally falls into three categories: personal, social, and historical. My dislike of cotton wool is personal and idiosyncratic (I really hate it). My taste in houses is undoubtedly social. The hardest taste to recognise *as taste* is at the historical level: the fact that nearly all of us in the UK are going to be eating some sort of manufactured cereal or bread for breakfast, which wouldn't have been the case a hundred years ago. In many instances all three of these levels are blended: the music I'm listening to right now, for instance, is a playlist I've put together specifically for when I work. It is music I've personally chosen. At the same time, I'm sure that someone could come along and probably work out that my choice in music is broadly typical for a man of my age, with my education, working in my sort of job! The historical level is partly revealed in the fact that I'm listening to music on my phone which is paired with a speaker. The historical is collective taste, generational taste. My mum just about got the hang of CDs, but mobile phones were definitely not her thing, and the idea of a Bluetooth connection would have seemed like black magic to her and not something to be encouraged. The relationship between taste and class mostly occurs at the social level, but it is shaped by these much more general historical changes as well.

The growth of consumer culture, coupled with new levels of affluence that allowed more and more people to access a new world of plenty, led many commentators to wonder if the class system in Britain was undergoing a fundamental transformation. The Labour Party, and others on the left, were concerned that the success of consumerism meant that their traditional working-class electoral base had somehow disappeared. The period 1951–64 found the Labour Party in the electoral wilderness as successive Conservative governments held power. The writer and political analyst Stuart Hall remembered the period as one of anxious questioning: 'Has the coming of the telly, the fridge, the small car, you know all these things, undermined permanently Labour's chance of winning ever again?'[4] In other words, had the traditional working class been somehow 'bought off' with consumer goods and the welfare state? Did they no longer see themselves as an exploited class, whose interests could be collectively represented by a political party? Something was going on, that was for sure.

Journalists, politicians, and sociologists faced new problems in discussing social class. Perhaps the most obvious was that class identity might not just be about income levels. This is Richard Hoggart writing in 1957: 'most steel-workers, for instance, are plainly working-class though some earn more than many teachers who are not'.[5] If class was not 'just' about income, then what was it about? The answers came in thick and fast: it was about community, about education, about culture, about accent, about *taste*. Did you leave school at fourteen or fifteen or did you stay on for qualifications? Do you get paid weekly in a small brown envelope or monthly? What do you call your midday meal? Do you eat your bread with margarine or only ever butter? What do you consider a good night out to be? The answers pointed to all sorts of different aspects of life. To employment, of course, and the money that came with it, but also to forms of leisure, to domestic life, to the upbringing of children, and so on.

At the same time, this golden age of affluence saw the emergence of various new kinds of jobs that seemed neither working-class nor straightforwardly middle-class. If you worked in the chemical industry or in an electronics factory, were you working-class because you worked in a factory, or middle-class because you were some sort of technician or engineer? And if you were a badly paid, low-level, administrator in local government, were you middle-class simply because you didn't wear overalls, but were expected to wear more formal attire? For many commentators and analysts, the language of working-class and middle-class, inherited directly from the nineteenth century, was no longer any good for describing a new reality. They sought new names for new classes: the technician class, the administrator class, and so on. Others thought that class itself was outmoded and that a new classlessness was becoming a dominant experience in welfare state Britain.

In this book I treat these debates as source material. What seems clear is that the absolutism of class categories no longer quite fitted lots of people's everyday experience. Certainly, many of the unequivocal markers of class were disappearing. The class system of upper-, middle-, and working-class, which was translated on the railways as 'first class', 'second class', and 'third class', ended in 1956. As the century progressed, the sort of spaces that might be emphatically working-class or exclusively middle-class gave way to the sort of experience that characterises air travel: most of us are stuck in coach. Yet this doesn't quite get, I think, what was happening to class, and how class was and is related to taste and consumption.

In the late 1930s a group of enthusiastic, amateur social scientists sought to study everyday life in Britain. The movement was called Mass-Observation and one group studied the industrial city of Bolton, calling it Worktown. One of the things that the observers noticed was how, during the week, the male factory workers would all drink in the public bar in the public houses, where beer was a penny cheaper, and where, if the fancy took you, you could swear and sometimes spit (a necessary by-product of working in a dusty mill). It was a male preserve. At the weekends, though, these same men would drink in the posher lounge bar where the beer was dearer and where swearing was frowned on because of the presence of women. For Tom Harrisson, one of the founders of Mass-Observation, this meant that class wasn't a fixed possession, but something that was actively negotiated and changed across the week:

> Broadly, we found the whole of Worktown went up the social scale at the weekend. On a weekday, anybody in Worktown wearing a bowler hat was either B class or a mourner. At the weekend, anybody could and did wear a bowler, and the visible class distinctions of Tuesday became inextricably confused on Saturday afternoon. Weekend Worktown was a place superficially populated by well-to-do middle-classites – on an ordinary weekday, a city of wooden clogs, grimy faces, manual workers.[6]

For all its insistence that class is based on male employment (a tradition that continues today) this does, I think, help us understand what has been happening to social class in the second half of the twentieth century and into the present. Class hasn't gone away – the gap between the wealthiest elite and what constitutes an average income has widened considerably – but it has become more complicated. What Tom Harrisson saw as the superficial changes in how people experienced class across the week became less and less superficial in the postwar period, as we moved from work, to home, to leisure activities. Class identity and class feeling was no longer the bedrock of experience. The old world of class arranged solely around employment, or even employment and education, was bound to be complicated by the arrival of rock 'n' roll, milk bars and cafés, subcultures, 'flat-pack' furniture, television, jeans, correspondence courses, leisure centres, and the Open University.

I'd argue that class is still one of the best ways of describing everyday experience within the last sixty years. To capture its changing nature, though, class needs to be wrestled away from a nineteenth-century flattening into three, or sometimes just two, monolithic categories. The difficulty is that we have become addicted to thinking of class as either working-class or middle-class, with the occasional nod to an upper class. This universal, old system has an amazing ability to pull everything into its orbit, to the point where things that were (at the time) an escape from these rigidly fixed class categories have since found their way back inside them. Many of the tastes that I'm looking at here, from the second-hand, well-scrubbed pine kitchen table to the Japanese paper lampshade, were an invitation to a loosening of traditional class culture. Many of these tastes purposely looked outside of Britain for inspiration and reference. They offered the promise of a loose bohemianism for many. A bohemianism at home and at leisure that was often at odds with the world of work. For many people today these items are solidly middle-class.

Taste is never reducible to class identity. Carpets and yogurt have their own sensual properties, and within a consumer society they come to us wrapped up in images of a better life. Advertising tempts us not just with new things, but with the promise of new ways of living, new ways of life. In this book, I will show you the sensual landscape offered by these new tastes, their attraction to many young people who were becoming adults through the decades after the mid-1950s. I want to capture something of the promise that this new emphasis on domestic life offered, to describe the pleasures of new foods and furnishings, new ways of socialising and imagining the future. With one eye on the environmental dangers and opportunities that this domestic consumerism also presented, we'll take a close look at adverts and promotional literature.

There is, of course, a gap between what tastes offer and the reality of what they provide: after all, we are talking about a commercial culture that always promises more than it could possibly deliver. (Do cigarettes, perfumes, chocolates ever make you more attractive in the way that advertising suggests?) During the UK's 'golden age of affluence', the social sciences and particularly sociology, a relatively new discipline in this country, took off. While this might seem to be a peripheral phenomenon, confined to university departments, it was in fact often central to how consumer culture was discussed and experienced in Britain. The 1960s and 1970s were the decades that saw a form of popular sociology filling the pages of newspapers (both broadsheets and redtops) and magazines (specialist magazines like *New Society*, of course, but also the new colour supplements that were accompanying weekend newspapers), as well as being the basis for many radio and television programmes. Sociology and sociologists were also portrayed in cartoons and in novels as good subjects for satirising modern life. Sociologists produced a popular literature of their own, published by the likes of Penguin founder Allen Lane under the iconic blue-spined titles of the Pelican imprint. These non-fiction books were relatively cheap, and could tell readers about affluent society, popular psychology, history, architecture and any other subject under the sun.

The focus of sociology was often on class and consumerism. The social scientists looked at the possibility that new classes were emerging by studying new patterns of work, new levels of affluence, and changes in urban living. Sometimes they wanted to name these emerging classes (the 'class of home-owners' or 'the administrator class', for instance), and at other times they were happy to call them the '*new* middle classes' or the '*new* working classes'. The question of how to get beyond a nineteenth-century understanding of class, of moustache-twiddling factory owners, of a middle class of socially aspirational professionals, and a mass working class of manufacturing employees is not a question that has gone away. In 2011 a large online survey (a survey conducted with 325,000 respondents) found that in twenty-first-century Britain there were eight classes (elite, established middle class, technical middle class, new affluent workers, traditional working class, emerging service workers, and precariat).[7] This book won't provide a new answer to these old questions, but it will trace a path though the lived confusions of class, of how a married couple, for instance, might disagree about whether they, as a couple, were middle- or working-class.

While social scientists were telling us that class experience was changing with affluence and consumerism, they were also using traditional ideas of class to define the meaning and measure of taste by reducing consumption to what they termed 'status striving'. By seeing taste as a vast competition for prestige, what was immediately lost was any sense of the actual content of these tastes and the feelings that might be associated with them. The only feelings that are regularly registered in the accounts of their findings are feelings of ambition and anxiety, a sense of superiority or worry. Social aspiration has always been awkward, subject to mockery, treated as rather vulgar, and so of course it is always other people who are obsessed with 'keeping up with the Joneses', never those giving their opinions, or analysing these opinions.

For this book, taste is not fundamentally about status striving. Yet it's also clear that the sense of social aspiration that newspapers and television comedies made so much of did affect the atmosphere and practice of taste. The widespread assumption of status striving added a layer of self-consciousness to taste, one that is still there today, to perhaps an even greater degree. My position on taste is relatively straightforward: as consumers, I think we like jazz or sushi (or whatever) on their own sensual terms for the pleasures they offer, and we also like them for the cultural worlds that they bring with them (a world of sophisticated cosmopolitanism, for instance, or authentic community). Much of this book is concerned with detailing the kind of social worlds that one strain of commercial culture offered to British consumers in the 1960s and 1970s. As well as enjoying our tastes, we can also be self-conscious about the class associations that go with them. We might like something *in spite* of the class associations that go with it. I think that this is often what people mean when they talk about 'guilty pleasures'. Sometimes our tastes are purposefully chosen to fit with how we would like to identify in terms of class, and this includes studious attempts to try and avoid specific class associations! To my mind, one of the key feelings associated with the tastes being examined in this book was a sense of lightness, of informal ways of socialising, which partly came from leaving an antiquated class system behind. But such feelings are also peppered with a sense that this 'classlessness' could easily be rebadged as a middle-class feeling, primarily available to those with the luxury of a securely middle-class upbringing.

Consumer culture was never likely to be the solution to the problem of living in a society structured around the unequal distribution of opportunity and resources. Consumption is more likely to amplify inequalities. Yet there is also a sense that the consumer culture emerging in the 1960s and 1970s had a social mission that connected it in part to the democratic impulses of the welfare state: bringing the 'good life' to the masses. People like the designer and retailer Terence Conran saw his role as belonging to the commercial wing of welfare society, of offering good design to all, under an ethos of democratic culture. I'm going to avoid passing judgement on this: I'm neither going to be wagging my finger at the thought of 'capitalism' offering a shop-soiled version of freedom, nor am I claiming that consumer culture should be seen as bringing about a democracy of taste. I am also not interested in positioning myself in relation to questions of whether such design is good taste or not. I'm much more interested in figuring out how these commodities were represented and experienced during a period that established so much of the domestic culture that we still live with. I'm interested in the desire for a cosmopolitan lifestyle that these tastes encouraged, even if it is based on a tourist approach to cosmopolitanism. I'm interested in describing how some of the new goods allowed people to alter their relationship to the past. I'm fascinated with how the world felt to people setting up home for the first time during this period of affluence, and how journalists and other writers imagined their lives.

As we wend our way through the history of some of the tastes that emerged during the period of the 1960s to the 1980s, we will encounter exciting new shops and magazines and the new styles of living that they were presenting. These tastes tell a story about some of the new feelings that were becoming prominent in Britain. I'm sure that at times it is a story that is focused on quite a small portion of the population (the young, those in Metropolitan areas, those in the South of the country, etc.), but it is also a story that comes to have a much wider resonance, and today is often at the base of an almost ubiquitous culture (the success of the duvet is one example of this, but so too are the hardwood floors, the mis-match seating, and bare-brick walls of so many bars, pubs, cafés and restaurants).

We will also look at how these feelings about taste and status were captured by novelists, playwrights, memoirists, and others. Here, for instance, is a nurse describing her domestic environment from the late 1950s:

> I was married in the 1950s and our first home was completely devoid of ornaments. Vases and knick-knacks given to us as wedding presents were soon hidden away and disposed of as quickly as possible. Our flat was decorated in what we considered to be the 'contemporary style', which as far as we were concerned meant two walls papered in stripes and the rest with spots!![8]

Many people, of course, were much less able to follow taste trends like this. If you were on the breadline, obviously a commitment to interior design would be unlikely. For many people, a mix-and-match aesthetic was the result of never quite having sufficient means, and never quite having the dedication or time for the sort of complete lifestyle that was often portrayed in magazines and became a reality for this nurse. For many people, including myself, taste and a lifestyle that might go with it, is a messy affair. I'd love to make homemade pasta and my own bread, but never quite get round to it. I'd like a more minimalist interior but live with four other people, a dog and a cat. This book is both about the image of what was considered 'tasteful' and fashionable, and about the compromised reality of how people go about fashioning their lives and lifestyles. One of the central elements of the book is the way that an aesthetic of inconsistency, or what the advice literature at the time called 'eclecticism', emerged as a way of mixing the modern and the old, the planned and the haphazard, the artificial and the natural. It was a lifestyle and an aesthetic that seemed to positively encourage a more *laissez-faire* attitude towards taste.

In combining promotional literature and imagery with popular social sciences, as well as memoir and fiction, I'm not intending to privilege one form of evidence over another.

They each tell their truth and they each only give a partial account of a world. The remembered experience is, for my account, not more or less real than the sort of consumer journalism comparing different brands of dishwashers. What is important to remember is that our reality has, since at least the 1960s, been fashioned in design studios, magazine journalism, advertising photography, and the retail trade. To say that such people trade in fantasy doesn't mean that those fantasies aren't a crucial element of our reality.

Behold, the duvet cometh ...

The world I'm going to show you is often stunningly ordinary. The examples of taste we will explore will include, quiches, mayonnaise, kitchen tables, carpets, yogurts, pasta, shelf units, and self-assembly armchairs. This is not going to be an account of the 1960s, 1970s, and 1980s that is focused on the kooky and the kitsch: no lava lamps here! It is the everyday things that are driving this revolution in taste and lifestyle. While little bits of London were swinging (as well as tuning in and dropping out), much larger chunks of the country were taking small steps towards a future less in awe of a Britain of stiff-upper-lips and minding your Ps and Qs. This is a period of affluence and opportunity, where a future might be forged in the white heat of technology. Where universities and colleges were growing in number and scale as more and more people could boast of having letters after their name. Where a multicultural reality was beginning to find a place away from the racist stereotypes of the media and the patronising treatment of the state. Taste and lifestyle might seem a side shown to these larger histories: in this book they get top billing.

I'm going to take you into the heart of this soft revolution by stalking the high street, watching new chains of shops and restaurants open (and sometimes close again), seeing new kinds of goods (duvets, for instance) taking over. We will meet TV chefs and newspaper cartoonists, journalists, and satirists. The soft revolution is displayed in full-colour ads and magazine editorials. It is also there to be mocked and knocked, in plays, films, and novels. We will be guided by the likes of Adrian Mole – an unreliable guide if ever there was one – as well as Posy Simmonds' Weber family, and we will take instruction from Keith Floyd and Delia Smith. We will seek advice from Terence Conran and *The Likely Lads*, and watch as Mike Leigh, Malcolm Bradbury, and J. B. Priestley try to make us cringe for having the slightly wrong taste.

1
Taste and tastemakers

Before we get to the nitty gritty of my story, I need to take a step back to show you why the word 'taste' is so central to its telling.[1] Taste is key to describing how the world feels to people. It describes the ordinariness of liking one colour more than another, one flavour of jam over another, as well as our ability to evaluate the quality of films, books, and music (sometimes confidently, sometimes not so much). It names our approach to fashion and design, as well as our ability to distinguish between sweet and savoury foods. It expresses our personality and our desires. It describes the popular styles of a generation, a period, a country. We say, sometimes blagging it, that the Victorians had a taste for corsets and crinoline. When we return from a foreign visit, we talk enthusiastically of the new tastes we have enjoyed, and weigh-up the characteristic tastes of the place we have just visited. Everything there seemed so different. The coffee tasted so particular; the adverts were full of unfamiliar products shown in unusual ways. Even the electric pylons weren't the same! We only realise how fully immersed we are in a set of tastes (our own, but also our national tastes and period-tastes) when we go elsewhere, either in reality or in imagination.

Dictionaries tell us that the English word 'taste' originally came from an old French word for touching and feeling. It seems striking to me that the bodily senses the word relates to are so intimate: unlike seeing and hearing you can't taste and touch from a distance, you have to get up close and personal. (In Shakespeare the word taste can refer to carnal knowledge.) Taste is also linked to the word 'test' – to test something out, to experience it through trial and error, through use. And, of course, we use the term to refer to forms of discernment, judgement. We say that someone has 'good taste' and imply that they seem to have an intuitive ability to pick out the best, the coolest, the 'right thing'. Taste is a small word to bring all that together: to link the senses, experience, and judgement. It is also a vital word for describing how we experience the world. Think back to your oldest memories, perhaps visiting grandparents. Don't you remember (or feel you remember) what the room was like, the atmosphere, how the food tasted. We might remember the feel of a cardigan, the 'give' of an armchair, the cold draft of a bedroom and the warmth of a kitchen. These memories might be full of love and joy, but perhaps also a slight queasiness: why was the room so hot? How long had that food been cooking? Taste is intimate, it is the world that we feel.

In this chapter I'm going to return to some of the age-old issues around taste. People have, for hundreds of years, recognised that taste is relative. In some countries dairy products are hard to find because they are felt to be slightly disgusting, while another country boasts over 400 different varieties of cheese. What is considered delicious, comfortable, polite, and beautiful differs from country to country and changes over time. We recognise that taste is governed by convention, and yet we also recognise how fundamental some of these conventions are. Taste gets under our skin, perhaps it is our skin. If you have grown up in a culture that finds milk slightly revolting you aren't going to suddenly find the coagulated and smelly version a delightful indulgence, even if you're visiting a country that ranks its blue cheeses as the height of luxury. On a more individual level we often say that 'there's no accounting for taste' when somebody likes something that isn't to our taste. That well-worn phrase can also suggest that taste isn't something that we can rationalise. You don't get very far trying to convince a small child that a broccoli gratin tastes better than a packet of Haribo fruit gummies. Better off just bribing them. (Or if that fails turn off the Wi-Fi.) But that sense we have, that taste is entirely subjective, comes unstuck when we find ourselves totally agreeing with the online reviews that detested the same rubbish film that we watched last night. The conflict between seeing taste as entirely in the eye of the beholder *and* something that can be judged will take us back to a philosophical topic that was widely discussed in the coffee-houses of eighteenth-century Britain. Our ancestors didn't sort it out, but they did clarify some of the issues at stake.

Two and a half centuries later the world is very different. The coffee-houses are still there but now they offer a bewildering variety of drinks and are often standardised across the globe as well-known brands (Starbucks, Caffè Nero, Costa Coffee). And rather than discussing politics and fashion the clientele is more likely to be busily scrolling through a virtual world. While eighteenth-century philosophers thought that we should consult a small group of taste experts to advise us about what was most polite, most sensitive, most witty, most fashionable, today we are bombarded with adverts, recommendations, warnings, and suggestions from every conceivable angle. Unlike the philosophers of taste who were writing in the 1700s, at the dawn of consumerism, where it was only the wealthy who had the luxury to fret about the style of their wigs, we live in the age of almost total consumerism where we all seem to be the target of taste experts and advisers. This chapter is going to take you quite quickly from the 1750s to the 1960s, to show you how taste continued to govern what it means to live the good life, and then to show you some of the major changes to the role of taste in society. The 1960s and 1970s, 'the golden age of affluence', is a period for new tastes and for new ways of seeing and selling taste, and its routes lie in the fashionable drawing rooms of eighteenth-century Edinburgh.

The eighteenth century is still with us

Taste, for the Scottish philosopher David Hume (1711–76), was a term that referred not just to our likes and dislikes or our judgements about beauty and ugliness, it also referred to our manners and behaviours. We have hung on to that larger meaning of taste when we say that what so-and-so did was in poor taste when we mean that they have behaved badly. The link between manners and taste is an important one to bear in mind in this book. In our current age we often treat manners as though they are separate from taste, but often the exact opposite is the case. The relationship between the tastes we enjoy and the manners we promote are often more implicit than explicit, but the link is there, nonetheless. Over the last hundred years, for instance, children's presence in the home has changed considerably. A hundred years ago, middle-class and upper-class society considered that good manners meant that children were to be 'seen but not heard', often simply 'not seen and not heard'. Today, in households with young children, their presence is everywhere: their toys are in the front room; the sound of their play animates the house. This isn't just a shift in what is considered acceptable behaviour for children, it is about how our front rooms have changed. They are no longer places of strict decorum but have become rooms where informality and relaxation are the name of the game. Kick back and hang out. And we have the furniture and decoration to go with it: the low-level settees and cushions; the large TVs; the lack of fragile ornament displays to break.

David Hume's 1757 essay 'Of the Standard of Taste' sets out what were then the main issues around taste. In many respects they still are. One interesting aspect of Hume's approach is that he keeps on moving between scales, between a group of friends, say, and the world at large. So, in explaining how difficult it is to imagine a coherent set of 'standards' (which is his topic) he mentions that even amongst a group of people who have had exactly the same education and have 'imbibed the same prejudices' there are often marked differences of taste (these might be the equivalent of having a preference for raspberry over strawberry jam, or a fondness for Handel rather than Bach in music, or arguing that one Bach 'Prelude' is better than another). On a global level taste takes on much more extreme variations. Hume, with an eighteenth-century frankness that today would be frowned upon, claims that 'we are apt to call barbarous whatever departs widely from our own taste'.[2] He means by this that travellers from Scotland to far-flung places in the world will often find the manners and customs of other people 'barbarous'. No doubt he has in mind reports by Christian missionaries on the 'savage' tastes of people who the West were in the process of colonising. But he also imagines how he would react to the 'barbaric' manners and tastes of his ancestors.

To imagine that everyone else's tastes are not quite up to scratch quickly brings about the realisation that such judgements can easily be reversed. Seen through the eyes of others it is now you who are the barbarians. It is you that smells a bit odd. It is me that eats in a revolting manner. And Hume recognises this. This will become the basis for an anthropological approach to taste: you can't measure taste against a universal standard, as different cultures will have their own rationales for what is polite, delicious, and beautiful. But what complicates this picture of 'each to their own' permissiveness is the sense that anyone might have about the rightness of their own tastes, manners, and customs. This is where 'feeling' comes into the picture. We might know that standards of taste can't be made universal, that they are relative, but that doesn't mean that we can easily feel this. I might *know* that in Japan blowing your nose in public is seen as deeply impolite, repulsive even, but because I don't *feel* this attitude it would be easy for me to forget if I'm visiting Tokyo, especially if I happen to have a cold.

In Hume's time the word for 'feeling' was 'sentiment' and Hume spends much of the essay explaining how sentiment and judgement are both distinct and related. For Hume, the ancient proverb *de gustibus non est disputandum*, which translates roughly as 'about matters of taste there can be no disputes', falls primarily on the side of sentiment. What you feel most intensely can't really be open to argument because I can't tell you that your feelings are somehow wrong (even if I think that they might be misplaced). In terms of feelings and sentiment there is nothing to argue about because there are no shared criteria for measurement. In the field of judgement, though, things are quite different. Here there might be lots to argue about precisely because there are some shared reference points. There are, for instance, lots of generally assumed common values. For Hume 'every voice is united in applauding elegance, propriety, simplicity, spirit in writing; and in blaming [...] affectation, coldness, and a false brilliancy'.[3] No one likes a show-off, and we all appreciate lively, elegant, and polite conversation! Elegance, for Hume, might be a universal mark of good taste, even though how elegance is interpreted is going to be open to lots of local variety (and the history of fashionable dress is certainly evidence of this). But there are also various criteria that might guide us in our evaluation. Just as we can differentiate tasteless, watery jam from a richer, fruitier version, so we can distinguish a well-told tale from one that constantly loses its thread.

Hume's approach to taste tries to knit feeling and judgement together, and to do this he argues for the importance of taste experts, or on his terms, critics. The big question facing a philosophy of taste is: why would you trust an expert in taste when so much of it relates to feeling? It is easy to see how we might *generally* benefit from listening to experts in all sorts of areas of life. We might, for instance, seek out the advice of a boiler fitter when we need a new boiler (assuming that they aren't working on commission). We would presume that they have much more extensive knowledge of different kinds and makes of boilers than we do and have a good sense of each one's reliability and efficiency. Couldn't we assume something similar about food, furnishings, and films? The least we could expect from an expert might be that they are familiar with lots of examples of the things they claim to have expertise in. We hope that a film critic might be able to tells us which horror films are the scariest and advise us about which thrillers are going to keep us on the edge of our seats. We might be sceptical if they had never heard of Alfred Hitchcock. For Hume, expertise in taste comes from having a good knowledge of the classics (work that has stood the test of time), as well as an apprenticeship in comparing and contrasting different work so as to develop a knowledge of how writing or music works – what makes it tick, what makes one piece more effective than another, and so on.

Music, of course, is not the same kind of thing as a boiler. Would we want our critics to think in terms of efficiency and reliability when it comes to films and food? And this is where Hume brings sentiment back into the mix. The best critics are not those that can dispassionately tell us which detective stories are best at keeping us guessing, but which ones combine originality and emotion, for instance, which ones keep us guessing while making us care about what we are guessing about. In other words, taste criticism is not the separation of judgement and sentiment but their combination. We don't, according to both Hume and common opinion, value critics that have no sensitivity: we want our critics to be moved, outraged, provoked, seduced, enthralled, entertained, even bored. And this is Hume's counter-intuitive point: feelings, the very stuff that makes taste so varied and so haphazard, are also what must be used to pick out the best from the rest, as long as it is also informed by some form of expertise.

Whether or not Hume is correct philosophically is less important to me than the way that he has identified the function of taste and criticism in modern life. Taste circulates not through dispassionate judgements but through feelings. It isn't the clear synopsis of the film that draws us to the box office or the Netflix selection but the adjectives that tell us that this film will have us rolling in the aisles or sobbing in our hankies. If we look at all the places where tastes are being promoted, we rarely see logical or reasoned persuasion, instead we see a world of feeling and mood, atmosphere and emotion. Take a look at any IKEA catalogue or recent recipe book and you see a visual world setting out to entice us, delight us, spark and intensify our desires. It is a world of amplified feeling. We want that sofa, or one like it, because it fits into a world of laughter and love, of relaxation and play. The feeling of taste is there in the descriptions, in the photography, in the way that goods are staged.

The golden age of affluence introduced us to a glossy, colour-saturated world of gadgets and gizmos, and open-plan living. The editorial columns of magazines and newspapers echoed with the snappy lingo of the advertising copywriter. The line between sales catalogue and journalism became blurred. The desire for instant gratification was intensified by faster forms of consumption: from fast food to flat-pack furniture. And everywhere images of a better life. And that life had everything to do with feelings: feelings of ease, of lightness, of spontaneity, of a wipe-clean future. Hume might not have had IKEA, or anything like it, in mind when he was thinking about taste in mid-eighteenth-century Edinburgh, but he certainly saw the importance of feeling as the essential ingredient that animates taste.

Hats, cigarettes, and electric guitars

Hume didn't have much to say about 'period-taste', even though he recognised that historical changes in taste were clear evidence that there were no absolute standards to taste. In this book period-taste is going to be crucial because, more than anything, it establishes some of the key feelings of a period. Our own period-tastes are hard to see because we are living within them, but you can get a sense of previous period-tastes in old movies and magazines: what would it have been like to talk in that way, to drive those types of cars, to live like that? Period-taste is the world that we swim in; it colours our perceptions and shapes the atmosphere of a time.

In the area of clothing, for instance, I only wear a hat when it is either very cold or extremely hot and sunny. That is my choice, and it doesn't tend to make me stand out. When I look at films and photographs from the 1930s, though, I notice that nearly everyone, men especially, are wearing hats whatever the weather: some wear bowler hats, others wear Trilbies, while others wear some form of cap. In the 1930s, my choice of not wearing a hat would have seemed odd, eccentric even. It would have been notable and viewed by many people as a sign of me being disrespectfully casual. Tastes in men's hats in the early decades of the twentieth century were governed by class, costs, and practicality, rather than by individualistic expression. A city banker might wear a bowler, a plumber a flat wool cap, and both might wear a different hat at the weekend. A Trilby might be a sign of professionalism for a doctor or a sign of respectability amongst Caribbean Britons in the 1960s, but it could also be worn in a different way by racetrack bookies and journalists. In the 1980s a Trilby, especially if worn towards the back of your head, could be a sign of young multicultural confidence amongst the Two-Tone ska revivalists. In twentieth-century Britain, taste in hats has a historical dimension to it so that we could say that Britain (like many other countries) changed from being a hat-wearing nation, where hat wearing was ubiquitous and unremarkable, to one where hats became the preserve of the fashionable or the professional, or associated with rituals (weddings, funerals, graduation) or protection. It is this dimension of taste that is so vividly historical, as one generation gradually gives up on the customs of their parents and adopts new ones.

The male mill workers from 1930s' Bolton expressed a complex social identity by wearing a cap during the week and a bowler at weekends, and they might also express their individuality by how they wore it, or by picking a specific style of cap. But they also demonstrate historical tastes simply by wearing a hat. This is the level of taste that is hard to see because it either seems so obvious or, from a distance, so quaint. It is the level of taste that is the taken-for-granted tastes of a generation. Hat wearing shaped how life felt: it made, for instance, the presence of class visible in a way that was lost when routine hat wearing ended. It expressed masculinity and femininity. The tastes that often go unnoticed are the ones that are the most ordinary. In the 1970s, for instance, social tastes might be exhibited by favouring the BBC over the available commercial television channel, and personal tastes might be exhibited, for instance, by a preference for watching magic shows rather than comedies, but what also needs to be recognised is the wide-spread taste for *watching TV* and the limited choice of programmes to watch. Part of what made the 1970s feel the way it did was the shared reality of television – the knowledge that nearly every twelve-year-old would have watched last night's *Top of the Pops*.

Another example of how taste functions at a general level can be found in smoking. Whenever I travel on old 'classic' buses (which is not often) I'm always amazed to find, not built-in ashtrays, but angled bits of metal designed for stubbing out cigarettes. Smokers would stub the cigarette out on the textured metal on the back of the seat in front of them and then let the cigarette end drop to the floor. Not only has our tolerance and taste for smoking changed in the intervening years (and smoking on buses, trains, airplanes, and underground railways were still an ordinary activity when I was in my twenties in the early 1980s) but so has our sense of acceptable ways of disposing of cigarettes. Changes around tastes in smoking are of course hugely important in terms of health (between 1950 and 1990 the number of male smokers dropped by 50 per cent with a corresponding drop in cases of lung cancer) but do they mean anything more than the fact that we have generally become healthier? If we listen to these two anti-non-smokers from the late 1930s, we can catch a larger sense of the ways that taste shapes experience:

> I notice I sometimes find myself inclined to 'look down' on non-smokers. This may be quite unreasonable; but on the other hand, I have noticed in many cases (by no means a general rule, of course) that there is something 'queer' about men (this does not apply to women) who are non-smokers. That is, they quite frequently have eccentricities, and even unpleasant traits, which are not so noticeable in smokers.

> I always feel that there's a milky babies' breath smell about a man who doesn't smoke; he seems to me not quite a *man*. He repels me in somewhat the same way as does a scoutmaster. Quite unreasonable of me, I know, but there it is – if a man hasn't the smell of tobacco about him he doesn't seem to me quite wholesome, and I can't like him no matter how admirable his character may be. By *like* I mean physical[ly] like. I may *admire* him for his qualities and manner, etc., but I don't want him *near* me. When I was a child I used to love the tobacco smell that clung to father's, uncle's, schoolmaster's waistcoat.[4]

These are not just opinions about smoking but bodily reactions to the absence of the smell of tobacco clinging to men. These responses tell us something about what was considered essential to how masculinity was felt and experienced in the 1930s, at least by some people.

A final example comes from the world of music. In the early 1980s a friend of mine used to regularly lament the fact that his aunt would never experience the joys of appreciating heavily distorted electric guitar music. His aunt (like mine) didn't have a taste for the sort of rock music that featured distortion and feedback. Their taste was more attuned to the melodies on the soundtrack to *The Sound of Music*, which was the best-selling UK album in 1965, 1966, and 1968, easily outselling the Beatles. The point is more substantial than it seems. This wasn't about preferences or about the snobbery that might look down on rock music because it could be seen as 'low' taste, for instance. This was about generational taste, period-taste. Our aunts just couldn't hear distorted guitars as music. To them trying to like Deep Purple or Black Sabbath or Slade or Suzy Quatro was like trying to enjoy the sound of lawnmowers and electric drills. It was hard work, and they were never going to hear it as music. In one sense it was as simple as that. People often talk about tastes as though the choice is one of liking classical more than pop, or real operas over soap opera, but culture isn't experienced from the outside, like a menu, but from the inside as a set of living feelings. Not to be able to feel distorted electric guitars as music wasn't a choice for our aunts.

Just from these examples it seems clear that taste isn't just about personal or social identity but also about larger historical changes: changing notions of what counts as musical; changing feelings towards tobacco smoke; changing practices of hat wearing. More recently we have seen historical changes in taste around kitchen waste: what for many was once a source of disgust has become part of an everyday routine of recycling. In an age of pandemics, our manners have been undergoing all sorts of changes: how close we stand to people, and how we greet someone has been changing. It might be temporary, or it might be the start of a more general change in manners and taste. While events like pandemics speed up the process of change, the larger historical changes around hat wearing or distorted music are often so gradual that they are barely noticeable as large-scale transformations of taste. We might also want to think about the importance of the infrastructures that are necessary for tastes to flourish. A hat-wearing society needs a millenary industry and millenary outlets. If a society at large is going to decorate their houses with wallpaper, then wallpaper needs to be made available and to be cheap enough for most members of that society to buy it. Different groups might then note their preference for flowers over stripes, an expensive brand over something simpler and cheaper, but unless the availability is in place, that preference amounts to little. The infrastructures of taste – the shops that supply us, the magazines that advise us, the adverts that seduce us – will be an important element of this book.

The rise of consumerism

One way of finding out about taste in any period is to look at its lifestyle magazines. In the eighteenth century, tastes and trends were written about in what we could call the original lifestyle publications in Britain – *The Tatler* and *The Spectator*.[5] These publications reported on public opinion, discussed the latest fashions and tastes, and wrote about culture – particularly how to recognise good writing and true wit. The journals were worried about the way that commerce was encroaching on art and concerned that art was becoming inferior because of the influence of money (a perennial issue across the centuries). In another sense, the journals were themselves an example of that commercialism. Taste – both in writing and in fashion – were frequently discussed, and *The Spectator* and *The Tatler* were clearly seen as arbiters of taste, to the point where a reader could mockingly write to

Mr. Spectator under the name of 'Jack Modish' proposing that the magazines should simply publish a pamphlet telling everyone (and especially those that don't live in London) what to wear and how to behave.[6] The complaint of a 'metropolitan elite' sending out fashion advice to the provinces echoes through to our own time.

In the second half of the twentieth century, the commercialisation of taste – both in the narrow sense of films, books, music, and in the broader sense of manners and fashions – would make the eighteenth century feel like a tiny echo of what was about to occur. What can we say about the changes in consumerism from the eighteenth century to the 1960s and 1970s? The period witnessed not only an extraordinary growth in the range of goods that became available, but also an almost unimaginable expansion in the way that taste was promoted. We moved not simply from scarcity to profusion in the realm of desirable goods, but from a small select band of taste-experts and tastemakers to a massive army of persuaders using every possible means to charm and seduce us. Advertising in the twentieth century became a profession, a skill, a whole way of communicating. It fed all sorts of new media – magazines, radio, television, and on to the age of the internet. We can see its glossy techniques in the photography industry and in the fizz and glitz of magazine editorials. It has crept into most corners of our everyday life as its algorithms chase us around the internet, and it is shaping our perception of what is cool and what is Instagrammable. In seeing this massive expansion of advertising and promotion we might want to ask not just how have tastes changed, but how has the *role* of taste changed over the years as consumer society took shape?

Writing in the mid-1970s, the journalist Jonathan Raban (a significant voice in this book) could describe the world of taste within the UK as an anxious maze:

> The leisure pages of the Sunday newspapers, fashion magazines, TV plays, popular novels, cookbooks, window displays all nag at the nerve of our uncertainty and snobbery. Should we like American cars, hard-rock hamburger joints, Bauhaus chairs … ? Literature and art are promoted as personal accessories: the paintings of Mondrian or the novels of Samuel Beckett 'go' with certain styles like matching handbags. There is in the city a creeping imperialism of taste, in which more and more commodities are made over to being mere expressions of personal identity. The piece of furniture, the pair of shoes, the book, the film are important not so much in themselves but for what they communicate about their owners; and ownership is stretched to include what one likes or believes in as well as what one can buy.[7]

It is a familiar refrain that bears the echo of Steele and Addison's magazines, as well as some of Hume's concerns. The sense that we aren't valuing something in itself, but only for its associations is a comment that will continually be heard within journalism and the social sciences, as well as within popular culture (the idea of 'keeping up with the Joneses' is often a theme within late twentieth-century sitcoms). There is, no doubt, another side to this. My sense is that consumer culture would hardly have been so successful if its major product was the feeling of an anxious, endless striving for something. This is consumer culture in a minor key.

Other writers – sometimes in the same magazines, or in novels and memoirs – have offered much more upbeat accounts of the role of taste in the postwar period. If taste can sometimes increase insecurity, then shouldn't we assume that it could also produce other effects too? Couldn't it also produce a new confidence for some, or amplify someone's sense of identity? Don't we also need to ask how taste has provided groups of people with a new-found confidence, and new-found visibility? If we look at the energy surrounding taste and the way it is used to perform innumerable identities, then to see it primarily in terms of anxiety might be over-simplifying its role. One of the stereotypical images that are offered of the middle classes, particularly the lower middle classes, is an anxious striving not just for conformity, but for 'good taste' (or 'well-bred taste') of a class slightly further along the social hierarchy. One of the stories that this book wants to tell is how a class – the new middle class – came into its own, not through the anxious mimicking of a 'higher' class, but through the making of a new class feeling, with a new set of tastes to go with it.

There is another shift that we can see as we move from the world of David Hume into the world of late twentieth-century consumerism. For Hume, refined and tasteful culture was a way of promoting 'higher feelings', of directing human urges and instincts towards finer sensitivities. By the time you get to the 1960s, taste is less concerned with this civilising mission, and more interested in a form of hedonism: of comfort, relaxation and letting it all hang out. When we think of the permissive society and its aftermath, when we think of consumerism in general, aren't we thinking of tastes that address our desires, our comforts, our physical worlds? The sense of morality associated with eighteenth-century 'good taste' is still there in the 1960s, but it plays a minor role. Even the language of practicality and efficiency around 'good design' is more tied to bodily pleasure than to morally superior tastes that are trying to keep bodily pleasures in check.

As well as recognising a shift in taste from a focus on fine feeling and sensitivity to one that emphasises pleasure, I think it is easy enough to see a shift in the kinds of items that are earmarked for discussion about taste and consumption. This is the journalist Robert Millar in the opening pages of his book on consumer culture and taste from 1963:

> What did we do with our evenings before the age of television? How did we manage to live without detergents, frozen food, plastic buckets, shirts which don't need ironing, materials which won't crease in the wrong places and keep creases in the right places, socks which needn't be darned, furs which look like furs but are not, laminated surfaces, scooters, spin driers?
>
> Were we really happy without stereophonic sound, Cinemascope, Cinerama, bottled suntan, machines which sell nylon stockings, coal and whisky, ball-point pens, powdered tea, instant coffee, transistor radio sets, electric clothes brushes, electric shoe polishers, electric toothbrushes, tranquillizers?[8]

The list of items is slightly different from Jonathan Raban's, but not much. While Raban is concerned that people are worried about what bags go with Beckett, highbrow culture doesn't get a look in with Millar (for obvious reasons: he is concerned primarily with highly visible commodity culture). Millar's list is probably closer to what most people were concerned with, and what most people were consuming. It is a world of taste that unlike Hume's is mainly about private life – it is aimed at our intimate domestic environments, and the watchwords are efficiency, convenience, and newness.

Lists will be a big part of this book. It is hard, I think, to write about consumer culture without making them. Instant soup might stand in for a new culture of convenience and mass production, but it only really does the job when it is connected to other items (electric kettles, supermarkets, convenience-stores, and so on). How could we think of the tastes of the 1960s and 1970s without making lists? It is the whole network of items that matters. I think that the changes in bedding – from sheets, blankets, and eiderdowns to duvets – is significant, but its significance is only really glimpsed when it is seen as part of a network that might include pasta, floor cushions, Pink Floyd, mineral water, salad, vegetarianism, CND, family planning, DIY, yoga, and yoghurt. One person's tastes might only include a few of these items and might also include items that seem to belong to a previous generation's taste; what matters is not how thoroughly a person inhabits a world of taste, but what that world of taste (however partially it is adopted) does for that person.

The duvet started to be adopted in the UK in the 1960s and by the end of the twentieth century it had become the ubiquitous taste for UK bedding. In the 1960s, duvets were rare in the UK: you would have had to send off for one, rather than being able to buy it from a high-street shop. In the 1960s those who were at the forefront of advising on bedding favoured duvets but recognised that it was going to be a struggle to get the British to go for them. For instance, the Council of Industrial Design (CoID, an important agent in advising on domestic design) published a series of small books on different rooms in the house in the late 1960s and into the 1970s. The entire series is about ease, comfort, and convenience. Good taste for CoID is never impractical, never something that you would struggle with. The book on bedrooms asks 'Why is bedmaking such a wearisome chore? Why not scrap all those separate top layers – sheets, blankets, eiderdown – and use one top cover only? With a fitted sheet below, one quick flip and the bed is made'.[9] Yet CoID is clearly arguing for a minority taste here. The author talks to a British bedding supplier about why duvets aren't more popular: 'if you tell an ordinary Briton that his bedclothes are not going to be tucked in at the sides he will start shivering before you have finished speaking', comes the reply.[10]

Perhaps if you were an early adopter of duvets in the 1960s you would also eat muesli and yogurt. Perhaps having a duvet was a status symbol. If so, it was a relatively well-hidden one. By the mid-1970s duvets were becoming much more common, and so too were items and practices that could loosely be associated with duvets – for instance Ski yogurts. I'm sure that the first wave of people who took up duvets and yogurts were probably young, thought of themselves as modern, and were relatively affluent. In this book I'm less interested in what these items 'meant' (how they functioned as symbols, for instance), than in how they felt, and what those feelings did for people. This is a good reason for keeping Hume in the back of our minds. Commentators on taste tend to favour tastes that can be seen as symbolic (a handbag that somehow symbolises a sympathy for Samuel Becket's writing, for instance), but what if we treated taste as an expression of feelings? For duvets this would mean trying to catch that new feeling of lightness, of casualness that was imbedded in having a duvet. At the start having a duvet would also include the feeling of letting go of a previous way of life. Not just letting go of the daily rigmarole of bedmaking, and the physical weight of blankets, but also the cultural feeling of bedding. For my parents' generation bedding was often a wedding gift and it was also something that was passed down from one generation to the next. As a child I slept under an eiderdown that had been my grandmother's. No children or grandchildren will inherit my duvet. Having a duvet would have felt like the past was slipping through your fingers – something to mourn perhaps, but also something to embrace.

From the small ads to the high street

New tastes require support – they need infrastructural support to take off! The growth in foreign holidays in the 1960s required an increase in the number of travel agents and travel companies offering package holidays. A desire for retro curios and eccentric trinkets was a boon to the second-hand furniture trade, turning many junk shops into something altogether trendier. One of the reasons why duvets were a minority taste in 1967 was their relative lack of availability – both on the high street and in the popular imagination. All sorts of infrastructures were involved in moving duvets from being a minority taste to becoming a majority taste: shops started stocking them; magazines began promoting them; bedrooms became warmer through central heating. In this book the most obvious infrastructure will be retailers. But another aspect of infrastructure that is equally important is the way that ideas, feelings, and attitudes circulate around goods. A shop might be brimming with duvets but unless you've got the desire for one you are not going to think of buying it. Attitudes and feelings about taste in the age of affluence most obviously circulated through advertising in newspapers and magazines, sometimes on television and in cinemas, and through books and brochures that set out to advise consumers. They also circulated more implicitly in novels and television programmes and in films. Often there were direct links between different elements: for instance, in the CoID publication on bedrooms Meade simultaneously tells her reader about the pleasure and practicality of duvets while also giving you the names and addresses of duvet suppliers.

If you look through magazines aimed at 'women and the home' from the end of the 1960s and into the 1970s, what routinely greets you when you first open them is a few pages of black-and-white classified adverts – some with pictures, some without. The small ads aren't the big full colour adverts that promote cigarette brands or big carpet manufacturers, but adverts for smaller retailers, who often work through mail order. In magazines such as *Homes and Gardens* and *Good Housekeeping*, adverts for duvets (usually called 'continental quilts' or some version of that; see figure 1.1) are found amongst adverts for 'Danish sisal

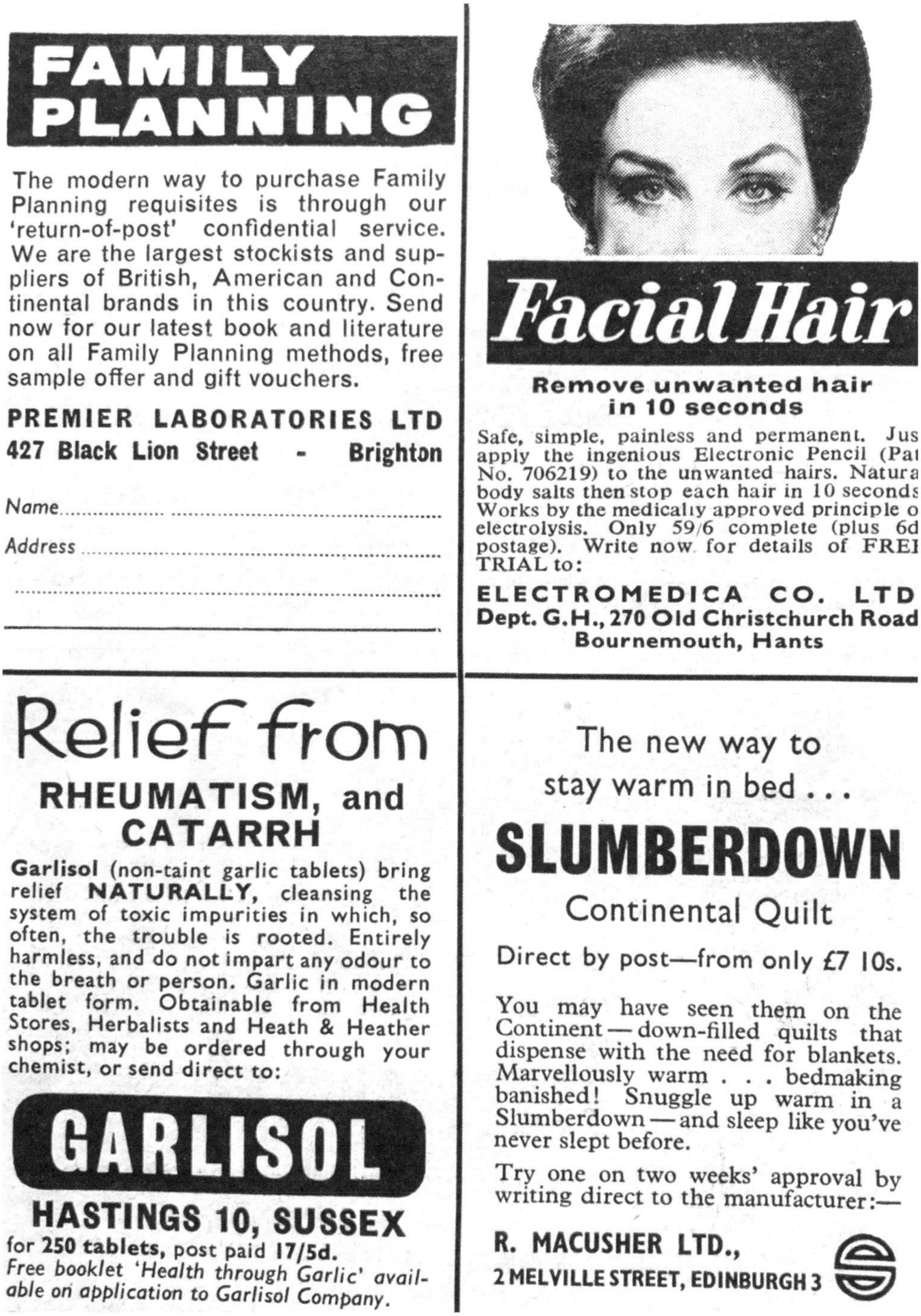

1.1 *Good Housekeeping*, January 1968, p. 12. Advert for a Slumberdown duvet carpeting', or furniture from the Scandinavian Room, and devices for making 'yoghourt' at home, as well as addresses to send off for family planning: 'the modern way to purchase Family Planning requisites is through our "return-of-post" confidential service'.[11] The main advertising business within these magazines can be found in the big colour spreads: persuading a readership that they should be spending their earnings on central heating, and that a dishwasher was no longer a luxury, but was now a necessity in the same way that a washing machine was. Central heating, fitted carpets, and dishwashers were the subject of large colour adverts as well as being the subject matter of articles discussing their pros and cons. The smaller black-and-white adverts tell another story: not of things that have arrived in houses around the country but of tastes that are on the verge of making into the mainstream of taste. The small ads show us small enterprises taking a punt on marginal tastes, hoping that they will become mainstream. Some do and some don't. Here, in small unobtrusive and unostentatious adverts you can glimpse a new world with slightly more sexual freedom, with Scandinavian bedding and flooring, and mail-order prophylactics. It is a little bohemia bubbling away beside the main tributaries of consumer culture. These are perhaps minor infrastructures, smaller networks working across the big names of mass retailers and manufacturers. A sign of emerging consumer interests as well as changes in social behaviour.

The various infrastructures for promoting taste are important to this book for reasons already hinted at: objects don't circulate alone, and the tastes of the emergent middle classes rarely single out objects as distinctive in and of themselves. One of the writers who clearly understood the interconnected aspect of consumer culture was the French sociologist Jean Baudrillard in his two books from this period, *The System of Objects* from 1968 and *The Consumer Society* from 1970. Baudrillard is brilliant in seeing consumption as something like an infrastructure of seduction. In *The Consumer Society* Baudrillard suggests that consumer culture was already, in the 1960s, working in a way that is so familiar to us today – a logic of association. Online shopping is today a 'personalised experience' where algorithms take data about our buying behaviour and try and predict what we might also be in the market for: 'people who bought this also liked these things', 'people like you also bought things like this'. Baudrillard thought that such associations were at the heart of what consumer society meant. This wasn't a world of individual items, but a world where commodities communicated with one another (your electric kettle connects to your instant coffee granules, which connect to the supermarket). It is also a world where a network of different items come together to compose a style of living (yoghurt, white paint, pasta, and so on).[12] Consumer society doesn't ask for loyalty to a company or brand, nor does it want us to stick to a strict set of objects. Quite the reverse, it encourages a degree of restlessness, of wanting the next item in an endless chain of association.[13] Although Baudrillard was writing about consumerism in France, what he had to say is also relevant to Britain.

Frank Trentmann writes that 'what the telegraph did for communication, the department store and mail order did for shopping: they compressed time and space'.[14] Department stores and early mail order meant that things from all over the world and from various times could be bought and brought to you with a degree of ease, as long as you had the money. Both the telegraph and the department store belong to the nineteenth century. So, what were the equivalents of the department store and mail order for the 1960s and 1970s? As we will see, mail order played its part in the lifestyle revolutions that I'm looking at (and so too did the department store). The history of everyday life doesn't work with the latest cultural technique obliterating what went before. The biggest change since 1945 in terms of how tastes were promoted has got to be television. Television was able to show us what instant gratification looked like on a nightly basis, and that seemed so much part of the consumer culture in the late twentieth century. The 1970s' family game show, *The Generation Game*, literally acted this out, when each episode would end with the winner having to memorise a vast selection of commodities rolling past them on a conveyor belt. The winning contestants had to reel the items off within a time limit and the ones remembered would be kept as the prize. The items made up a litany of must-have commodities for the lifestyle culture of the 1970s: fondue sets, soda-syphons, electric tea-makers, sunlamps, salad bowls, and always topped off with a cuddly toy. But it is hard to see the 1960s and 1970s as a straightforward connection between a form of communication and a type of shopper. In the 1960s, communication and retail merged in significant ways: advertising became a dominant art form; magazines and newspapers blended commodity seduction and investigative journalism in almost untraceable ways; TV, even when it was not actually playing adverts, seemed to be advertising. That was its register. Today, of course, things are very different again, and we would need to start with the intermeshing of online communication and shopping: algorithms and identity; mass reviewing and influencers; celebrity culture and social media.

'The tuning of my sentiments ...'

Jenny Diski's memoir, *The Sixties*, starts with an act of self-creation – through make-up, through clothes, through attitude. The year is 1967, Diski is nineteen years old, and is recreating a 'look' that had enthralled her as a young girl when she practiced ice skating with a much older girl who was dressed entirely in black. When Diski asks her why she dresses in black, the older girl answers with what was probably a well-rehearsed reply: 'I am in mourning for my life'. In 1967 Diski finds an 'utterly black' crêpe dress in the 'swirly art deco, black and gold interior, dim lights, loud psychedelic pop music, feather boas' of the shop Biba, in London's Kensington. When she tries on the dress she sees 'the image of my marvellous skating girl appear in the icy glass'.[15] Later on, she itemises the films she watched, the books she read, and the music that she listened to and danced to during that decade. She reads Thomas Hardy, Dostoyevsky, Nabokov, Pablo Neruda, the Beats; she watches Hollywood and British B movies, and the New Waves of Godard, Antonioni, Pasolini, and others; and she listens to Mingus and Monk, Dylan and Baez, the Stones, the Animals, and the Kinks. This music, she writes, 'all either accompanied me from the beginning of the decade or had emerged by the middle of it and were essential: the rhythm inside my head, the beat of my heart, the tuning of my sentiments'.[16] That phrase – 'the tuning of my sentiments' – feels like it is directly channelling David Hume. As she notes, she also spent 'an inordinate amount of energy worrying about my hair and shortening my skirts'.[17]

A sociologist of taste could use the information about her cultural consumption for placing Diski, probably with some degree of accuracy, within a milieu and a class (the bohemian wing of the middle class, say). This same sociologist could probably calculate the amount of cultural 'capital' (or cultural status) being amassed in establishing her tastes, and the sort of flexibility it would give her as she moves through a classed society. The sociologist might catch a sense of a striving, a refusal to enter a world already moulded around class values and gendered preconceptions and they will also have an inkling that this attitude is available to her partly because of the privilege of her background. Sociologists go for the bigger picture, but this doesn't tell the whole story. We miss how taste matters if we don't also see if from the inside, if we don't catch the way our tastes tune our sentiments, the way our hearts beat to the rhythms of the things we love, the things that move us. If taste sociology has, on the whole, been interested in how taste functions as a sign of status, in a jockeying of social positions, then I am more interested in how taste can be used to understand historical experience from the 'inside'. This doesn't mean ignoring Diski's cultural privileges (including the fact that her ability to pop into Biba is a result of her location), but it does mean being attentive to the feelings which finding that 'utterly black dress' invoke, being alive to the world that make-up, clothes, films, furniture, and fashion can create for us.

Taste, as a way of doing cultural history, offers, I think, a number of fruitful avenues. It gives you access to the way that history is lived, intimately and emotionally. To get the fullest sense of this it is important to hang on to the idea that taste operates at different levels, and that the same taste can be simultaneously personal, social, and historical. Buying a duvet in the 1960s might be a personal choice because you are attracted to this particular item; it can also be seen as social choice, perhaps connected to a liking for Scandinavian style social democracy, and it is also part of a historical shift towards more informal styles of living. All three levels show us elements of what the past felt like. What conjures up the past most vividly are often the feelings we have around taste experience – the time when your mum first buys you something that allows you to feel as if you too are involved in the process of self-creation (a pink shirt with a pear-drop collar in my case), that first record that felt alive with the blush of new ways of living (David Bowie's *Ziggy Stardust and the Spiders from Mars* on my sister's recommendation). There are delicious expectations here as well as a myriad of potential pitfalls – the disdain of elders, the mockery of peers, the ability or lack of it to confidently wear that shirt – no wonder we often associate the most intense feelings of taste with the delirium of youth. Getting a duvet or eating a yogurt can't compete with the intensity of a pink pear-drop collar shirt or your first brush with Bowie, but it is part of a continuum and needs to be understood in terms of feeling.

The scale of taste that is most often written about today is probably the social level. In some ways this level has most reason to concern us, as the English artist Grayson Perry evocatively put it, 'we learn the texture of our place in the world from the curlicue of a neck tattoo, the clank of a Le Creuset casserole dish, or the scent of a mouldering hunting print'.[18] Class distinction is played out, to some extent at least, through material goods and the practices that go with them. In 1899 the economist Thorstein Veblen claimed that a leisure class distinguished itself through a display of 'conspicuous consumption' which emerges from 'conspicuous leisure [that] grows gradually into a laborious drill in deportment and an education in taste and discrimination as to what articles of consumption are decorous and what are the decorous methods of consuming them'.[19] The well-to-do learn how to acquire the most tasteful items and to have the most tasteful interaction with them (to eat slowly, for instance). According to a sociological perspective the dominant classes display their superiority through their taste and through a set of associated cultural practices. The dominated classes, who don't have the economic, social and cultural resources to compete, are refused access to this world of taste. To paraphrase the French writer Pierre Bourdieu, taste provides the feeling of togetherness by uniting you with those who share your preferences and values, but, perhaps more importantly, it also feeds the feeling many people get when they are moving from one social class to another that they will never quite be part of the club, that they will never quite fit.[20]

Accounts of taste might, for instance, put a good deal of emphasis on whether you like 'wearing silver instead of gold, or listening to Bach rather than Wagner or Pearl Jam rather than Elton John' because such choices 'go to the core of who we are'.[21] Tastes are intricately connected to feelings, and the feelings that they convey are varied in the extreme. What we like, what we choose, might evoke feelings of pride, excitement, comfort, nostalgia, love, ease, but also anxiety, embarrassment, even shame. The same tastes might produce contradictory feelings for the same person in different situations. The music you listen to, the food you eat, the way you decorate your rooms might produce feelings of ease and pride most of the time but might suddenly become a source of anxiety when you invite a new work colleague home. What will they think of me when they see my extensive collection of China dogs? We have tastes for ourselves but most of us find it hard to escape the feeling that judgements of taste can be made about us. This is where taste is most affected by social judgements: will we be seen as 'classy' or merely aspirational?

My challenge in this book has been to follow taste from the inside. I have tried to see how particular sets of tastes functioned, to see how they felt, and how they attracted people to them. And to see what became of those people who took up these new tastes. To many people these were the new middle classes. To get inside the tastes of the new middle classes in the late twentieth century, we will start by visiting one of its key locations: Habitat.

2

Instant good taste: the Habitat story

The first Habitat shop opened on Monday 11 May 1964 at the junction where Fulham Road meets Sloane Avenue in London's South Kensington (figure 2.1). The 'Home' section from the *Sunday Times* had announced the opening the day before: 'Tomorrow morning, on the stroke of half-past nine, a heavy nine-foot tall oak door will pivot open and another new London shop will be in business'.[1] You get a sense of the style of the place from the door alone, with its herringbone pattern of oak slats and the door pivoting rather than being hinged. This was a shop that was sure of itself and its style. The shop was designed primarily by Oliver Gregory, who was part of the Conran Design Group, working with Terence Conran, who was the impresario overseeing the whole Habitat endeavour. Instead of using window displays to promote specific items, as was customary in department stores, the vast plateglass frontage allowed unimpeded views throughout the ground floor. The shop was laid out with 'quarry tiles on the floor, whitewashed brick walls, white-painted wooden-slatted ceilings, and spotlights'.[2] It felt a bit like a fashion boutique, but this time with furniture, bedding and kitchenware. Parts of the tiled floor were covered with sisal matting, other parts with simple monochrome carpeting. Cool jazz provided the soundtrack for improvised and informal living.

The ground floor displayed furniture and textiles as well as selected items of crockery and lighting (figure 2.2). The basement was dedicated to kitchenware and general domestic odds and ends. The journalists reporting the opening of the new shop described its interior:

> The impression on first going through the huge, light wood door is very pleasant. Grey haircord carpeting and buff tiles on the floor, untreated blueish-grey bricks or pine panelling or rough textured white plaster on the walls, and a herringbone ceiling of white-painted wooden slats. This provides a restful, neutral background for the simple furniture spiked with splashes of brilliant colour.[3]

The shop opening was reported widely and journalists like Anne Donaldson commented as much on the ambience of the shop as what it sold. Some months later in an article for *House Beautiful*, Anne Barrie continued this focus on the mood of Habitat:

2.1 Habitat, Fulham Road, London, May 1964

> In the store's airy, grey-carpeted interior, simple bentwood and cane chairs, flank deep, plushy sofas: sturdy dining tables in scrubbed natural pine are set with enamel mugs, a bright red coffee pot; bolts of fabric sit easy to see and to feel, on shallow pine-plank shelves. And all the time music swirls softly from an unseen gramophone. The atmosphere is at once both gay and restful – and somehow faintly seductive.[4]

The shop was selling more than domestic goods and modern design; it was a theatre of consumption. The sense of seduction, of an atmosphere of relaxed energy, was crucial to its performance and staging of taste.

While journalists tended to be enthusiastic about the ground-level display, they were positively enthralled when they went downstairs (figure 2.3). This is 'Our Woman's Editor' from *The Financial Times*:

> Heavy porcelain cooking ware from France: [...] Scrubbable butchers' blocks for large kitchens or garden eating: fabrics, pots and pans, shopping baskets, teak chests and lovely deep-pile rugs for barefoot sybarites, to quote Habitat: miniature Thai oil lamps, and warm pine kitchen units: all these, and literally thousands more original, simple but sophisticated, wares from any country that makes them best will keep you walking around the shop wishing you had left the cheque book at home.[5]

2.2 Habitat, Fulham Road, London, 1964. Ground floor window display – Chesterfield sofa and bent-cane, fan-back chair

The breathless listing of goods is a hallmark of the flurry of reports of Habitat's opening. But why? After all, don't most shops have a lot of items in them? And wouldn't any department store at the time also have had a similarly desirable range of goods?

It seems that what was so enticing about the shop was its light, informal atmosphere and the careful selection of items. Today, we would probably say that the selection of goods was curated. This is the *Sunday Times* picking up on the distinctive orchestration of desirable things:

> Habitat will sell not simply china, glass, fabrics, carpets and furniture – but a whole *look* in furnishing. The chances are if you like one thing, you're in the right mood and will like the lot. The stock isn't new, it's not trying to be. It's the pick of the furnishing pops all under one roof. As our photographer Terence Donovan said, 'It's the sort of shop where you go in to buy a skewer and come out with a butcher's block tucked under your arm.'[6]

This is the key to Habitat's success, and what makes it so central to the story that this book tells. Habitat wasn't about 'statement furniture' (though there were items that could fit that description) and nor was it about promoting a precise aesthetic form, but it also wasn't a shop trying to cater to all and every taste. It would become known as a 'lifestyle' shop, selling items that seemed to conjure up not just a look but a way of living. As Donovan says,

2.3 Habitat, Fulham Road, London, 1964. Basement displays

one thing leads to another: you want a pasta jar (a hard-to-find item in Britain in 1964) and you find a rug and you want that too. Each item is part of an ensemble that doesn't necessarily belong together as a consistent design. In this it was unlike G-Plan furniture, for instance. The ensemble connects as part of a way of living a more informal, improvised, and spontaneous kind of home life. Habitat revelled in inconsistency, pairing old-fashioned furniture classics such as Chesterfield settees with plastic tables. And it was inconsistency that helped amplify the feeling of informality: consistency seemed to insist too much on rules, on planning.

The shop wasn't just selling bean bags and pickling jars, they were selling moods and feelings. What Habitat offered wasn't just a selection of desirable items, but new ambiences and attitudes, a new scene for living. As we will see, something of what is suggested on the floors of Fulham Road's Habitat was also taking place on a much larger scale inside houses and within neighbourhoods across the UK during the 1960s and 1970s, and to a large extent is still with us today. We can get a better sense of that way of living by looking more closely at the way that this first store was set up and designed to function.

The can't-wait-to-get-it-home feeling

The *Sunday Times* provided a photograph of the main movers and shakers of this new venture (figure 2.4): the three directors pictured were Philip Pollock, who also had a foam furnishing company called Aerofoam (which formed the basis for a series of seating concepts sold by Habitat), Pagan Taylor (nearly always referred to in the press as ex-top-model) and the furniture designer Terence Conran (who at the time was manufacturing furniture as well as running a design company). Pagan Taylor was the managing director of the Habitat store. Catherine Currie and Sonja Jarman are named as joint managers, and Caroline Conran (Terence Conran's wife) is pictured without a working title (though she was heavily involved in setting up the kitchen departments of the store and writing publicity copy). It was Pagan Taylor who came up with the name 'Habitat' when looking for a word to replace 'home', and journalists at the time were quick to pick up on the way that habitat referred to the *natural* home of plants and animals. The term 'natural' is used throughout Habitat promotions: natural woods, natural materials, natural finishes, natural choice.

The overall feel of the new shop can be found in three overlapping elements: the eclecticism of the chosen goods; a sense of immediacy that was unusual in furniture shops; and the informality of the shop itself. Simply put, the aim of the shop was to bring the fast rhythms and spontaneous desires of the fashion industry to the much more staid and slower rhythms of the furniture and furnishings trade. The shop was going to be somewhere where young people might hang out. In Conran's words 'the bright young chicks have got to have a

2.4 'The people behind Habitat', photograph in the *Sunday Times*

red Magistretti chair the way they've got to have a Sally Tuffin and Marion Foale dress'.[7] Quickening the pace of furniture retailing and intensifying the desire for household goods was at the heart of Habitat, and as the business grew it would be at the centre of various innovations, such as 'quick assembly' items and 'Habitat by post', as well as the cultivation of what Habitat called 'that-can't-wait-to-get-it-home' feeling.

For at least a year before the opening of the Fulham Road shop, Taylor, Conran, and others had been scouring Europe and beyond for stock. Paper 'globe' lampshades were sourced from Japan, chairs and tables from Italy, wooden furniture from Scandinavia, fabrics from India, cookware from France, enamelware from Poland, and so on, as well as lots of items from across the UK:

> most of the items are British – a rare tribute when design is the criterion, though happily less rare as the years go on – but the panel shopped also in France, Italy, and Scandinavia, and as far away as Japan. No matter where they come from, though, there is this natural feeling, epitomised by country pine kitchen units and rush-seat chairs.[8]

One of the key elements was finding the sort of goods that professional chefs would buy: standard, hard-wearing, and unfussy. As Conran's biographer reports:

> For cookware, Terence turned to France for his inspiration. He had long been fascinated by a small shop in Soho called Madame Cadec, which sold French-made professional cookware. It was where the best restaurants shopped. Pagan Taylor knew a place in Les Halles in Paris, called Dehillerin, which wholesaled *matériel de cuisine*, so Terence, Caroline and Pagan went off and bought pepper-mills, pâté moulds, copper pans, pots, salad bowls and shakers, cook's knives, carafes and legumes sieves.[9]

The selection of goods demonstrates an attraction towards a certain kind of cosmopolitanism, but one marked by a dual sense of both being extremely modern and at the same time, completely timeless. The modernity was suggested by Scandinavian bentwood furnishings and Italian lacquered chairs, while the timelessness was found in products inspired by a generalised global peasant culture: rough matting, earthenware, Rattan basketware, and wooden spoons. (This was, of course, a peasant life of the imagination: an easy life in a land of plenty with all the hardship magically removed.)

What Habitat did was offer its customers pre-selected items rather than choice: instead of inviting customers to choose from a range of teapots as a department store might, it offered one, and that was a distinctly old-fashioned dark brown glazed earthenware teapot ('Granny's old brown teapot' as the first brochure would put it). The teapot wasn't any old teapot, it was – within Habitat's imagination – the *sine qua non* of teapots. It was a teapot steeped in teapot-ness. Such items seemed to suggest that variety (certainly in teapots) is unnecessary and that some objects have achieved their correct form and any alterations are simply fussiness. As Fiona MacCarthy pointed out, the originality here is not in the object but in making such objects easily available in one place: 'Here, pre-assembled and impeccably displayed, were all the things the design pundits had hunted for and gloated over all these many years: workmen's mugs and rustic cooking pots and sturdy peasant furniture, baskets, cheap pub glasses, butchers' aprons, wooden toys.'[10] Given that Conran's aim was to bring the tempo and energy of the fashion industry to furnishings, this aspect of the shop might seem odd. Presumably if you buy the 'ultimate' teapot then there is no need to change it a couple of years later, unless, that is, the idea of a teapot changes or tea drinking goes out of fashion.

Habitat was pointing in two directions at once: towards innovation and towards the ideal object. With its aims to match the fashion industry, Habitat promoted what the design critic Reyner Banham called the throw-away aesthetic, which both Banham and Conran saw as a liberation within design: 'people are not so ready to invest their all in one good piece and have it hanging round their necks for ever more'.[11] On the other hand, they are pushing the 'age old' – the only butcher's block you'll ever want or need, the one that will never go out of fashion. As well as selling 'with-it' tables and chairs, the majority of Habitat stock included the sort of objects that a child might draw in their pictures of home life. The gingham tablecloths and wooden spoons are part of a vernacular culture which, by 1964, were more likely to be found as illustrations in picture books than on the high street. To find these items would require searching junk shops or finding them in barely surviving hardware stores.

The idea of pre-selection was intended to bring together the sort of 'finds' that a shopper might chance upon in a small-town ironmonger, say, or in a furniture shop in a provincial Italian town. But instead of undergoing the long hours needed for the lucky find, this had now been successfully outsourced to Habitat. For Pagan Taylor the 'find' was at the centre of Habitat: 'Every big store has its quota of "finds" – beautiful, useful things for the home – but not everyone has the time or the experience to uncover them. We are determined that each item in Habitat will be a "find" in itself'.[12] Habitat, then, was nothing but finds. And this sense of turning happenstance into convenience is another aspect where the tempo of shopping is speeded up: 'We hope we have taken the foot slogging out of shopping by assembling a wise selection of unusual and top-quality goods under one roof. It has taken us a year to complete this pre-digested shopping programme'.[13] The pre-sorted, the curated, offers an immediacy to taste; here is everything you could hope to come across in your search, all collected together with no distractions. Taylor admitted that taking the hard work out of taste could sound like a bad thing: 'friends are already describing this operation as "instant good taste". I don't like the phrase, but I suppose it is roughly descriptive of what Habitat aims to do'.[14]

The dynamic between new, innovative seating, for instance, and age-old 'rustic' objects was played out in the way that the shop was organised. For furniture, the layout was set up to mimic the arrangements that might take place in homes across the country (an aspect of display that would be fully realised by IKEA whose displays look like sets for TV dramas). In contrast the 'standardised objects' (the age-old wooden spoons, and the like) would be displayed as if they were still at the warehouse: stacked up in what Habitat would call 'dump displays' (figure 2.5). This is Maurice Libby remembering the Habitat display ethos: 'None of us could understand why there were these enormously deep shelves that were eighteen inches deep and three feet wide. Terence would go into a kind of trance trying to convey to us the unbelievable thrill he'd had in the big French wholesalers. We didn't know what he was talking about. He said, "I want this whole shelf full of glasses," and I realized he meant all the same'.[15] This is an aesthetics of abundance, combining the large-scale repetitiousness of industry with goods often associated with handmade craft.

The design journalist Fiona MacCarthy recognised immediately that what was so seductive about Habitat were the new rhythms it bought to domestic shopping, rather than the relatively ordinary objects that were for sale:

> Conran has perceptively exploited urban restlessness. In Habitat, things happen almost anywhere you look. Glasses and steak knives and cooking pots pile up: dozens of dolls sit in pyramids of chairs: folksy wicker baskets tilt from side to side with loads of striped and checked and flowered Conran hurdy-gurdy fabrics. The merchandise is ordinary and fairly cheap. But its setting and its build-up, the frenzy all around it, makes it seem more covetable, gives it its mystique.[16]

As the writer Barry Curtis put it, the shop 'combined the informality of the boutique with the abundance of a warehouse'[17] and this new energy brought a new lease of life to objects that might otherwise have appeared old-fashioned and drab. The dump display is the warehouse mystique that MacCarthy describes, and it suggests that items have achieved, if not their ideal form, then their most 'tasteful' state. Objects are selected because they *feel* right: the almost kitsch attraction to 'Granny's old brown teapot' becomes newly energised when it combines the singularity of the lucky find with the appeal of mass standardisation.

Habitat was aimed primarily at a young clientele who were being initiated into a world of understated and affordable furnishings as well as the moods and behaviours that went with them. In naming this clientele in 1964 Habitat were keen to tell us who they were in broad, dynamic strokes. Their first press statements name them as 'young moderns': 'We aim to reach the young moderns with lively tastes – and we don't believe they will be confined to the professional classes'.[18] The nuance here is telling: the young moderns may or may not be from the professional classes, but they will have lively tastes. The class dimension of this is uncertain but is clearly not addressing a traditional middle-class audience, if by traditional we mean a class of professionals with the opposite of 'lively tastes'. Everything is set up for the young moderns who are coupling-up and settling down: 'we believe young marrieds be prominent among our customers and special help and advice with wedding lists is available. An H.P. scheme has been devised to help couples setting up home for the first time, to equip their household with the best possible items on the easiest possible terms'.[19] These 'young marrieds' who are also 'young moderns' are being invited by Habitat to a style of life: 'we don't claim to have a monopoly of goods which cannot be found elsewhere', says Pagan Taylor. 'But we do believe that we have assembled the pick of

2.5 Dump display of the chicken brick

the props for comfortable, elegant living from a wide area, in a way which has never been done before'.[20] Modern, elegant, comfortable are the watch words for the young people addressed by Habitat in 1964.

I will have more to say about the class dimensions of who all this is aimed at as we go through the book. For the moment, though, let's go with 'young moderns' as the audience and clientele for this taste, but with a sceptical sense that these young moderns are a little unknown, a little unfocused as a group. They are, to some degree at least, socially mobile – either slipping down (purposefully or not) from their parents' class (or at least shrugging off elements of that culture with its aspirations of heavy furniture and durable style) or finding themselves in a new and different world from a previous generation. This was, after all, for many people just that – 'a different world' – with new kinds of work in new industries (chemical and electronics) and occupations such as social work and the expanded world of teaching. An expanding middling world of technicians, of nurses, of social workers, whose class identity can't simply fit with the nineteenth-century world of either working class or middle class. Whatever the actual clientele of Habitat in 1964, the shop in Fulham Road was an immediate, albeit moderate, success. Soon though, it was going to be everywhere.

Taking over the high street

The rise of Habitat was exponential and with that came various changes in direction. Habitat quickly moved from being a boutique operation to becoming a chain store, the equivalent of a supermarket of furniture and household goods. In 1964 Conran described Habitat 'as the Mary Quant of the furnishing world';[21] by the 1970s he was comparing Habitat to the supermarket chain Sainsburys.[22] In December 1970, the *Guardian* ran an article titled 'The Marks and Sparks of instant furniture?' with the by-line by Richard Carr on 'the future of Habitat, a retail business which, for a certain section of the middle class, has become a way of life'.[23] Changes in scale allowed Habitat to increase its range of goods, to provide new ranges of items, and to spearhead what was to become a flat-pack revolution.

The second Habitat shop appeared in central London, on Tottenham Court Road next to the furniture store Heals towards the end of 1966. Whereas the Fulham Road shop had been relatively small, and was in what was then a residential district of London, the new shop was much larger as well as being in a district famous for furniture, where a shop like Habitat could expect a high level of passing foot traffic. The new shop introduced important new items alongside what was already familiar in Fulham Road. The *Observer* immediately smelt the 'packeted Provençal herbs, pungent and aromatic' and noted the 'colourful square floor cushions for lounging on, moulded fiberglass low tables by Magistretti in shiny black, white or red, and a marvel of a construction in a soft hide science-fiction chair from Finland which spins round at a touch and seems to support you floating in space'.[24] It might be the bright red fibreglass table that tempts you into the shop, but it is more than likely that it will be an item of cookware that you will leave with (paid for or not).[25] The new

Tottenham Court Road store vastly extended the emphasis on the kitchen, introducing the terracotta 'chicken brick' (figure 2.5) ('it's a new idea over here but the Italians have been doing it for centuries') as well as range of grocery items; 'a collection of essential aids to cooking on sale from the marble-topped Herb and Food counter. There will be good olive oil, leaf gelatine, rock salt, and other useful things that are hard to find'.[26] The Tottenham Court Road store also introduced a new mezzanine area dedicated to high-end electronics: stereo music systems by Braun and Bang & Olufsen, and portable mini-TVs by Sony.

After that, new shops came in thick and fast. In 1967 two new Habitats arrived: one in Manchester in September and another in Kingston in November. By 1975 there were twenty-five shops, fairly evenly spread across England (including Birmingham, Bolton, Coventry, Leicester and Liverpool), with one in Scotland (figure 2.6). Further shops were added in Scotland (Edinburgh in 1978, Aberdeen in 1981) and in Wales (Cardiff in 1976). By 1985 there were fifty stores in the UK, twenty-three stores in France and Belgium, and a further eight shops in Japan and eight in the USA (trading under the name 'Conran'). In some respects, the mid-1980s marks the high watermark of Habitat as well as the beginning of a slow decline in its fortunes: the fifty stores that were there in 1985 would become thirty-seven stores by 1993. Between these two dates, a new force in domestic retail came to Britain: 1987 is the year that the first IKEA arrived in the UK.

Journalists had picked up on the similarities between IKEA and Habitat from the early 1970s and saw Conran as copying the older Swedish company in his expansion of the brand: 'Though Conran started out with the idea of selling his own furniture on his own terms, he now sees Habitat as an organisation with a much larger role, indeed as a kind of

2.6 Habitat in Glasgow

Marks and Spencer of the furniture world. In Sweden such a position is held by IKEA'.[27] The move from boutique to household name also required a change in production and a greater emphasis on flat-pack furniture:

> just as M & S [Marks and Spencer] sells garments under its St Michael label which are made by independent manufacturers but to its own, tightly controlled standards, so Conran is now looking for a group of furniture manufacturers to work with him in the same way. They will be asked to produce furniture to his own designs which will be knocked down, packed flat and sold largely by mail order.
>
> The furniture must be flexible, so that ideally its components can be used in several different ways, and similarly the production lines must be able to handle both small batches and long runs, so that they can respond quickly to the changing pattern of orders. The aim is to cut the high retail mark-up.[28]

As a business venture within the furniture trade Habitat was a radical departure from the usual way that furniture was sold in Britain.

It is the innovations of flexibility and speed that are particularly worth noting. The first of these is the way that Habitat offered a variety of ways for their customers to communicate with them about purchases. 'Habitat by phone' was one part of this. In 1969 Habitat had an ill-fated (and very short-lived) merger with the stationary retailers Ryman, and that same year they introduced a 'Habitat by Post' service, which also kickstarted the much more extensive and complete use of catalogues: 'Next month, Habitat by Post, one of the glossiest mail order operations to date, will be launched. From now on you will be able to order your complete tasteful bentwood environment without leaving your trendy bentwood rocking chair'.[29] Again, the mail order business was not new, but it was an important aspect of Habitat's new scale. The expansion via mail order was an outcome of the acquisition of the furniture manufacturers Lupton Morton (the one positive outcome of the Ryman merger) who specialised in office furniture and relatively cheap flat-pack furniture aimed at students, who represented an expanding market.

In retrospect, acquiring Lupton Morton was decisive for Habitat. It was Lupton Morton's experience in making furniture that could be assembled at home or in offices that would make a significant contribution to the shape that Habitat would take in the 1970s. Lupton Morton was also responsible for one of the most popular ranges of cheap furnishings in the 1970s – the Campus range – which could be sent by post to your home or picked up from Lupton Morton's Wallingford warehouse in Berkshire, which would become the site of Habitat's largest 'out of town' store. In a press release from 1970, Habitat announced their new range of 'KD' furniture: 'This is the first time ever, anywhere in England, that a chain of retail stores is offering a large range of KD furniture packed flat in "carry-homeable" cartons, for customers to satisfy instantly that "can't wait to get it home feeling"'.[30] KD stood for 'knocked down' furniture that could then be reassembled with QA – quick assembly. The terminology never really caught on, and this way of producing and selling became better known as 'flat pack' furniture. It is all about a feeling – a 'can't

2.7 That 'Can't wait to get it home feeling', Habitat catalogue, 1980

wait to get it home feeling' (see figure 2.7). 'The first Saturday our Manchester store had its take-away section', writes Habitat's publicity team, 'ten three-seat sofas plus lots of other packaged furniture were carted away by instantly satisfied customers'.[31]

If Habitat began life as offering 'instant good taste', it would spend the next two decades working out ways to increase the speed of immediate gratification. As the number of stores mounted up, the size of them increased, with more and more offering 'carry home' furniture. In a world dominated by online stores like Amazon it is hard to recapture what this new form of instantaneousness must have felt like. Before Habitat existed, buying new furniture in Britain meant visiting a shop, often with only a few items in store, getting an appointment with a salesman (and they were mostly men) who would take you through their catalogue. Once you had chosen your item or items you would have to wait for them to be built, which might take weeks or months. Habitat's flat-pack furniture came with the energy of the immediate. But the feeling of 'nowness', of immediacy, wasn't just an aspect of a new mode of buying furniture, it was there in the chairs, tables, and sofas.

These, too, had a feeling of immediate presence, of belonging to the moment rather than to a tradition.

Catalogue culture

The changing character of Habitat was easy to see in the way it promoted its wares and communicated its specific attitude to modern life. Publicity is key to any retail enterprise, but it was especially crucial to the growth of Habitat. The very first brochure for the shop was a large, folded broadsheet produced in 1966 for the opening of the Tottenham Court Road shop. In monochrome, it boasted hand-drawn illustrations by Juliet Glynn Smith and typed copy by Caroline Conran (figure 2.8). The graphic style was faux-naïve while the writing was jokey: 'what a grind – pepper mills from France'; 'a battery of best birch spoons'; 'get stewed up with this black iron casserole'. The mood was light and folksy.

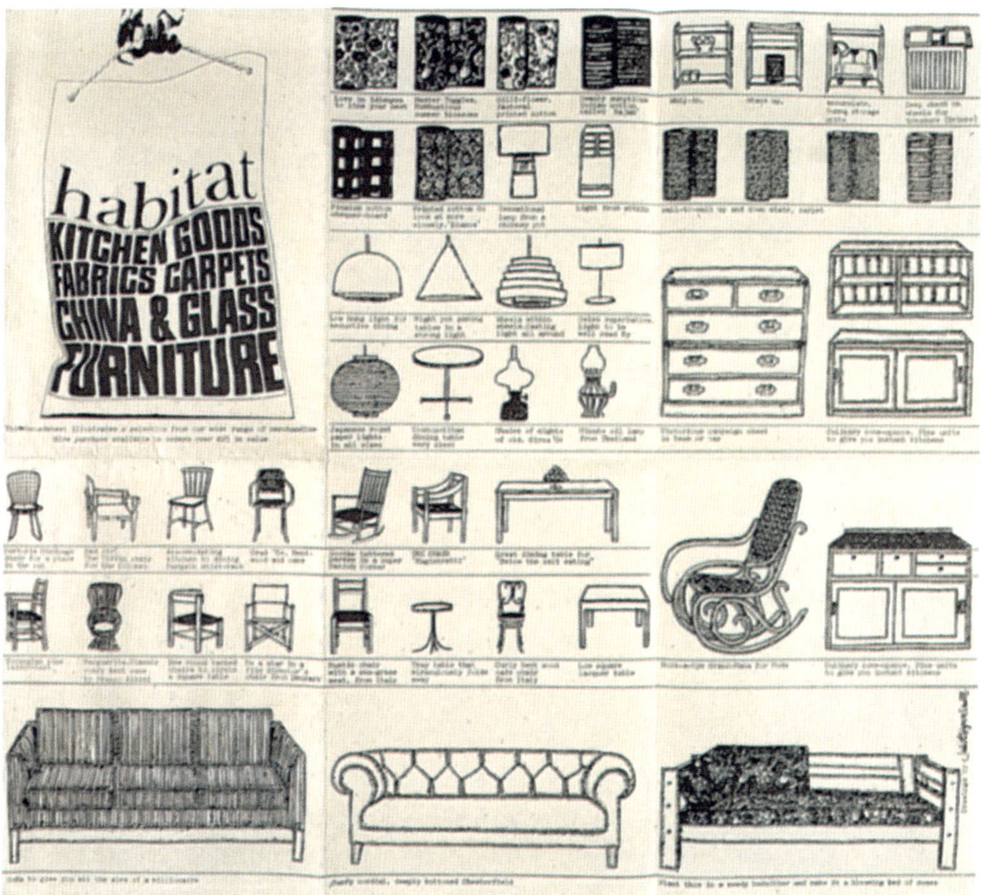

2.8 1966 Broadsheet brochure by Juliet Glynn Smith and Caroline Conran

It looked a bit amateur, a bit crafty. The 1969 union with Lupton Morton led immediately to the *Creative Living* catalogue, which was prepared for the mail order aspect of Habitat, but also led to what from 1971 became an annual catalogue (figures 2.9 and 2.10). This was a much glossier and professional affair, part way between a compendium of available items and a lifestyle magazine offering advice, design ideas, and dream images of a life of youthful sensuality. The catalogue became a way for Habitat to stage its idea of the 'good life' in a way that would capture people's imaginations more fully, away from the shop.

Just as the opening of each new store became an event to be discussed in newspapers and colour supplements, so too did the release of the annual Habitat catalogue. In February 1973 *The Times* could announce that 'this week saw one of the eagerly anticipated events in the British furnishing calender [*sic*] – the appearance of the new Habitat catalogue', and would go on to describe its contents: 'this year it contains – quite apart from the equivalent of a magazine full of merchandise and furnishing ideas – an eight-page, illustrated stitch-by-stitch guide to making home furnishings: blinds, curtains, loose covers, bed covers'.[32] The annual Habitat catalogue was a mixture of interior scenes featuring Habitat furnishings, photographs of individual items, examples of textiles and wallpapers, and various 'advice' sections. These advice sections were often 'how-to' guides (for instance 'a guide to baking bread', 'making good coffee', 'the art of tempura', 'how best to use your lighting', and so on) but could also include articles with a historical flavour such as 'A Look Back at the Bauhaus'.[33] The 'how-to' guides tended to mix the promotion of Habitat items with more general information. If the annual catalogue was an institution by 1973 (part of the British furnishing calendar), then it had worked fast, because the 1973 catalogue was only the third catalogue produced in the classic annual format.

Across the decades, the catalogues demonstrated changing fashions in both home-furnishings and in the art of publicity. As historical documents, they chart the comings and goings (the durability or not) of household fashions: the longevity of wooden spoons, for instance, and the much briefer life of smoked-glass coffee tables. They also show the changing market position of Habitat. It is, for instance, noticeable that as IKEA began to dominate the household goods market in the UK (by the early 1990s), Habitat rebranded itself again as a 'designer-led' high fashion shop and it did this by redesigning the catalogue. By the end of the 1990s, the Habitat catalogue looked more like an up-market design magazine than the classic catalogues of the 1970s and 1980s: gone are the glossy pages and the photographs brimming with goods that could be purchased at the stores; in its place, are matt pages of studied 'coolness', where the images themselves are stylish, often with a shallow depth-of-field that emphasises, for instance, the gloss of an old wooden floor rather than the commodities being sold.

The 1970s and 1980s was the period when Habitat had its strongest presence within domestic retailing in the UK and when the catalogue held its biggest cultural importance. As soon as the catalogue achieved its mature form in 1971 (with full colour photography, tableaux of domestic interiors, domestic advice sections, and miscellaneous photographs of

2.9 The Habitat annual catalogue 1971, Winter/Autumn supplement

2.10 From Habitat, Autumn and Christmas Catalogue 1971. The foreground features Scoop seating and Magistretti tables. The background includes 'basic' range desk and drawers, with two hard plastic wall pockets on the back wall. The duvet on the bed would still have been a novelty in 1971

household items), it was being promoted as something more than a catalogue of retail items. With the launch of the second annual catalogue in 1972, Habitat announced: 'Last year we gave away nearly 800,000 Habitat catalogues. They've become well-thumbed, worn-out collector's items, used over and over again as a definitive guide to home furnishings'.[34] By 1981, by which time the catalogue was no longer free, but could be purchased in any high-street newsagent (as well as in the stores), Habitat were selling 1,125,000 catalogues annually, and it was clear to Conran that 'the catalogues are also bought as a glossy interior design magazine providing new ideas'.[35] In this sense the catalogue comes to be seen as a 'lifestyle guide': a resource for learning how to live the life being promoted by Habitat. It is therefore a key site for finding the characteristics of that life.

The catalogue takes the various items that can be bought at Habitat and weaves them together into a world. A world of taste and feeling. It is a sort of living demonstration of what life could be like if you took the furniture out of the virtual world of the shop and into reality. For example, in the 1977–78 catalogue, the stage sets for living the Habitat life are found both in the clean, neutral spaces of the contemporary interior but also in the rural settings of Southern France (figures 2.11 and 2.12). While the duvet-wielding man and the manicuring woman might not be the same people participating in the al fresco dining scene, they exist in the same Habitat universe. There is an implied continuity between the getting ready for work in the first scene and the fun times being had in the second scene. The catalogue invites us, the reader, to make connections between the images. The preparation for the working day is actually not an overture for work (that wouldn't be fun), but a prelude for a life of spontaneous sociability and easy living outside of working hours. Housework, like making beds and cooking, are miraculously shrunk into momentary displays of sensual enjoyment, while the labour of washing, changing duvet covers and preparing food are easily forgotten. The classroom or the newsroom, the hospital or the laboratory are, of course, not there (we wouldn't expect them to be). Work, even domestic labour, is invisible. The only time we see it is in the home office (figure 2.13), and there the main form of work seems to be graphic design, probably a commission destined for a Habitat catalogue. In the world of Habitat, home isn't a haven for relaxation and renewal, a neutral zone away from work. Here home is everything – it is where you can be you.

The Habitat effect

Habitat helped to change the landscape of taste within the UK, particularly in the 1960s and 1970s. To what degree it is hard to say. There was obviously a class dimension to this which changed across the years: its reach was broadest in the late 1960s and through the 1970s and into the 1980s when Habitat was still growing and before it began to reassert itself as a high-end design shop as it competed with the roll-out of IKEA outlets from the end of the 1980s. This is not to say that Habitat and its catalogues dictated what a country (or a section of that country) thought of as good or bad taste, but that it made a certain taste or set of tastes newly and widely available. Habitat can be thought of as a purveyor and conveyor of taste; it produced a new domestic imagination. It wasn't a design revolution, but it was part of a taste transformation, and the difference is important. But it did more than fill houses with goods, it altered how people felt about furnishings irrespective of whether they were actually bought from Habitat. Looking back from the present it is impossible to look at this uncritically; after all the very idea of bringing 'fast-fashion' and

2.11 Habitat catalogue, 1977–78, p. 80, 'with duvet, sheet and pillows in Kimono, a grey and cream check with more than a whisper of Oriental charm'

2.12 Habitat catalogue, 1977–78, p. 96, 'Folding chair/cane seat. Tablecloth, tile print'

2.13 Habitat catalogue, 1975, p. 45, 'A very professional draughtsman's table or drawing desk. Lay the top flat and use it as a table'

the 'throw-away aesthetic' to the world of furnishing is environmentally disastrous. But my approach is less about judging the environmental ethics of the new tastes and more about seeing how these new tastes changed what it felt like to live in modern Britain.

The great project of Habitat (at least in its years of growth) was about extending an idea of 'good taste' to a much larger demographic than had previously been the case. Such a process could be called a *democratisation of taste*, but we need to tread carefully here. What we may be seeing is not something 'democratic' (whatever that could mean in this context) but a general expansion of the way that class and taste are being connected. If nothing else, Habitat was an enormously profitable enterprise with a vested interest in trying to expand its clientele. Taste, in the world of Habitat, can be seen as an active ingredient in both broadening and loosening the *feeling* of class for an expanding middling class. That class (potentially at least) could stretch from the young aspiring offsprings of the working class to those floating within the broad category of the middle classes. It did this by focusing on the domestic front as *the* realm for social life, and the realm of social identity.

From the perspective of Habitat, the project was presented as something that was socially progressive. Talking in 1964, Conran would claim that:

> five years ago, good taste meant a rosewood dining table, eight dining chairs and rosewood sideboard to match, costing £600. If you couldn't afford that, you simply didn't have good taste. But all that is changing now. Today good taste can mean a simple wooden table and half a dozen bentwood chairs, for as little as £50. Suddenly, it's within everyone's reach.[36]

In 1964 £50 was not a negligible sum. More importantly, and as we have already seen, the idea of 'good taste' has always been a deeply contested terrain. While Habitat did, particularly in the 1970s, provide inexpensive goods that were associated with 'good modern design', for those whose idea of 'good taste' meant Queen Anne dining tables and eighteenth-century hunting prints, Habitat would never be good taste. It would never reach those for whom 'taste' meant solid comfort and continuity, who associated taste with tradition (working-class traditions, or middle-class ones). Yet this shouldn't stop us recognising the social ambitions of Habitat and looking more broadly at the sort of changes in sensibility that the chain was involved with.

For Conran, the shop was on a mission: 'My whole attitude to life was [...] why shouldn't design be something that is available to the entire community? The mood in England in those postwar years was that we had an opportunity to reshape the world'.[37] The question of who was included in 'the entire community' is answered in 1973 when Conran is responding to criticisms that the shop was aimed primarily at affluent young 'trendies':

> Many people still think of Habitat as a shop for the young – or even just the higher-income-bracket young. 'Certainly our customers are much younger than the majority of customers in other furnishing shops', says Mr Conran, 'but we particularly dislike being thought of as a young "trendy" organization. We would much prefer to be thought of as High Street furniture store selling good, solid-citizen furniture'.[38]

It is hard not to catch the scent here of the same postwar spirit that established the welfare state. The difference is, of course, that while the National Health Service, was a non-profit, public institution, Habitat was a financial corporation answerable to shareholders and the requirements of capitalist expansion. Yet to ignore the rhetoric of 'solid-citizen furniture', or to see it as merely marketing talk would be to miss something essential to the Habitat sensibility, namely its refusal of a world of 'high-style' in favour of something that felt more sociable, more in tune with the practical life of people. This is Conran talking in 1968: 'if high-style design does the job as well as the traditional shape, but 95 times more expensively – what is the point of buying high design? [...] Perhaps this is why Habitat kitchen basements tend to look rustic'.[39] The rustic, for Conran, was a commitment to 'solid-citizen furniture'. Whether the 'rustic' that was peddled by Habitat was experienced as authentic or not (and this will be something I'll come back to), what matters here is that it was treated as a way of living the 'solid-citizen' aesthetic. Critics like Fiona MacCarthy didn't buy it: 'The debt to Arts and Crafts was altogether obvious. But where Arts and Crafts were genuine (or almost), this was phoney: a brilliant and timely commercial pastiche'.[40] For MacCarthy, the counterfeit ruralism of Habitat was something to critique; for one section of the buying public, it was something to embrace.

Paradoxically there is an aspect of the Habitat look which the Habitat shops would never be able to cater for. To get the look meant including things that weren't new, it meant including the obviously battered and discarded. This is the aspect that requires you to go out scouring junk shops and markets. This part of the look can be reproduced on a much tighter budget. This part of the look is an aesthetic of austerity that was often deployed (through necessity as much as through specific choice) by a poorer, bohemian class who were squatting and setting up communes, who were living austerity as a calculated refusal of the sort of commercialism and consumerism that Habitat represented. This 'look' is another dimension of the taste promoted by Habitat. It was there not just in the apartments of the young moderns but could be found in all sorts of more experimental modes of living.

When the Manchester branch of Habitat (the first branch outside greater London) opened in 1967, the *Sunday Telegraph* assessed the growing impact of the brand:

> It seems difficult now to recollect what the furnishing scene was like before Terence Conran and, later, Habitat arrived, so much do they now [... form] part of what is best in our current design world. Without being particularly avant-garde or wildly inventive they have supplied the sort of simple, cheerful and bright furniture, fabrics and other merchandise that was so hard, if not impossible, to find before. There is nothing 'difficult' about Habitat merchandise – it never takes the breath away or has one wondering whether it is in advance of its times. It is, on the whole, immediately pleasing and eminently liveable-with.[41]

That sense of immediacy and ease, of cheerfulness and simplicity is crucial to Habitat's success. It is also key to the social world that Habitat tastes wants to produce: a world of cheerful informality.

The Habitat effect reached far beyond the legions of loyal shoppers, and beyond the enthusiastic readers of the annual catalogue. The mid-1970s marked a moment when Habitat was still expanding rapidly and innovating consistently, and before the turn to a Laura Ashley-directed conservativism of the 1980s that echoed the rise of Thatcherism and the 'right to buy' housing policies. Three writers in particular offer useful cultural assessments of the Habitat effect in the mid-1970s. The first is the novelist Angela Carter, who draws out the social implications of Habitat, the second is the design educator Peter Lloyd Jones, and the third (though I will discuss his assessment at other points in this book) is the travel writer Jonathan Raban.

Angela Carter's essay was written for the magazine *New Society* (a magazine designed to popularise social science for informed social commentary)[42] and treats the shop as a thoroughly social phenomenon. While she mainly sees Habitat as symptomatic of a new order of consumer culture aimed at social advancement and pandering to a narcissism, she also notes how different the shops were from what went before:

> The shops are the antithesis of the department store, with its hushed decorum and imposing, beadle-like, senior counter-jumpers, where merchandise is mediated between the firm and you by supercilious assistants who fetch items from locked glass cases, items known only to themselves, and spread them out on counters which mark the division between buyer and seller with absolute precision. There is no sense of a ritual exchange in a Habitat shop.
>
> The staff, usually young, wearing name tags, negotiate with the informally clad customers on friendly, easy terms. Merchandising is democratised. There is music, a pleasant sense of subdued bustle. Everything for sale may be felt, handled, touched; no locked showcases. The goods are displayed with such reckless prodigality it is easy to forget they have to be paid for.[43]

This new informality in shopping is hard to see as distinct or revolutionary today. It is how we expect shops to be. It is only, perhaps, when we stumble into a high-end jeweller or an exclusive art gallery that we catch a whiff of what furniture shopping used to be like.

The casual informality infusing shopping was part of a broad social change that probably affected most people but was experienced most keenly by some of the middle classes. 'Habitat purchasers', wrote Carter, 'are not over-awed by their own dining-room suites. They will live *with* their furniture, not alongside it – as my mother did. My mother always thought her mahogany table was too good to use *as* a table. It inhabited the rarely used dining-room like a rich lodger'.[44] This sense of furnishing not being part of everyday life is not something that would be said about many objects in a working-class household, though it is certainly applicable to the idea of a parlour 'kept for best'. Carter is making a deliberate point that something is happening within middle-class culture, which might include an expanding lower middle class imagined as the new middle class. Living 'alongside' the furniture of a house is to treat it primarily as a symbol of something (of tradition, of family, of status); to live with your furniture is to be drawn into their sensual world. It might be a world of rush matting and rustic pots, or it might be a world of floor cushions and Provençal herbs. What I think Habitat did bring about for many middle-class households was a shift from the home as place of endless rules about manners to a space where the emphasis was on informality and improvisations. Of course, there is nothing to stop dictatorial dads demanding obedience to some arcane set of rules of behaviour when a child is sprawled out on a bean bag rather than sitting upright at a desk. But my guess is that it is harder.

The other writer worth noting here is Peter Lloyd Jones who was, at the time, head of Three-Dimensional Design at Kingston Polytechnic (which would become Kingston University in 1992). He will go on to write *Taste Today*, but in 1977 he is arguing something similar to Angela Carter: he is noting how Habitat is draining the pretentiousness out of furnishings:

> the overall perkiness disarms that element of portentous self-regard which often makes 'high' design difficult to combine easily with the more prosaic bric-à-brac that most of us live with. No doubt the market for this kind of merchandise *is* found predominantly among limited sectors of the new middle class but, for all that, the new trendies are not simply the old social climbers. The game is more open than that.[45]

There will be more to say about 'the new middle classes' throughout this book, but here let us note that traditional associations of taste are wearing thin. For example, in modernist design the high-minded aspects that used to drive design are less important now: a Breuer chair, for example, no longer has the weight of design hygiene behind it and all the morality that goes with that. And those furnishings that are passed down between generations, insisting on cultural continuity, have become outdated and unnecessary in a world of modern, cheap, accessible goods: furniture can have the look of tradition without the ageing that goes with it. Habitat hasn't the weight of high design nor the depth of the sort of cultural heritage noted by people like Richard Hoggart about traditional working-class interiors. This is furnishing that has lost weight, has become culturally thinner. But if that suggests a loss of tradition, there was also another way of looking at this, as something like a liberation, a lightness. It is a move from a hierarchy of taste to something more horizontal – a cultural flattening. This is furnishing that isn't an end in itself but is part of a new way of living.

The sense that Habitat was everywhere is, of course, a mistake. What matters for this book is that Habitat allowed one particular class or group to become visible in new ways. We could say that Habitat was a response to changing class identities. Or we could say, more strongly, that it had a hand in changing those identities. We can say that a section within society no longer had the aspirations of the old middle classes who sought to mimic upper-class tastes. The new middle class – those who liked wine but would never think of decanting it – were being fashioned in the same cauldron that was producing Habitat. Habitat was never a solution to class culture – it could never simply overcome it – but it could be a testing ground for seeing how far class culture could and had changed. For some it was not too far at all. As one correspondent to the *Guardian* put it:

> I hate to be just an old left puritan but the assumption that Habitat (or its emulators) has found its way into all our homes is the kind of fatuous thing that could only be written by a comparatively rich, middle class southerner (or someone affecting that style). To call Conran (talented though he may be) a 'good revolutionary' is the kind of cant that deepens divisions whilst pretending to be all things to all men.[46]

Other writers were more snobbish about Habitat and described it as a 'Mecca of nouveau-riche good taste'.[47] Conran's assessment of Habitat a few years after opening it is probably right:

> I opened Habitat in 1964 to sell my furniture and practical decorating ideas to an energetic enterprising section of the public which had previously been overlooked. These people want well-made attractive furniture at a reasonable price, which is related in feeling to the informal lives they lead and the places they live in. They accept the fact that their lives and tastes will change.[48]

Habitat features throughout this book. But for now, let us move on and look more broadly at how a 'good life' that Habitat was contributing to was being imagined and realised in the 1960s and 1970s.

3
The good life

The historian and magazine editor, Juliet Gardiner, grew up in the market town of Hemel Hempstead, in Hertfordshire, during the late 1940s and 1950s, and left home when she was sixteen to live in Bristol. In 1961, at the age of seventeen, she married the journalist and future Conservative politician, George Gardiner. In 1963, the young marrieds bought a small house in Blackheath, in London. It was on a Span Housing estate similar to the houses in figure 3.1. It was here that Gardiner felt she had become, in some vague, unspecifiable way, middle class. Span Housing combined a sense of moderate or light modernism – flat roofs, no decorative features – with the garden city ethos intended to encourage neighbourliness, such as shared front gardens. The Gardiners moved into an estate with 'graphic designers, an academic, teachers, social workers (senior pay grade, presumably), a solicitor, a Labour MP, a couple of businessmen, an accountant, a potter and a boat designer'.[1] Some of these professions were securely middle class in the 1960s, while others – graphic designers and social workers – hadn't yet gained the patina that went with 'proper' middle-class professions, and instead suggested the more uncertain status of the new middle classes. But what adds to the ambience of the estate was the fact that all the householders were young, and that they all had a similar interior design style.

The way that Gardiner describes the life of the Span Housing estate suggests that all the occupants shared similar tastes:

> we borrowed each other's sewing machines and ran up curtains. Eschewing pelmets in favour of Silent Gliss near-invisible rails, we chose plain linen or folk-weave striped fabric from Heal's or Dunn's of Bromley, or Lucienne Day fabrics [...] or hung white Venetian blinds which were a chore to dust. We saved up for sturdy, rush-seated lacquered Italian Magistretti chairs, rescued the scrubbed pine kitchen tables our mothers had discarded in favour of wipeable patterned Formica – at least I did.[2]

We will need to come back to this discarded pine kitchen table in more detail in a moment, but for now I want to note this mixing of old and new – new modern fabrics; old, discarded tables. As we have already seen with Habitat, the taste that is emerging in the 1960s for the 'young moderns' is far from narrow: it works to incorporate the old with the new, the age-old wooden spoon with the immaculately new. The incorporation of the 'old' is an

3.1 Span Housing Estate, Blackheath

important feature: 'many of us could not entirely disregard the charm of Victoriana – in strict moderation – with the odd cachepot holding a palm rather than an aspidistra, even a pair of white Staffordshire dog figurines, which I still treasure but which were hard to place since there was no call for mantelpieces in a Span house'.[3]

This eclecticism will be central to understanding the tastes and lifestyles of an expanding new middle class. One of the things to note is that Staffordshire dog figurines and cachepots aren't there as *antiques* (the sort of thing that Angela Carter's mother might have shared a house with), they are there as a bit of fun, a charming addition, an eccentric conversation piece. This is not to say that they couldn't also be antiques, but they don't function in this way, either in monetary terms or in terms of the sort of reverence that the word 'antique' might suggest. The Victoriana that the 'new moderns' particularly went for includes old enamel adverts promoting Bovril (also known as 'beef tea'), Colman's mustard, and Wills' cigarettes, as well as various brands of tea, which gave off a whiff of colonial era kitsch. But if Victoriana could supply the bric-à-brac, it couldn't supply the main 'look':

> most of us painted our interior walls white, with an accent colour in each room – though some found it a bridge too far to move on from magnolia. Thames Green, a sludgy greenery-yallery colour – as the name suggests the polluted Thames would be – was the colour du jour, followed by 'moody aubergine'. Or we covered a wall in hessian and bought a colourful Casa Pupo Spanish rug, or a pile rug with a design of circles and squares which owed a nod to the paintings of Joan Miró or Kandinsky, to lie on the polished herringbone parquet floor with underfloor heating.[4]

Victoriana, or the inclusion of other period elements – which in older houses would include picking out and emphasising what estate agents would learn to call 'period features' – was not intended to make the home look Victorian: it was there precisely to dent the clinical blankness that was often associated with high modernism. The moderate modernism favoured by Habitat and their enthusiastic clientele made an optimistic nod to the future, which was offset with the inclusion of a purposefully quirky past. The eclecticism espoused by Gardiner and her cohort, simultaneously sought to avoid the overly deodorised world of modernism, without allowing the musty smell of heritage much houseroom.

Gardiner's memoir also recounts the relationship between this interior look and the sort of holidays that they went on. They, like many other middle-class young marrieds, were starting to holiday in France, and part of the pleasure of such trips would be bringing 'finds' home:

> We would come back with strings of garlic, blue enamel house numbers, wine glasses, carafes, Provençal earthenware casseroles [...]. So we were more than ripe for Terence Conran's Habitat when the first one opened in the Fulham Road in 1964. Its most famous early merchandise was undoubtedly the earthenware chicken brick, which was to become a symbol of what we imagined was a new idiom of continental peasant cookery, using dried herbs and creating what was known as *jus* rather than making Bisto gravy to accompany every meat dish to add a ubiquitous flavour to mince.[5]

The sort of shopping sprees that Pagan Taylor and Terence Conran had undertaken to collect items for Habitat was a scaled-up version of what young people, particularly those who wanted to embrace a world geared to informality, pleasure, and continental rhythms, were already doing. Driving to France in French cars – Renault 4s and Citroën 2CVs – feasting on fresh baguettes, unusual cheeses, and plenty of cheap wine and then returning with a haul of authentic goods was what the summer was all about. Well, it was for these young moderns. For these people, who had already experienced a different lifestyle in France, Italy, or Spain, going to shop in Habitat wasn't necessarily a totally new experience, but it was a convenient one that was new to the British high street. But Gardiner's experience, particularly in incorporating Victoriana and old scrubbed pine tables, suggests that Habitat was never going to be able to supply the full feeling of this taste. It would need something else. And this is what Conran partly supplied in 1974 with the publication of *The House Book.*

The 'good life', as it was being imagined in the 1960s and 1970s, set about delivering a taste for domestic ease, for authentic foods, for accessible fashions, even for hobbies that had once seemed to belong only to the well-heeled, to as many people as possible. It saw itself as a democratic mission. And as a mission it had the potential to alter how class and gender were lived. It was a democracy of sorts: all that was required was a home of your own and a belief in consumerism – oh, and a well-paid job. But even if you didn't quite have the house, the belief, or the job, versions of the 'good life' could still be approximated.

Rustic, modern, eclectic

There was always going to be a contradiction between modern retailing and the sort of rustic-urbanism taste that was emerging in the 1960s. Looking back on Habitat, Terence Conran remembers that 'we were keen to show that the Habitat lifestyle was not about buying everything new and from us, but also about mixing things and expressing one's own personality'.[6] For Habitat, as a shop, 'mixing things and expressing one's own personality' initially meant buying a plastic table *and* a traditional butcher's block – a combination of two seemingly dissimilar worlds of taste. But the encouragement to scour second-hand shops and flea markets was also evident when the colour catalogues started appearing after 1969. The catalogues staged the new commodities in real and studio settings, and accompanied them with old clocks, 'junk' ornaments, houseplants, and other items that might suggest 'personality'.

The solution to the contradiction posed by Habitat – namely that it was offering mass-produced items to a taste that was being schooled to value the original find – was reconciled with *The House Book*. In many ways the theme of the book was not simply about how to make liveable spaces within a house, but how to take a house and remake it as a house of taste. What was implicit here was that if you were going to take this project seriously you needed to *own* the house you were living in. While there were certainly aspects of Habitat taste that could be achieved in rental accommodation (and the success of the Campus line of cheap furniture that Habitat offered in the early 1970s was certainly testimony to this), the more extensive taste that was going to be detailed in *The House Book* definitely required ownership and the book offered practical guidance and actual addresses and telephone numbers for securing a mortgage, hiring a surveyor, and so on. Ownership was not simply to do with financial motives, but also to do with the kind of remaking that was often necessary for all but the most modern housing. The sense that Habitat (or any other retailer of modern lifestyle furnishings) could only ever be a *part* of a total look, and that houses themselves might require seriously refurbishing and de-furbishing to achieve the required state, was recognised long before *The House Book* was published. This is the *Telegraph Colour Magazine* in 1968, with a feature article on Terence Conran and his success with Habitat, and showing the reader how to get that Conran look:

> The furnishing format is deceptively simple. The rules are essentially commonplace and quite safe. First, degut your house regardless of its architectural style – although obviously, good architecture counts when exposing the structural shell. Then mix old and new, junk shop finds with modern design (Conran's, of course) and set it off against white paint, natural floors and existing proportions. Don't obscure window frames with curtains, or clutter walls with hefty cupboards.[7]

If you were renting, then degutting would have resulted in the police being called in. As we will see in chapter 5, degutting was exactly what the people who would be known as gentrifiers were doing. The *Telegraph* article shows us that the Conrans were experts in buying rundown houses in up-and-coming neighbourhoods and turning them into desirable properties. *The House Book* was useful to someone seeking to make a living from house restoration at a time of rising house prices, but it also offered ideas to anyone wanting to get the modern, informal look. It catered for those with a terraced house in Bolton or a squat in Bromley. It spoke to those totally committed to fashioning an interior haven, but also to those who couldn't fully embrace (for lack of finance or lack of commitment) the Conran aesthetic but wanted the relaxed, informal *feel* that was associated with Habitat living.

Terence Conran's *The House Book* began life as a training manual for Habitat floor staff who had little experience in interior design and needed guidance for suggesting ways that customers might achieve the 'look'. It turned into a vast publication that spawned a raft of other publications.[8] *The House Book* was a kind of textbook for the design messages already spread effectively by Habitat shops (and by their more up-market spin offs, such as the UK Conran shops) and by the Habitat catalogues. It carried with it a vast ambition:

> The House Book is for everyone who would like to make the most of where they live. There are over 1000 beautiful colour pictures to give you ideas, backed with solid facts and diagrams so you can put them into practice: it could save you pounds. It is such a compendium of information and ideas that anybody setting up house should have one.[9]

It was for everybody and anybody.

The House Book was an immediate success, going on to sell more than two-and-a-half million copies in multiple editions and various translations. It existed in dynamic tension with Habitat, primarily because it seemed to encourage what we now call recycling and upcycling, and refused the off-the-peg interiors championed by Habitat and its annual catalogues.[10] While there were examples of interiors fitted out with brand-new furnishings, the emphasis was much more on the 'lived-in' feel of more weathered furnishings and kooky knick-knacks. One of the lessons that *The House Book* taught was to delight in the battered, the old, the discarded. And one of the most significant examples of revaluing the old and the battered was the 'well-scrubbed' pine kitchen table.

Perhaps as significant as popularising duvets, the taste achievement that should be most associated with Conran was a basic revaluing of the rudimentary and battered pine kitchen table. Something fundamental happened to this table as it moved from being a piece of furniture that would have been discarded by Juliet Gardiner's mum, to something that could be enjoyed by young moderns for its authenticity, something that could give sensual pleasure because of its cracks and stains and not in spite of them. During the 1960s and 1970s the battered pine kitchen table moved from being an item associated with the poor and with utility, a table associated with a bygone age of 'below the stairs' servants, to becoming the basis for a new lifestyle based around unfussy cooking, informal eating and easy sociability. In this way it is probably the preeminent example of Angela Carter's idea of pieces of furniture you live with rather than alongside.

The House Book constantly stressed the sensual pleasures of surfaces and fabrics, the delight in lively things. Explaining how to get the 'farmhouse' look, *The House Book* explains that:

> Brick, slate, wood and tiles are used in conjunction with new, man-made materials all over the house; kitchens with traditional central tables are no less friendly if they also contain washers and freezers. Rush-matting and cane-seating are part of the farmhouse style. Natural wood, especially pine, belongs to it, but never fake pine plastic laminate. Part of it, too, is the sort of furniture that was once found in the servants' attics or below the stairs in the kitchens and pantries.[11]

I think one central aspect to the success of the tastes that Habitat and Conran championed was the way it promoted sensual pleasure rather than symbolic meaning. This doesn't mean that these interiors couldn't also function symbolically, and function in terms of status; there is a sense that as soon as we are asked to 'read' someone's taste, we would usually think symbolically (what does this table stand for, what does it mean?). Yet the durability of the 'well-scrubbed pine kitchen table' (and it is as popular today within middle-class bohemia as it was when *The House Book* was at its most influential) is because it isn't just a symbol of informal sociability, it embodies it and helps perform it. It is a piece of furniture that enhances sensual pleasures and easy sociability: there is nothing to cry over when wine is spilt on it, nothing to feel precious about when it is kicked and chipped. It's a full-bodied table with none of the anaemic qualities of a 'designed' table.

The weathered kitchen table takes pride of place in *The House Book*. It is the first colour image in the book, and it is given a full page (figure 3.2). The page is titled 'Style/1'. The photograph is captioned with the following words:

> The hub of the farmhouse is its kitchen, and the hub of that kitchen is the table: old, huge and scrubbed, a reminder of endless gargantuan meals that have been prepared and eaten there. Here, all abiding warmth and comfort comes from an Aga recessed in the beautiful old chimney breast – such a welcome for a farmer returning from his fields – or a fugitive from the city rat-race.[12]

Just as the writing wants to evoke culinary memories – real or imagined, it doesn't seem to matter – the image emphasises the table as having a history (the picture draws attention to the table's edge and its notches and splits) and a practical life (the scattered arrangement of onions, mushrooms and peppermill, and the cooking and consuming utensils all point to gustatory pleasures). *The House Book* reassured its readers that they didn't have to live on a farm to enjoy the idealised ruralism associated with the 'farmhouse style'. The pine table can be a sensual refuge for fugitive stockbrokers and city lawyers *and* standard furniture for idealised farmers and farm labourers.

The book covered all areas of interior decoration and design, as well as supplying information about DIY, loft conversions, gardening – anything related to the spaces of domestic living. It is a huge volume, and I can only scratch the surface of it here. In some respects, it continues the work of the Habitat catalogues by supplying tableaux that emphasise the

3.2 The hub of the hub: 'Farmhouse Style', *The House Book*, p. 9

social life of furnishings, but this time all of them are 'actuality scenes' (albeit ones that have been thoroughly manicured for their photogenic qualities). The book sets out to both promote diversity of styles and suggest that the reader should think of interior design style within six modes: Farmhouse; Townhouse; Country-house; Mediterranean; International; and Eclectic. The book in general seems to mostly supply images that strive for a mix of

Farmhouse, Townhouse, Mediterranean and Eclectic. Within each style there is a loose attitude that strives to be easy-going about the mixing of elements. This idea of 'soft-eclecticism' is at odds with the way that 'eclecticism' (or a 'strong-eclecticism') is set up as the most difficult of styles for the reader to achieve, one that requires something like design 'genius' (the main example offered is David Hockney's living room):

> This style [eclecticism] is highly personal, and the mark of people who are supremely confident of their own taste. They may be, and usually are, associated in some way with the arts, and it is they who are the creative innovators, discovering, as it were, the styles that in a short space of time are imitated, simplified and absorbed into styles that will be generally accepted.[13]

No doubt such prose is designed to flatter the diligent consumer who has been absorbing the lessons of Conran and Habitat. Anyone who has paid attention to the catalogues and the shops would understand that the simplified light-modernist seating supplied by Habitat's 'basic range' could fit with an old Victorian birdcage from the local junk shop. The soft eclecticism is much easier to achieve than Conran makes out, though as we will see in the next chapter it requires a certain degree of 'flair' (whatever that turns out to be). While strong eclecticism might involve placing different design styles together – an eighteenth-century-style Chesterfield sofa next to a Wassily chair designed by Marcel Breuer at the Bauhaus, for instance – soft eclecticism could be much more easily and cheaply achieved.

The soft eclecticism promoted by *The House Book* is not simply about combining notable styles, it is also about decorating different types of housing with a style that mixes 'country kitchen' and 'uncluttered informality'. Commenting on a picture of a 'farmhouse kitchen' *The House Book* tells us: 'this kitchen could be equally at home in a cottage or a modern tower block of flats'.[14] Eclecticism is an attitude that allows the interior to have little or no relation to the world outside: it is an aesthetic that is literally cut off from its environmental reality (of town or country, high-rise or cottage). Chapter 5 shows that this is linked to larger changes in urban living, and how useful this idea of eclecticism was to the changes taking place within inner-cities when properties that had been identified as outdated, or even as 'slums', were remade as desirable homes.

The style (or the style of multiple styles) of eclecticism provides the perfect settings for the social informality that *The House Book* and Habitat were promoting. The pages that show us Terence and Shirley Conran's own domestic environment are a good example of what it could look like. The Conrans' home shows us eclecticism as a way of life as much as an aesthetic choice. Figure 3.3 lets us into the Conrans' kitchen; the caption in *The House Book* reads: 'In the Conrans' basement kitchen, a long narrow table seats eight and (a very important point) this still allows room for comfortable circulation, even when all the chairs are occupied'.[15] The signs of easy living are everywhere: from the supine cat stretched over modern work surfaces to the vast Welsh dresser at the back; from the mismatched chairs to the overflowing bowl of bread rolls in the foreground; from the wire cradle of eggs to the stuffed carpet bag on the table. This is the Habitat imagination at its most vivid and it

3.3 The Conrans' basement kitchen, *The House Book*, p. 219

is, paradoxically perhaps, empty of nearly anything that could be acquired from Habitat (the cupboards and drawers underneath the cat are from Conran's Summa range which were available through Habitat). It is the result of acquired learning, rather than simply acquired commodities. In this kitchen it looks as if the occupants have momentarily left the room, and forgotten to push their chairs in. Soft eclecticism becomes the name for a form of unstuffy social ease. Underneath the red tablecloth in the foreground lies, I'm sure, an old, well-scrubbed, pine kitchen table.

If the kitchen picture asks us to imagine an informal and convivial life, then the picture of the living room (figure 3.4) gives us another stage for this lifestyle and a range of people to enjoy it with. In the kitchen, a lively ambience is suggested by the eight dinner guests who have just left; in the 'living-room' a different mood pervades: 'The living room has to be both private place for being peaceful in, and public platform where you can sparkle when you are, as it were, at home to the world. It must be a place where you can relax, and it must, moreover, enable you to recharge your energies'.[16] Figure 3.4 shows Conran at home

3.4 The Conrans' living room, *The House Book*, p. 187

with his three children, and with Caroline Conran perched on a table. There is a Richard Smith artwork on the chimney breast (an artwork that is a mixture of abstract art and soft furnishings) and placed around the room are various found objects that are often seen in Habitat catalogues (the antique telescope, for instance). In *The House Book* the photograph is captioned: 'Comfort, controlled casualness, flexibility and prettiness; the Conrans' living-room scores high on all the important points without being over-designed'.[17] 'Controlled casualness' is, perhaps, the phrase that comes closest to naming both the interior style and the lifestyle that goes with it that *The House Book* encourages; it sounds contradictory and ambiguous, like 'studied informality' or 'rehearsed spontaneity'. It is something learnt in a way that hides its learning. Readers of *The House Book* might not be able to emulate the scale and lavishness of the Conrans' living room (they wouldn't be able to afford the Richard Smith artwork hanging over the fireplace, for a start), but they could approximated the look in any modern flat or terraced house (with knocked-through rooms, of course).

Eclecticism is the stamp of the home owner's personality on what might otherwise be standardised good taste: natural finishes, modern furniture, and so on. Eclecticism is one way of facing up to a consumer culture where the products are mass-produced. The furniture bought from a high-street shop like Habitat (or IKEA) is replicated in any number of homes. Consumer culture, though, is built on the idea of choice and a high standard of living rather than just on standardised living. It was standardised living that the Euro-American Cold War warriors claimed was the problem in communist countries. To stop people from recognising too quickly that aspects of consumer culture could end up making everyone's lives look the same, tastemakers needed to reintroduce a sense of individuality and eccentricity to ideas about taste. Conspicuous eclecticism was not so much an 'anything goes' aesthetic as an insistence that personality could be expressed by displaying quirky objects. One example offered by *The House Book* is of a wall covered in pairs of gloves – gardening gloves, winter gloves, various professional gloves, etc. – which is explained with the information that 'there is a growing tendency to mount collected objects of strange provenance side by side on vertical surfaces'.[18] Eccentric displays are not about financial value nor are they in the slightest bit functional (they are often about defunctionalising functional objects), they are there instead to assert the personality of the occupant. A democracy of good taste might require mass-produced furnishings, but you could still be idiosyncratic, kooky.

The House Book showed the reader the vast array of possibilities for a modern, eclectic look. In many ways, the rooms shown in such lavish colour were primarily a stage set for new ways of domestic living, new forms of sociability. And this required a new sort of person – someone able to rustle up delicious food for a spontaneous meal with friends, someone who doesn't have to plan ahead when entertaining at home. Informality was the key, but informality had to be learnt. The 'dinner party' – in its various formats – would be at the heart of the social life of the new middle classes but it would have to be wrestled away from its roots in formal dining and to do this required new cuisines that, like the well-scrubbed pine kitchen table, seemed to insist on sensual pleasure, authenticity, and unfussy preparation. Key to the modern informality were tastes that were distinctly unfamiliar to most people who had grown up in Britain before the war.

Bistros in Bristol and Pizzas in Plymouth (and everywhere else)

Juliet Gardiner's trips to France were part of a new culinary détente that the British new middle classes were brokering with mainland Europe around food. Gone would be the commitment of a traditional middle class to the overcooked recipes of the English public-school kitchen, with its masochistic love of overcooked cabbage. The good life for the new middle class would be lighter, looser, and less flatulent. The good life that was being offered by *The House Book* was based on a refusal of stylistic purity: it could breezily accommodate both the cool permissiveness of Scandinavian furniture and the quaint allure of Victoriana; it could combine the sleek industrialism of a modern fridge with the rustic quirkiness of a rough earthenware pot. But if purity wasn't an overarching value of the new middle classes, then an idea of authenticity was, however approximate the version might turn out to be. A sort of 'borrowed authenticity' would be the defining characteristic of the food culture that was feeding this emerging class. And it was borrowed authenticity that Gardiner was bringing back from the South of France, and that others would be buying from Habitat, or stashing in their suitcases as they returned from Majorca or the Algarve. They were bringing their Provençale casserole dishes and their newly acquired desire for Mediterranean nonchalance back to a world that still treated olive oil as something to be used for dislodging stubborn ear wax.

On 1 April 1957 the BBC's current affairs programme, *Panorama*, reported on the spaghetti harvest in Italy and Switzerland. The programme recounted how an exceptionally mild winter and an early spring was producing a bumper crop of spaghetti, and how spaghetti farming in Switzerland was much more of a family affair compared to the plantation scale of spaghetti farming in Italy. The report explained how the uniform length of spaghetti was 'the result of many years of patient endeavour by plant breeders'.[19] The programme showed us spaghetti trees with strands of spaghetti dangling from the branches, and how the pickers laid out the spaghetti in the sun to dry. It is perhaps surprising to see the BBC going to such lengths to play an April Fools' Day prank, but of more interest here is the idea that the BBC could assume that so many people in the UK, if not most, would actually fall for it.

The charismatically tipsy restaurateur and TV chef Keith Floyd, who started running bistro-style cafés in Bristol from about 1967, remembered that in the early 1960s he 'never knew how to cook spaghetti. How did you get it into the saucepan? It was hard and came wrapped in blue waxed paper. We soaked it in water to make it soft, we broke it up in bits. It was a long time before I learnt you just pushed it gently down into the boiling water so that it curled around the pan'.[20] The education that taught Floyd about pasta and omelette cooking was undertaken in very select pubs (the forerunners of today's gastro pubs), cafés and bars that were being influenced by the writing of Elizabeth David. It was David who inaugurated the postwar interest in Mediterranean cooking through a series of books that began in 1950 with *A Book of Mediterranean Food*, followed by *French Country Cooking* in 1951, and *Italian Food* and *Summer Cooking* in 1954. *A Book of Mediterranean Food* described an opulent culinary life that could be found on the shores of the Mediterranean. This was a life that was only enjoyed by the British upper classes before the war, and much of the pleasure of reading the book in 1951 must have been the disparity between the lavish recipes of garlic-infused meat on the page and the reality of austerity Britain where meat was still being rationed. David's books evoked a world of sunlight and sensual pleasure that was gradually becoming an annual possibility for more and more people as austerity gave way to affluence by the second half of the 1950s. Rather than directly influencing the British palate through often elaborate recipes, David's early impact took a more tangential route through chefs and restaurateurs, including people like Terence Conran, for whom she was a heroic figure.[21] It was her 1960 book *French Provincial Cooking*, as well as her food journalism at *The Spectator* and elsewhere, that made her a more mainstream influence.

One of her themes in the early 1960s was culinary authenticity and her persistent complaint was the bastardisation and adulteration of Mediterranean food culture when it crosses the channel to the British Isles. In an article in *Punch* from November 1961 she bemoans the fate of the notoriously fashionable quiche Lorraine:

> You could hardly go out to a cocktail party without somebody tipping you off about the delicious *quiche* they made in the penthouse restaurant of the new block at the far end of the Finchley Road. At the dinner-table grave discussions would arise as to the proper ingredients of a *quiche* and the desirability or otherwise of putting cheese in the filling. [...] By the time our aspiring cooks had absorbed instructions to make this French regional dish with a prefabricated pie-shell, a couple of triangles of processed cheese and a tin of evaporated milk, nothing much of the original remained. The Lorraine part had got away from the *quiche*, and with it the charm and glamour.[22]

Her writing often exudes a showy, aristocratic air (the cocktail parties, the penthouses), but her complaint was a common one. The charge of inauthenticity is the bread and butter of food journalism, which has a kinship with travel journalism: no modern food journalist worth their salt is going to champion a high-street curry house in Britain when they could be reminiscing about the authentic biriyani they ate in Dhaka.

If the 1930s and 1940s witnessed specific taste wars around the social differences between butter and margarine,[23] then the 1960s and 1970s saw something similar taking place over the differences between salad cream and mayonnaise. My mother, who was born in the 1920s and stoically remained 'traditionally middle class' throughout her life, was a devotee of salad cream, and probably had a social (and mildly xenophobic) aversion to mayonnaise, vinaigrettes, and salads that deviated from the strict triumvirate of tomato, cucumber, and lettuce. For Elizabeth David, my mother had acquired this taste partly through culinary training:

> By the thirties there was already a vast public brought up in the belief that mayonnaise was a sauce which could only be produced in a factory, which contained no olive oil – and tasted mainly of acetic acid. And that is what, by the sixties, when they see mayonnaise announced on a menu, the great majority of people expect. It is not unnatural that they should be suspicious and indignant when confronted with the authentic sauce. Like most tastes, that for olive oil and mayonnaise made with it is an acquired one.[24]

While my mother didn't acquire a taste for olive oil and mayonnaise, many people did. They acquired it via the restaurants and bars that took a version of David's teaching to heart, and they acquired it through newspapers, magazines, and recipe books.

The novelist, Len Deighton, offered regular readers of the *Observer* a useful schooling in French cooking. Deighton had picked up an interest in cooking from his mother and from a string of holiday jobs in restaurants. He had also started collecting cookery books, including those of David's, and because he didn't want to ruin his expensive books by actually using them while cooking and because he had studied illustration at the Royal College of Art, he had been producing visual notes about particular dishes and processes that he then pinned up in his kitchen as cooking aids. These drawings formed the basis for his cook strips that appeared first in *The Daily Express* (for a few issues in 1961), and then weekly in the *Observer* from 1962 to 1966. The published cook strips formed the basis of books that Deighton published in 1965: *Len Deighton's Action Cook Book*, and *Où est le garlic: Len Deighton's French Cook Book.*

An early strip tells the reader how to make mayonnaise and its garlicy variant aioli. Hand-made mayonnaise, olive oil, and garlic were ways of distancing yourself from a more constrained version of middle-class life, while also signalling a distinctly non-working-class approach to cooking. When the mayonnaise recipe was republished in book form Deighton added some more information about how to acquire olive oil: 'the finest, first-pressing oils are very often obtainable from wine merchants. If you buy in bulk, the cost of these very high-quality oils will be no more than that of the less good ones bought in small bottles'.[25] Olive oil was not an easily accessible commodity in Britain at the time and easier to get in tiny bottles at a chemist than in a grocery shop (hence Deighton's advice). While Deighton's cook strips did include such familiar standards as 'English Trifle' and 'Tripe and Onions', their primary aim was to encourage readers to develop a Mediterranean palate through recipes for 'Cassoulet', 'Coquilles St Jacques', and 'Boeuf Bourguignon'. Deighton's food strips were an invitation and incitement to embrace a 'new' continental and cosmopolitan food culture, even if some of the recipes were unlikely to have mass-appeal: the strip for the week following his mayonnaise recipe, for instance, was for 'Cervelle de veau au beurre noir' (calves' brains in a black butter sauce).[26] Not one for the faint-hearted.

The combination of 'borrowed authenticity' and a continental sense of sociability also accounts for the success of PizzaExpress. The changing food landscape of the UK in the decades from the 1950s to today is one that moves from scarcity to profusion (food rationing that was first brought in during the war actually increased when the war ended in 1945 and only stopped in 1954). If today we expect to be able to go for a pizza or find a good Indian restaurant in every town and city in the UK, then this is partly due to changes in food culture that were first established in the 1960s. The Indian restaurants that drew on the well-established presence of Indian food in port-cities in Britain took on a new visibility

3.5 Len Deighton Cook Strip from the *Observer*, 15 July 1962, p. 23

in the 1960s, but apart from a few exceptions they never promoted themselves in terms of authenticity. Indian food culture in the UK was exceptionally accommodating to the strange demands of white customers.[27] PizzaExpress, though, modelled itself on an idea of authenticity. The founder, Peter Boizot, opened the first restaurant in 1965 and by 2021 there were 470 PizzaExpress restaurants in the UK. The first one (figure 3.6) appeared in Soho's Wardour Street and what set it apart from all the other places where you could eat pizza as part of a general Italian meal was that it had an authentic pizza oven. At first Boizot wanted to create the full Pizza Rustica experience of Naples and Rome, where people either carried their pizza slice away with them or ate within the restaurant standing up at a counter. I guess he decided that you can have too much authenticity. Especially in drizzly London.

Boizot opened a second PizzaExpress in 1967 in Camden, and it was here where the blueprint for all future PizzaExpress franchises was developed. The restaurant was designed to offer a flavour of the Pizza Rustica, while combining different forms of sociability. At the centre of the PizzaExpress experience was the drama of the pizza itself: 'In the middle of the floor space was a big bright red counter, behind which pizzaiolos would

3.6 The first PizzaExpress opened on Wardour Street, Soho in 1965 (pictured 2015)

work like beavers to toss pizzas high into the air right in front of the customer'.[28] The snaking counters that characterised PizzaExpress restaurants allowed customers to watch and talk to the pizzaiolos, most of whom were brought over from Naples. The counter created an island of production in a sea of consumption and pizzaiolos were encouraged to be as flamboyant as possible in their pizza making. Away from the noisy pizza-making island were booth-style tables with their own acoustic environments: 'The tables themselves were circular, and were littered with devices to aid with acoustics'.[29] For Boizot 'the result was a fast, casual-style restaurant'. It was both noisy – mimicking the noisy sociability of the Pizza Rustica – and yet retained a quiet intimacy around the table.

The restaurants also included live music and the first Soho restaurant opened a jazz club in the basement. There is, of course, no direct relationship between jazz and pizzas, and yet the sort of thematic improvisations that were such a key part of 'modern' jazz (and, to some extent part of the 'trad' jazz revival on the 1950s and 1960s too), seem to share something with both pizza making and the feelings of spontaneity and improvisation which characterised the tastes that both PizzaExpress and Habitat were keen to promote. The recipe of taking a well-known and well-loved composition – something from Rodgers and Hammerstein, for instance – pursuing the possible byways of the tune, developing musical flights while also maintaining a recognisable melody line, echoed the way that the two chains gave us new twists on traditions. At any rate, both the shops and the restaurants often played Miles Davis and John Coltrane on their house music systems.

The sense of 'borrowed authenticity' finds its source material in Spanish, Italian, and Greek tavernas, in French bistros, and smoky Harlem-style jazz clubs. What is being borrowed is not just a way of eating or of music making, but an ambience, a sociability, a feeling. Whether it was real or imagined is less crucial here than recognising the desire for a more relaxed form of sociability, and how this contrasted to the brittle propriety of manners and emotional reserve associated with the traditional British middle class. The imagined *joie de vivre* that might or might not accompany calves' brains in black butter is what is important. It is the presumed easy-going permissiveness that was associated with the Mediterranean that mattered, not the everyday reality of Catholic conservatism and low wages that was presumably an unavoidable reality of much Mediterranean life. It was the spontaneity and improvising that mattered for jazz in the UK, not the actuality of the colour bar. This, of course, didn't discount the association of these cultural forms with political radicalism, which might include the Campaign for Nuclear Disarmament (CND), protests against the war in Vietnam and against apartheid in South Africa and, other forms of political protest.

The sense of an easy, informal, and sensual life required a set of objects, images, and practices to make it real. So, when Keith Floyd decided to change the menu of the café he was running in Bristol in 1967, and to shift the focus from Spain to France, what was needed was a dramatic shift in the supporting cast of objects:

> So out went the Spanish bullfight posters, in came the Toulouse-Lautrec. [...] Out went the Denby cruets, in came the peppermills and little plastic boxes of French sel de mer. Out went the ketchup stained raffia place mats, in came the checked red and white gingham tablecloths. Out went the hand-thrown pottery ashtrays from the hippy in the garage down the road and in came Ricard and Pernod ashtrays. Out went the Denbyware bowls and in came the Le Creuset. Out went the uneven hand-thrown plates, in came large white gleaming discs of porcelain.[30]

The swapping of raffia and gingham may seem more-or-less incidental compared to the changes that brought in 'le menu du jour at 9s 6d, French onion soup or pâté maison or crudités, boeuf bourguignon, moussaka or coq au vin, fresh fruit or cheese or chocolate mousse',[31] yet this is all part of a sensual scene that could speak broadly of a new relaxed world of pleasure, leisure, and sensual enjoyment. The good life that was being produced by broadening the culinary repertoire seemed both endless (Spanish tapas, Italian pizzerias, and so on) and a consistent rejoinder to an inherited world of stuffy dining clubs or austere canteens. Both the details and the continuity matter. The differences between John Coltrane and Acker Bilk matter, but the very fact that both seem to resonate with an ease and lightness not found in an older, stuffier culture that would favour the seriousness of orchestral classical music, matters more.

Looking backwards to look forward

The logo for PizzaExpress was designed in 1967 and remains the same today. You've probably seen it: the restaurant's name is in a circle of swirls that resembles a pizza as seen from above. But what is most striking is the font of the lettering and the way that the swirls mimic the Art Nouveau style from the end of the nineteenth century. The pretend-authentic Neapolitan pizza brand name is framed within the stylisations that explicitly borrowed from Japanese culture to produce a visual impression of decadence and what, at times, looks like a mood of dulled intoxication. You can find the same use of Art Nouveau's graphic flourishes in the decorative designs used by the clothes store Biba, but you will also find a host of other retro styles there too: Edwardian, Art Deco, Victoriana, and so on. And rather than rustic authenticity, the stress is more thoroughly on stoned boredom and opulent decadence, or at least that's where Biba ended up. In some ways, the aesthetics of Biba was a world away from Habitat: if Habitat was all about natural surfaces, light, air, and exposed brickwork, then Biba was characterised by lacquered screens, reclaimed stained glass, and dark interiors where pungent perfumes hung in the air. And yet they shared a similar ethos of eclecticism, a dedication to instant gratification, and a refusal to 'bother' shoppers with sales assistants: 'I wanted the customers to feel at home, not hounded by sales assistants'.[32] Both suffered from extensive shoplifting.

Biba started out as 'Biba's Postal Boutique' with the idea of selling inexpensive boutique-style clothing – designed by Barbara Hulanicki – by mail-order. After some early attempts through the *Daily Express*, the *Evening Standard*, and the *Observer*, the breakthrough moment came when the *Daily Mirror*'s fashion editor Felicity Green contacted Hulanicki for a feature she was writing on women and the fashion business and thought that the newspaper could also promote a custom-made item of clothing that Biba could sell via the newspaper. The bespoke *Mirror* dress was a shift of pink gingham called, for obvious reasons, 'Barbara' (figure 3.7). The feature and the advert for the dress ran together on 1 May 1964, ten days before Habitat opened its pivoting front door. Felicity Green portrayed Hulanicki and Biba's Postal Boutique as a thriving business (which, at the time, it wasn't) and promoted the dress and kerchief as a bargain (which it certainly was):

> If you are in the market for something cool and shifty … If you like the idea of the headscarf to match … If you feel twenty-five bob isn't a fashion fortune – and it isn't … This is your dress, with its figure skimming lines, softly rolling neckline and keyhole back. It has been designed and made specifically for the *Daily Mirror* by Barbara Hulanicki.[33]

Over the next few days, Hulanicki and her husband and business partner, Stephen Fitz-Simon, collected thousands and thousands of orders from their PO Box. Biba was up and running.

Biba soon became a physical boutique when it opened a shop later in 1964 in Abingdon Road in Kensington, but it also continued to sell clothes by mail through the *Daily Mirror* and through magazines like *Honey* and later through its own catalogues. Dresses were sold through print media as 'Biba's Bonus' with adverts such as 'make the most of the little girl

3.7 Biba 1964 gingham dress for *Daily Mirror*

look in smock of dark brown chalkstripe blended wool'.[34] The 'little girl look' would be a continual feature of Biba, to the point where they even named a room the 'Lolita Room' when they opened as a vast department store (called 'Big Biba') in 1973 after a merger with Dorothy Perkins. You can get a sense of the pace and energy of the initial Biba phenomenon in this excerpt from a roundup of Boutique culture from 1965:

> Barbara Hulanicki and her husband Stephen Fitz-Simon started it [the Biba shop] last October. The whole thing began as a hobby with a small mail-order boutique and snowballed. When they were still only vaguely talking of the shop they came across just the place and clinched the deal. Barbara and her design partner, Ann Behr, collaborate over the clothes; try to get at least one new thing into stock each week. Probably the cheapest boutique of all – some dresses are only 19s 6d, and the most expensive clothes no more than £7. Many regular customers [...] come in several times a week to buy clothes to wear that minute.[35]

Habitat's 'can't-wait-to-get-it-home-feeling' was trying to approximate this 'clothes-to-wear-that-minute' immediacy. This was fast fashion at its fastest. In 1967, talking to Jonathan Aitken about Biba's success and the sort of customers they attract, Hulanicki describes the life cycle of her clothes as being miniscule: 'after a month's wear a new dress is an antique'.[36]

What journalists picked up on at the time was a sense that the tempo of fashion was becoming faster and faster, but also that some young people were prepared to spend a considerable portion of their income and their time on clothing. In his article about the new fashion culture in London in the 1960s, Aitken interviewed various Biba shoppers:

> I spend about £8 here each week – it's my weakness, I suppose. Yes, it is a lot considering I earn only £13, but then I save up all my luncheon vouchers and sell them off to the greedy boys in the office, sometimes my dad gives me a quid [a pound] or two when he's had a good night at the dogs, and sometimes I get something off my boyfriend as a present.[37]

These Biba shoppers were often office workers, or worked in new 'light' industries, or were shop assistants. They were part of a class that might be called 'salaried workers': they didn't undertake manual work, but they also didn't have the sort of qualifications that would mean that they would ever join the professions. The 'salaried workers' would include secretaries, clerks, and technicians. These were the potential recruits to the new middle classes, the people who weren't hamstrung by respectability, who embraced the world of the 'young moderns'. But the price of fashion and the low wages for clerical work meant that some Biba shoppers were holding down two jobs: 'I couldn't afford to buy any clothes at all on my salary as a secretary after paying the rent and all that. But I do three nights a week as a waitress, and this brings me in about six quid clothes money. It's worth it to look good the other four nights'.[38]

By the time Aitken interviewed these Biba addicts, the shop has moved to much larger premises (figure 3.8). Biba promised the young salaried masses 'the democratization of style'[39] because it had turned the elite world of boutique fashion into something that was

3.8 Shop manager Elanor Powell in front of Biba, Kensington Church Street, 1967

available to nearly anyone. This was boutique style as mass produced commercial culture. And even though Biba was based in London it had – through its mail order side, and because it was being written about in the national press and in lifestyle magazines – a much wider reach. It was also true that those finding their fashion kicks in the boutiques of Kensington or Carnaby Street in Soho were not all young women and were not all Londoners:

> Yes, sure I come here every week. From Birmingham, in fact. Well, I do have to get up at six in the morning, which is two hours earlier than I normally do, but then my clobber matters to me whereas my work matters only to my boss. I always buy something that's new in style, the very latest. In Brum I've got quite a name for being well dressed.[40]

The accessibility of fashion for young people is an ambiguous phenomenon. Hearing the voices of the 'switched-on' and the 'with-it' it is hard not to hear the excitement, the sense of a new confidence in the business of self-creation. And yet there is, at the same time, an undertow that seems less amiable, more malevolent. Perhaps it is the stoned boredom (figure 3.9) that at times looks almost deathly. Perhaps it is the frenetic turnover of looks, which suggests that however hard you try, being 'with-it' is ultimately impossible in consumer culture. Perhaps it is the slightly creepy Lolita-ness of it all.

Biba didn't have the staying power of Habitat or PizzaExpress. By 1975 it had imploded. In part this was because of Biba's appetite for expansion. As they moved to ever-larger premises the range of Biba goods grew exponentially:

> Different facets of the Biba image are strikingly displayed on three floors, which take in pricier fashion creations, children's wear, men's wear, rows and rows of women's clothes, undies,

3.9 Poster for Biba cosmetics

> boots, bags, hats, gloves, and now make-up. Biba's household goods include satin sheets, lamp shades, waste-paper baskets and wallpaper – all displayed in sumptuous splendour against the background of ostrich-feather bouquets.[41]

The Biba look was given to everything from children's pyjamas to paint. Even things that might seem allergic to a Biba-style makeover were fair game – dog food, chickpeas, and marmalade all got the Biba makeover. When the end came, the obituaries knew that something significant had passed: 'For a decade Biba has been a byword for style to every platform-heeled, denim-hugging London dolly. The Biba look was unmistakably urban and unique – 1920-style slinky dresses, surgical boot footwear, satin lampshades and feathers with everything'.[42] It was a taste that was endlessly derivative and yet strikingly recognisable with a 'colour palette of browns, maroon, orchid, amethyst, plum, and "dirty" pastels'.[43] Perhaps the *Daily Mail* got it right in its obituary: 'One of the most dazzling success stories of the Sixties, to many girls Biba was more than a shop – it was a whole way of life'.[44]

Dump the spectacles and make the girl cook the meal

Changes in taste are not just the shifting sands of fashion that leave the seemingly more fundamental aspects of social life unaltered. In many respects, taste constitutes the very stuff out of which we make our everyday lives. To adopt specific tastes can have an impact in all aspects of our life. The author of the cartoon strip recipes for mayonnaise and calves' brains in black butter sauce is probably better known to you as a thriller writer. Len Deighton published his first novel, *The IPCRESS File*, in 1962. In 1965 it became a film with Michael Caine taking the lead role (the unnamed narrator of the novel became Harry Palmer in the film). It's an anxious, slightly trippy film. The obvious context for the story was Cold War paranoia (it is a story about CIA operatives in London, about brainwashing, and about shadowy agencies purported to come from Albania), but it is also a story about class and taste. Harry Palmer is an ex-army sergeant who had had his fill of privately educated toffs during his National Service. Now he is part of a world of civil servants, espionage, and intelligence. Old school ties exist, but so too do computers. He is a womaniser, who eats Italian food, drinks Italian coffee, and smokes French cigarettes. He also cooks. The cooking was a shock to the US studio, who on seeing the rushes of Caine, the new anti-hero, making an omelette for his romantic date, reportedly told the director via telegram: 'dump Caine's spectacles and make the girl cook the meal. He is coming across as a homosexual'.[45]

Len Deighton and Michael Caine worked together on the set, with Deighton teaching Caine how to crack an egg one-handed, and how to make an omelette the French way. The two men got on well and remained friends after filming. They had a similar background: Deighton was the son of a car mechanic and a cook, Caine the son of a market porter and a cleaning lady. Both had undertaken military service: Deighton in the RAF, Caine in the British Army. Deighton and Caine's careers can't simply be described in terms of social mobility, where they left one class (the working class) to 'jump' into a ready-made middle class. For many ordinary people, war and military service pulled the rug from under the class system. What at one time had seemed like innate breeding, looked, on closer inspection, more like in-breeding. Their journey of working-class emigration fashioned new class identities in its wake, and it did so partly through the work of taste. What the US producers saw was gender and sexual confusion.

The same year that the film came out, *Len Deighton's Action Cook Book* was published. The cover looks like a direct rejoinder to the Hollywood executives. Here, a lilac-shirted man with a holstered pistol is preparing a plate of pasta, while a nightie-clad woman tousles his hair. Calling his book 'action cooking' plays with the idea of action movies, but Deighton was a man in tune with the artistic avant-garde too, and the title was also a reference to art, to action painting – to a world of spontaneity and living life in the moment. The book looks two ways at once. To Hollywood and the excessive masculinity of the action man. And to Paris and the left-bank existentialists, hurling paint at a canvas in an attempt to pluck meaning out of nothingness. Neither might seem the natural home for a working-class man in Britain. Neither Michael Caine nor Len Deighton's journey of social mobility tells us much about what is happening to class in Britain in the 1960s in demographic terms, but it does suggest that movement across classes also entailed changes in the way gender and sexuality were perceived.

Deighton's overlapping practice of writing thrillers and writing recipe books didn't redefine masculinity, but they subtly alter its representation. Recipes and cookery journalism in the postwar period were often aimed specifically at women, as a way for them to maintain a home where the man went out to work and the woman stayed home to look after the house, the kids, and the husband. Deighton's book was aimed at men, but it was also a commitment to a culinary world of French cuisine, wine, and buying unusual ingredients that would require regular trips to a delicatessen. We can get a better sense of how Deighton's books rework masculinity in the name of new class identities if we look at the novel that the film drew on.

The IPCRESS File takes something from the biography of Deighton in as much as it shows us class mobility in action. The unnamed protagonist in the novel is a style-conscious intelligence officer with working-class roots, who through a grammar school education has become part of an officer class that he despises. What gives him an identity throughout the book is a pervasive hatred for the public-school educated and superciliously privileged people he works with. The scorn he directs at these leading members of the establishment is two-fold: they don't have the hard-won street smarts of the non-entitled, and more pertinently, they don't have good taste. Here is the anonymous protagonist approaching the house of a high-ranking civil servant in the leafy Home Counties:

> It was a small converted farm-house with a décor that writers on women's magazines think is contemporary. Outside the mauve front door there was a wheelbarrow with flowers growing in it. Fixed to the wall was a coach lamp converted to electricity, not as yet lit. I knocked at the door with, need I say it, a brass lion's head knocker. [...] Dalby opened the door and tried to register surprise on his bland egg-like public school face.[46]

Dalby's class is etched on his face, or more accurately the lack of etching, the blandness, is itself (in Deighton's novel) a class characteristic. But more crucially it is the way that Dalby reveals a lack of personality by deploying every cliché of the 'farmhouse look' without any twists. For Deighton's protagonist this is not 'instant good taste' but off-the-peg, traditional middle-class taste without much care or thought, and without personality.

It is notable that unlike the 'angry young men' writers of a previous generation, Deighton's protagonist doesn't distinguish himself by insisting on an older stereotype of working-class masculinity (hard-drinking and fist-fighting): instead, it is his sarcasm, cosmopolitanism, and sophisticated tastes that stop him becoming like one of the upper-middle-class administrators he despises, but who he is now associated with. His tastes offer a tangent, taking him to a world unlike both his working-class past and the world of the entitled posh boys he works with. It is a sociable, sensual, and intellectual world:

> I walked down Charlotte Street towards Soho. It was that sort of January morning that has enough sunshine to point up the dirt without raising the temperature. I was probably seeking excuses to delay; I bought two packets of Gauloises, sank a quick grappa with Mario and Franco at the Terrazza, bought a *Statesman*, some Normandy butter and garlic sausage. The girl in the delicatessen was small, dark and rather delicious. We had been flirting across the mozzarella for years.[47]

Deighton, Caine, and the new middle classes were subtly shifting masculinity for the new middle classes, not in a manner that necessarily empowered women (heterosexual conquest is still the underlying goal) but with a new and more expansive idea of what masculinity might entail. Now, men could be interested in Mediterranean food and have opinions on styles of décor, and remain 'reassuringly' heterosexual, whatever the Hollywood executives thought.

The consumer society that was emerging in the 1960s put a high premium on lifestyle: the more people who could become involved in lifestyle culture, the better it would be for a consumption-based society. If more men could get interested in fashion, in cooking, in taking holidays abroad, then the consumer base was expanding for a significant range of commodities. Similarly, if leisure activities once reserved for the wealthy could be made accessible to a broader constituency, then this again was a way of expanding the consumer base. One notable example of this was the *Daily Mirror*'s intervention into the elite world of sailing. In 1963 they advertised a boat that could be made from a kit, could be lifted by one man, and could fit on the roof of the smallest of cars (a Mini of course). This was the Mirror Dinghy (figures 3.10 and 3.11) designed by Barry Bucknell (presenter of a popular TV programme showing viewers how to undertake various domestic DIY projects), Jack Holt (a yacht designer), and Bernard Hayman (editor of *Yachting World*). If you had £15 for an initial deposit (followed by twelve monthly payments of £4 5s), then you too could spend your weekends 'messing about in boats' and drinking at the sailing club. The *Daily Mirror* announced the boat in February 1963: 'Ahoy! You can make it for yourself for £63 11s. Here she comes – the *Daily Mirror* FUNBOAT! UP go the red sails, WHOOSH goes the breeze, OVER goes the tiller – and skimming and scudding into YOUR life and mine comes a brilliant new boat with built-in thrills and pleasure'.[48]

Making it yourself kept the price down (it was £95.11s if you bought it finished and ready for sailing), and the emphasis was fun and family life. But if you wanted to take sailing seriously this was also a possibility:

> Why a Daily Mirror Dinghy? Because the Mirror believes that more and more ordinary folk should be able to enjoy the health and happiness that a good boat has been bringing hitherto only to the wealthy. What kind of a boat is it? Big enough for the average family of four to go cruising in (10ft. 10in. long); light enough for one man to lift (90lb.); small enough to go on top of a baby car; easy enough for a beginner to sail, yet good enough for regatta racing.[49]

By April 1963 there was already a Mirror class regatta in Wraysbury near Windsor. Here 'sparetime sea-dogs who can hardly tell a jib from a mainsail', and 'families who had built

3.10 and 3.11 The Mirror Dinghy from the brochure, 1963

the boats in back gardens, spare bedrooms and even the front parlour' could compete in Mirror-class races.[50] By March 1964 there were 1,200 dinghies in existence and yachting experts declared it as 'the fastest growing class of dinghy ever'.[51] The introduction of the Mirror fundamentally changed the class dynamics of sailing, and democratising this leisure

pursuit was the conscious intention of the *Daily Mirror*. But as a lifestyle it was more than a way of taking part in an elite activity, it was a way of having a slice of 'the good life' – and that good life included fun, freedom, and a sense of autonomy:

> Imagine a boat of your own! A passport to freedom. [...] Soon you're afloat in your own boat, sailing away from it all. You don't need a licence. You don't need a number plate. You are free. That's why sailing is Britain's fastest growing sport. Difficulties need not stop you if you want a boat of your own. One Essex man built his in the lounge of his upstairs flat and 'launched' it through the window into the street on ropes. Burly miner Brian Taylor put the finishing touches to his dinghy at the bankside of the River Medway, pushed off with minutes to spare and came third at a race meeting.[52]

As with all the tastes that animate this book, we can look at the taste for sailing a Mirror Dinghy within the context of changing class dynamics, as well as on its own terms. We can get a strong sense of how taste is lived – the exuberance of living the good life, of participating in what had once been off-limits and unthinkable – of sailing close to the wind, of participating in a world where there are new phrases to learn, new skills to practice. To see taste just as a 'game of positioning' (keeping up with the Joneses) misses much of what makes taste matter, and what makes it important for looking at changes in social life. This isn't to suggest that taste is all plain sailing: the hurt that may come when wealthy sailing club members regard your new dinghy with disdain is real. That disdainful look is a real buzz-kill. But the buzz is there still in the rush of water and wind and the excitement of sailing your Mirror Dinghy.

Recruiting more people to the pleasures of interior design, sailing, fashion, and cooking as a leisure activity meant that there were suddenly a lot more consumers interested in buying all sorts of new (and old) goods. But these changes also made a big difference to the ways in which class and gender were expressed (and, as we will see, how ideas of 'race' were repressed and obscured). These were changes that allowed new class identities to emerge, which also had consequences for how men and women pursued their gendered roles. The growing market required more and more people to take an interest in lifestyle. Television and radio were often crucial here: cooking programmes, holiday programmes, and DIY programmes all come under the umbrella of lifestyle television. But a much older platform, namely print media, was a crucial recruiting tool too, particularly in the form of the new Sunday colour supplements that emerged in the 1960s.

4

Colour supplement living

In Angela Carter's account of Habitat, she connects the furnishings they sell, not just with forms of decoration, but with other tastes and with other forums of taste. Looking at a relatively plain, unfussy range of seating (various sizes of sofas and an armchair) that Habitat produced in the mid-1970s, she writes:

> But if I can easily imagine myself sitting on a piece of the William range ('Craftsman-built furniture which has a solid frame of beechwood'), reading the *Sunday Times* colour supplement, waiting for my Elizabeth David lunch to be ready, I can't imagine, say, a Rembrandt on the wall opposite, even if it were an unframed repro pinned up as casually as all hell.[1]

Some tastes gel, others don't. Habitat can connect to Elizabeth David, and it can connect to the *Sunday Times* colour supplement, but for Carter this scene can't include a Rembrandt in the mix – there isn't a natural bridge from the chair to that sort of picture. Of course, Carter isn't imaging that sitting on a William sofa with a Rembrandt poster on the wall – 'pinned up a casually as all hell' – is an impossibility, simply that it doesn't fit the selection of tastes that make up the world of Habitat and its associated styles. Given that a general eclecticism is the 'style of no style' that Habitat is promoting, it is worth pausing for a moment to try and think what Carter could mean here. Is it the look of the Rembrandt that wouldn't fit? Or – and this is where my inclination heads – is it because Rembrandt seems to demand a different kind of attention, or a different attitude of looking? A Rembrandt is never going to have the lightness of feeling which characterises the other elements. She seems to be saying that however casually you might pin up a Rembrandt poster, the Rembrandt poster itself can't support casualness – it is just not that sort of image. A different lifestyle if you will. Which might also mean that we could take casualness and lightness as the connecting thread that draws together an Elizabeth David lunch (or a Len Deighton one more appropriately) with a colour supplement from the *Sunday Times* and a soft furnishing range from Habitat.

We've already looked at how Mediterranean food and the theatrical flair of PizzaExpress supports the sorts of casual sociability that was becoming popular in the 1960s, and we've briefly seen the way that the sort of clothing produced by Biba supported a more immediate sense of fashion and being 'with it'. This chapter turns to phenomena such as the *Sunday Times Magazine* and other 'colour supplements' that started to appear in the 1960s, as well as lifestyle magazines more generally. These aren't simply more items on the list of things that have the same feeling of controlled casualness. These magazines and other lifestyle magazines offered a way of knitting tastes together, and of linking taste to other aspects of the world. These lifestyle publications aren't just another stopping-off place on the itinerary of commodities; they provide a privileged view of how that itinerary is orchestrated, how it functions, and how it connects and disconnects to the larger social world.

Life in full colour

The first edition of what would become the *Sunday Times Magazine* appeared as the *Sunday Times Colour Section* in February 1962. The *Observer* and *The Daily Telegraph* would follow in September 1964 with their own colour magazines. These supplementary magazines, which today seem so central to the idea of a weekend newspaper, were initially prepared as a bonus gift. The newspaper reader would feel that they were getting something for nothing (and a relatively luxurious gift at that) with the inclusion of this full colour magazine. The economic truth, though, was the other way round. It was because these colour supplements were attractive to advertisers, who would pay premium rates to have full colour adverts sent into the homes of a section of the public with the most disposable income, that they were attractive and lucrative for newspaper proprietors. As well as the colour supplement magazine arriving as a free gift, the reader – primed to inspect their high-end offerings – is simultaneously being delivered as a gift to the advertisers.[2]

The first issue of 4 February 1962 established a format that has been loosely but consistently followed throughout the ongoing history of the colour supplement. The cover shows a photo-shoot of the model Jean Shrimpton wearing a Mary Quant dress, photographed by David Bailey, who was himself in the process of becoming an icon of 'Swinging London'. In the grid of images one rectangle is given over to the footballer Jimmy McIlroy, who was at the time taking the football club Burnley to the FA Cup Final that year in May (where they would lose to Tottenham Hotspur). Inside there is a James Bond story by Ian Fleming titled 'The Living Daylights', and an investigation of the city of Lincoln as a microcosm of Britain, illustrated with a photo-essay that combines images of residents (referred to as 'the Teenager', 'The Coffee Bar Owner', and such like) with quotations about their life and attitudes. The Jean Shrimpton cover-spread acts as a trailer for a two-page article on Mary Quant with a picture of Quant and more images of Shrimpton modelling various Quant garments. There is advertising by various advertisers including one for G Plan Furniture. There is a set of feature portraits of people 'who represent today', which includes Jimmy McIlroy, alongside an artist (Peter Blake) and a sociologist (Alan Little, who we will meet again in chapter 6). The editorial piece – which gives the magazine its strapline of 'A sharp glance at the mood of Britain' is by Tom

Stacey, who was a foreign correspondent working for the *Sunday Times* and had been heavily involved in reporting on the process of decolonisation, primarily in various parts of Africa, particularly Uganda. 'The changing mood of Britain', as the article was called, looked at Britain as it was becoming a post-imperial country, and asked how it was facing up to its new identity. Stacey, who would, a couple of years later, try to get elected as a Conservative MP, paints a picture of the postwar mood as both complex and perplexed. After 'winning' two world wars as battered victors, Britain, according to Stacey, faced a diminished place in the world:

> Twice we have come through as the exhausted and half-sorrowing victors, emerging without vengefulness, but – if with any emotion at all besides profound relief – only with a mild bewilderment at our diminished power in the world and at what sometimes appears to us as the fertile discarding of the mighty offspring of our former kind of national ideal, our empire.[3]

This mood of bewilderment, confusion, puzzlement is something we will see at work again in Ruth Glass's account of gentrification in the next chapter.

This first colour supplement established a number of conventions and rhetorical strategies that would be deployed and developed over the years. First, of course, it is worth noting the importance of images in these magazines. While the 1950s and 1960s saw the increasing use of images throughout daily newspapers, in the colour supplements every story, *every* feature is accompanied by an image, and often the image takes up much more magazine space than the writing. The relationship of images to text in these magazines is borrowed from the conventions established in women's magazines and in black-and-white pictorial weeklies such as *Picture Post* (1938–57). In tone and content, the colour supplements would run various types of features and stories. There would be social issue stories, which tend to demonstrate their seriousness by using black-and-white photography, as well as the sort of cultural stories that might feature actors, artists, politicians, designers, and so on. Fashion spreads would become a regular feature, as would articles on home décor and holiday destinations. Cooking also routinely featured. The advertising tended towards products that imagine a lifestyle of affluence: banking, international travel, cars, and alcoholic drinks (usually spirits), and cigarettes. Often the adverts that on first flush seemed to be selling exotic beach holidays turned out to be selling spirits: Bacardi advertised extensively in the supplements with images that pictured sumptuous beaches and relaxed tropical life. Of course, this should come as no surprise, as most advertising by the 1960s presented the commodity as a magical route to a better life. The road to the good life was paved with perfume, booze, cars, and cigarettes, and ended up in a tropical paradise.

These are general conventions rather than hard-and-fast rules. The tendency across all the magazines was to use celebrities, or potential celebrities (people in occupations where celebrity status is often a goal), wherever possible. So, while the *Observer*'s colour supplement for 23 October 1966 would bear the title 'The class war 1966', suggesting a social issue enquiry into the state of the class system in Britain, it featured seven portraits

4.1 *Observer* colour supplement, 7 June 1970

asking relatively famous people to reflect on what class meant to them. To investigate class and status, the magazine talked to the TV playwright Dennis Potter, whose father was a coal miner: so rather than interview a coalminer, the magazine opted for the famous son of one. A quick look at the cover from the *Observer* colour supplement from 7 June 1970 (figure 4.1) offers a good example of the variety of these magazines and the way that they often blended genres. The main feature is on the composer Benjamin Britten, but the focus of that article, and the visual interest in the images within it, is on the Suffolk coast, the Snape Maltings and the Aldeburgh festival. The article reads as a contribution to Suffolk tourism rather than an attempt to describe and explain Britten's approach to music. In this way – in its focus on tourism and leisure – it connects to two of the other items shown on the cover: an article on Portugal's Algarve coast and another on how to make mayonnaise. Portugal, in June 1970, was still undergoing 'national dictatorship', which for decades had been overseen by António de Oliveira Salazar (prime minister from 1932 to 1968).

The article makes no mention of the dictatorship, but instead celebrates the delicious wines and foods that can be found in the Algarve for amazingly low costs.

The single image on the cover that is in black-and-white depicts the black New York actor Barnard Boston and his white 'English' wife Gudrun (her surname might well be Boston too, but the article doesn't mention it).[4] The article inside has the title 'Would you let your daughter ... ' and is by the exiled South African communist journalist Lewis Nkosi. It is a wide-ranging article discussing sexual desire and race, and looking at how the conditions of interracial love change in different areas around the globe (from Wolverhampton to Johannesburg). It offers a nuanced discussion of how wealth, tradition, and interracial desire are connected. While the images show us the famous and the would-be-famous, the emphasis of the article is often on interracial relationships amongst the working class. We see Michael Pratt, famous for playing a TV detective in the show *Randall and Hopkirk (Deceased)* with his romantic partner, the Indian actor Chitra Neogy; but we don't see the English Asian bus drivers and farm workers in Nottingham who were interviewed for the article, though we do hear their words.

The colour supplements described a modern world, filled with social problems, and also gave you a means of escape – into the world of interiors, holidays, cuisine, or fame. One solution to poverty, racism, crime, and all the other ills that the colour supplements regularly covered (for the affluent reader, at any rate) was to escape, either literally or in the imagination, to that deserted Barbadian beach for a Bacardi or two. And if that wasn't available, then there were endless possibilities for conjuring up a world free of conflict, where easy going conviviality could be achieved through homemade mayonnaise and photographs of that cheap holiday in Portugal. As Marc Boxer, the first editor of the *Sunday Times Magazine*, put it when he was reflecting on the allure of the colour supplements in 1985:

> Newspapers are about the world out there: an objective and masculine world, gritty and grey and above all immediate. Magazines at their best are more seductive, intimate, subjective. They are instant nostalgia, almost your autobiography in advance. You could have that kitchen, travel to that beach, cook that meal wearing that shirtwaister dress.[5]

The colour supplement shares the tempo of the times: its beat is 'instant nostalgia'. You read about the Algarve and already you are imagining the holiday snaps you will have taken.

The world of colour supplements didn't exclude the more masculine newspaper world, but what it did do was provide access to the 'seductive, intimate, subjective' world *within* the general ambience of that world. The colour supplements recruited relatively affluent men and women to 'lifestyle' culture as a general interest. What had previously been the preserve of women's magazines, particularly those magazines that centred on advising the reader about domesticity and family life, was placed as a central concern for any weekend broadsheet newspaper reader. The colour supplements expanded the reach of that arena of women's magazines which was concerned with what quickly became known as 'lifestyle'. The term lifestyle – with its associated compounds of 'lifestyle-advice', 'lifestyle-choice' – became a watchword in the 1960s and 1970s for the way that fashion, advertising, and consumption were becoming central ingredients to the way people lived. For those most critical of consumer society the term became associated with the superficiality of modern life. We, however, can use it as an umbrella term for taking taste seriously as part of everyday life.

Fashion, flair, and dishwashers

Today, lifestyle publishing might cover anything from so-called 'shelter' magazines to much more specialised publications aimed at specific practices such as wine tasting or mountaineering. The genesis of lifestyle publishing can be found in magazines aimed specifically at women, and today gender is still a defining characteristic of lifestyle publishing.[6] It was the insistent focus on homes and housework, with regular features on cooking, fashion, and home décor within women's magazines, that provided the Sunday colour supplements with the format to link newspaper journalism to expensive advertising. One of the most successful women's magazines of the postwar period was *Good Housekeeping*. The magazine was started in the US in 1885, and the UK version was published from 1922. In 1924 the Good Housekeeping Institute was established as a way of providing independent consumer advice, much of which was then passed on through the magazine. The 1920s saw a flurry of magazines emerging aimed at middle-class women in Britain who were having to get to grips with the new reality of the middle-class, 'servant-less home'. Such magazines offered advice on housework and took a quasi-scientific approach to home management. They were often evangelical about the benefits of any appliance (electrical or not) that could be called 'labour saving'. They relied heavily on advertising revenue to make money. Such magazines have always provided a training in domestic consumer culture, with editorial articles routinely cultivating precisely the same ground as the adverts that are also being featured. There are often whole sections of these magazines that discuss new commodities describing their various qualities, which are then amplified elsewhere in the magazine in specific adverts. It is hard to tell which bits are advertising and which are not.

Looking at some lifestyle magazines from the 1960s and 1970s gives a sense of taste's role in consumer society. What is crucial here is to look, not just at the specific tastes that were being promoted by the magazines, but at the historical changes they were acknowledging and enacting. As pointed out in chapter 1, to get a sense of the social function of taste we can't limit taste to the scale of individual consumer choices, or even the scale of what's 'in' and what's 'out' for particular social groups; we need to also get a sense of the larger historical scale of taste, and how it shows us changes in the way we live. Taste is not simply about the promotion of certain kinds of attitudes and styles, it is also about what doesn't need promoting, what is taken for granted, taken as read. When a magazine like *Good Housekeeping* began, it was addressed matter-of-factly to women who were married, who were thinking of getting married, or who perhaps were widowed. What today reads like a zealous paean to heterosexuality and marriage was the taken-for-granted world of the 1920s (as far as mass-market magazines went, that is). The same is true of the relentless whiteness that was a feature of the magazines before and after the Second World War.

By the 1960s and 1970s we can see changes in who the magazine was addressed to: for instance, there is much more emphasis on the trials and tribulations of marriage and the realisation that an increasing number of marriages would end in divorce. Articles on sexual and other problems within marriage became a regular feature.[7] But in terms of heterosexual assumptions the magazine didn't change significantly. In its idea and idealisation of the housewife there are many features of the *Good Housekeeping* world that in the early 1960s looked uncannily like the 1920s. For instance, in their 1963 book *Setting Up Home*, the *Good Housekeeping* team still lay out an extensive routine for the wife to follow in terms of housework, with a daily round of chores, as well as weekday variations (washing on Monday, 'main bedrooms, spare room as necessary' on Tuesday, and so on), only this time there is some variation in households where the wife also goes out to work. Then the husband helps with the washing up after the evening meal, and 'deals with the sitting-room grate, if necessary'.[8] This minor variation points to two changes that were important for these decades: more and more women were working, and there were fundamental changes occurring in domestic technology (grates might not need dealing with, grates might not even exist in many homes).

It is at the level of general assumed taste, rather than specific tastes, that magazines like *Good Housekeeping* work. Specific magazine adverts say buy *this* make of carpeting, *this* style of central heating. It looks as if the magazine is all about these different makes and styles. But what is less obvious is the way that the magazines have been persuading us that central heating and fitted carpets are now something that every home must have. By changing the assumptions of what is seen as a necessity or a necessary luxury, these magazines work together to produce changes of a general nature in the world of taste. Lifestyle magazines lay out the pattern of what a home requires in the first place to be a modern home. This work can be seen as a two-stage process: the first stage consists of introducing something new, which readers might feel is new-fangled, expensive, and unnecessary, and making it part of the furniture. The second stage consists of simply assuming that this is now just a normal and essential part of homelife. At this stage you can debate the available options. Today a magazine doesn't need to discuss the usefulness of a mobile phone. By the late 1960s fitted carpeting was fully established as part of the normal landscape of the house.

In the 1960s there were lots of devices and forms of comfort that, while available, were not yet standard and ubiquitous elements of a house. The magazines were busy turning what might start off as unnecessary luxuries into must-have necessities for modern living. In looking back over many years of a magazine you get the feeling that they're often running long term campaigns to introduce new goods and tastes into the home. By the early 1970s

Good Housekeeping had pretty much established central heating as a necessity for any home. It wasn't easy. The fortunes of central heating are patchy: in their 1963 book, *Setting Up Home*, for instance, *Good Housekeeping* begin a section on heating with the assumption that 'in this country, where periods of very cold weather are generally short-lived, it is usual to rely on central heating for background heat only and have radiant heaters for "topping up" when required'.[9] If you were lucky enough to have central heating, you wouldn't be daft enough to actually use it to heat the house, just to take the frost off the insides of the windows. By 1967 they were still busy promoting central heating as something that wasn't entirely 'usual'. Under a heading 'Central heating: the luxury you can afford', the Good Housekeeping Institute produced a long article on the various types of central heating and the benefits and drawbacks of the different systems. They might have been undecided about which system was best, but they were certainly not undecided about the benefits of central heating. In one section subtitled 'Four families in search of comfort', the reader is told that 'All had their individual preferences. All found their lives with central heating a great improvement on the old cold days. We asked them to tell us about it – snags and all'.[10] The magazine recognised that not all its readers were going to have central heating or be in a position to install it, so the following month they ran a section on free-standing heaters, but even here the reader was still being persuaded of the benefits of central heating: 'Winter's coming, and if you think there's time to waste before warming up you're acting like an ostrich! These Institute-picked auxiliary heaters won't produce the same effect as full central heating, but each will do a marvellous job of providing warmth when – and where – it's wanted'.[11]

If the taste campaign for central heating was nearing its final victory in the late 1960s, the campaign to get the dishwasher treated as a normal part of the house was only just beginning. Consumer culture is faced with having to navigate a contradiction. To change general taste for new forms of technology you have to change something from being a luxury to a necessity, but you also want to maintain that what you are getting is still luxurious. With the central heating campaign, you could see this being negotiated by the phrase 'the luxury you can afford'; with the dishwasher, something similar was also taking place. One advert that ran in *Good Housekeeping*'s competitor magazine, *Homes and Gardens*, in the late 1960s argued that 'If you think a clothes washer is a necessity, why call our dishwasher a luxury?'[12] *Good Housekeeping* again used the Good Housekeeping Institute to test out various machines under the statement: 'Never has there been a more universally hated chore than washing-up. Yet of all the labour-saving devices, the automatic dishwasher seems to cause the most controversy. Can it really be a matter for debate?'[13] A few pages later there is an advert for the Kenwood automatic dishwasher. After naming all its attributes (it's efficient, it's fully automatic, it holds plenty, it fits in anywhere, it's economic) the dishwasher addresses the magazine reader directly: 'your servant madam'.[14] The work that lifestyle magazines undertake is to give the reader a taste for something, whether that thing is convenience, luxury, efficiency, or what have you. Most often it is for something dressed up as a necessary luxury.

Lifestyle magazines like *Good Housekeeping* also teach taste in a more ambient way. No editor of a lifestyle magazine in the 1960s and 1970s was going to lay down a set of foundational style rules in a way that might have been possible thirty years before, because one of the aspects of the consumer culture in the age of affluence is the massive expanse of eclectic tastes. Instead of promoting certain styles, what was being promoted was an attitude towards taste and style. As a reader you were being encouraged to want taste, not a particular taste, but taste in general and by the bucket load. And, of course, what that attitude actually consisted of was necessarily open: it was up to you, with the help of advertisers and magazine advisors, to fill it. 'Getting taste' – becoming a person of taste – was, for the lifestyle magazines, a particularly vague affair. Good taste, in the tautological way of things, was about liking tasteful things.

In the January 1968 edition of *Good Housekeeping* the magazine ran a feature on 'Furnishing with flair'. Here 'flair' describes an attitude towards taste that *Good Housekeeping* wants the reader to embrace. We all need a bit of flair, a bit of panache. The article focuses on the interior design journalist Mary Gilliatt, who had just published a book on *English Style*, and looks at how Gilliatt decorated her own cottage. Each photograph by Michael Boys is accompanied by editorial copy showing us how Gilliatt has 'flair'. For the photo of the hallway (figure 4.2) the copy reads:

> Flair is: establishing a mood as soon as the front door opens and setting the scene for the rest of the house; painting hall walls a warm topaz yellow to lead the way for hot colours to come; running sisal carpet through in the kitchen-dining room for common sense and continuity; furnishing cheaply and sturdily, so the children of the house can feel at home too.[15]

For the image of her living room (figure 4.3) we are told that:

> Flair is: daring to be different; painting the beams white and the walls dark instead of the conventional vice versa; whitewashing the fireplace instead of leaving red brick; putting a Mexican bark painting above it instead of a hunting print; preferring a modern Conran chair and a Datum table to the inevitable antique.[16]

What would we learn from this? There are some practical tips about how you might achieve continuity from room to room by the use of flooring (the sisal carpeting, the colour schemes), but the main advice is to feel confident about your tastes. But if you were confident about your tastes, you wouldn't be in the market for advice. Flair is bold taste, unconventional taste, confident taste, daring taste. How do you get it? By being bold, unconventional, confident, and daring – by having flair. Tautological arguments about taste are the bread-and-butter of lifestyle magazines. The reader is left to learn 'flair' by seeing an endless display of examples of it. We learn flair by copying it (never the boldest decision you could make) or by hoping that your choice of canary yellow floor paint and maroon walls is going to wow everyone.

Two months later the magazine ran a feature on 'the country style', which echoes and pre-empts *The House Book*. Here we see examples of country style kitchens. The feature is

4.2 and 4.3 Mary Gilliatt's home photographed by Michael Boys for *Good Housekeeping*, January 1968

4.4 Michael Boys photograph for *Good Housekeeping*, March 1968, 'Make Mine Country Style', featuring Sumna storage units designed by Terence Conran

promoting a 'look' that mimics elements associated with rural cottage kitchens: 'natural' flooring rather than lino, for instance. The hook of the article is two-fold. The rural look is promoted as an alternative to the industrial look of many modern kitchens, which are often an assembly of gadgetry. The second aspect is more of a puzzle: if the rural look is associated with weathered and worn materials, with ancient floors and passed-down furniture and fittings, then how do you fabricate that look from scratch? Here *Good Housekeeping* is primarily teaching taste to its readers through example, and the examples come with prices and addresses for attempting the same look. At heart, then, lifestyle magazines have a conflicted approach to taste: on the one hand they seem to be encouraging self-confidence and self-belief; on the other hand, they are establishing the conditions whereby mimicry is really the best, sometimes the only, policy.

The article on the 'country style' tells you why you might need to get the look and then shows you how to accomplish it. The photograph showing you a 'country style' kitchen (figure 4.4) is accompanied by the following copy: 'not all modern kitchen furniture looks clinical. Since the scrubbed pine revival, more manufacturers have come to appreciate the sympathetic appeal of wood. This solid pine table by Conran has waxed legs, but the surface still likes an old-fashioned scrub'.[17] We are told who has made the main elements of the kitchen, which in this case is primarily Terence Conran, and we are told how much they cost and where to get them. We are also provided with a host of alternative design firms making similar items. The Japanese-style paper lampshade and bentwood chairs are not itemised in this way but are obviously crucial to the 'look'. Practical guidance is mixed with the sort of ambient learning from example that is used to sensitise readers to what is appropriate within a particular look. You can't go wrong with a Japanese paper lampshade. As in *The House Book*, the reader is encouraged to look to fashionable design names and standard forms of furniture but is also given suggestion for how the aged look might be accomplished at minimal cost (though with maximum effort). Not everything will have to come from furniture shops. Accompanying another image, we are told that while it looks old this 'kitchen is in fact very new; it's the materials used that are old. The units are topped with black marble slabs, originally acquired with washstands attached. But the unit fronts are ordinary tongued-and-grooved pine, and the "antique" hinges came from the local builder's merchant'.[18] The country style look produced for the modern home will also benefit from recovered materials: 'the floor was only laid last year, but looks genuinely mellow because the bricks are old. Most demolition contractors sell them for about £2 a hundred, and they're well worth seeking out, because new bricks are coldly uniform in colour and texture'.[19]

A new kind of magazine for the new kind of woman

Magazines like *Good Housekeeping* and *Home and Gardens* studiously avoided the world of news and politics. They remained steadfastly within the domestic realm. The colour supplements altered the terrain of lifestyle publishing by blending investigations into social issues (poverty, racism, war, famine, and so on) with a steady stream of high-end advertising, and features on holidays, cooking, and fashion. If the Sunday supplements brought more men into conversations about lifestyles and taste, then there were other magazines emerging that wanted to bring the so-called masculine world of news and politics to women's magazines. One such magazine was the monthly publication *Nova*. The first issue was published in March 1965, with the subtitle: 'A new kind of magazine for the new kind of woman'.[20] In September 1965 the subtitle changed to: 'For women who think magazines don't understand'.[21] The form that the Sunday colour supplements had developed, which brought together issue-based journalism with the new consumer society (with its endless seductions for increasing comfort) was dramatically amplified in *Nova*. But it was also challenged.

In the run up to the first publication, the team behind *Nova* produced a dummy edition to entice high-end advertisers. In this they set out the ethos of the magazine:

> There's a *new* younger generation of women with us. New in *kind*. A generation that won't fit into the old socio-economic groupings. Women with new standards, new ideas, new spending patterns and new power … *Nova* is a new kind of magazine for women. It starts from the proposition that there is a new kind of woman. She's young, alive, and aware, a product of the changes in the material and social conventions of the post-war world. She's a woman with a wider horizon of daily living, and with a little more knowledge, a little better taste, and wider interests than ever before … *Nova* will be her magazine. It will help her to live a more satisfying life, for it will understand her outlook, reflect her way of life, and refuel her interests. It will be modern, like her; frank, like her. It will set demanding standards, like her. It will look as up to the minute and arresting as she does.[22]

The focus on taste was elaborated through highly inventive fashion spreads, which were the visual centre of the magazine, as well as through regular food articles by Elizabeth David and Prue Leith, and articles featuring interior designers such as Max Glendinning and Zeev Aram.[23]

Like any lifestyle magazine, it relied on advertising revenue to survive, and the advertising was specifically aimed at what the magazine described as the AA market (Above Average Intelligence, Income, etc.). The magazine regularly ran adverts for Harrods and Aston Martin cars alongside more mainstream adverts for cigarettes, make-up, perfume, and Tupperware. But what made the magazine stand out was its visual aesthetics and its thematic articles, which broached topics such as women's prisons and skinheads. Of particular note was *Nova*'s approach to sex: 'Until *Nova*, women's magazines had traditionally been coy about one huge area of women's lives – sex. *Nova* was the first to cover the concerns that were also the issues of female liberation – orgasm, contraception, abortion, marriage, childbirth, parenthood, and how to get men, how to keep them and how to enjoy them'.[24] The mixture of aspirational advertising, trend-setting tastes, and editorial articles addressing social and personal issues meant that the magazine was (like many women-centred lifestyle magazines) constantly encouraging women to become 'superwomen': to have more, to care more, to have better orgasms (and more of them), to have more success at work, to be better dressed, better parents, to enjoy life more, to undertake constant self-improvement. One of the things that distinguishes *Nova* was the magazine's self-consciousness of the impossibility of these demands:

> One woman in her day plays many parts … and the silly thing is that the more she does, the harder it is for her to get any kind of notice taken of it at all. Even five years ago a girl who left her children with an au pair and went out to work found herself at the receiving end of a lot of heavy criticism … but she did get a lot of grudging admiration as well. People told her crossly that they didn't know how she did it, and certainly didn't expect to be asked to dinner, or to see her at the hairdresser's. Now it has become more or less acceptable, it's suddenly no longer clever, and the poor girl is expected to entertain lavishly, have fascinating hobbies, and probably build a house with her bare hands in the long empty evenings.[25]

Of course *Nova* is complicit in the process of setting unattainable expectations, but it is knowingly complicit and can also satirise how female 'liberation' can slip into a constant feeling of under-achievement.

Nova's politics were progressive in a loose, un-programmatic and non-aligned way. It was generally against all forms of bigotry and on the side of permissiveness. It also tended to treat new social phenomena with a depth and a matter-of-fact seriousness that was often missing in other magazines, which might opt instead to sensationalise or demonise. For instance, in an issue from May 1973 the magazine covered a new phenomenon that was emerging in the US – marriage contracts. In a long-form essay (roughly 7,000 words spread over nine pages) the article explored a form of contract that was being adopted in the US for couples wanting to pursue more egalitarian forms of marriage. Rather than being the more recent 'prenuptial agreement' aimed at the distribution and apportioning of assets should the marriage fall apart, these contracts were primarily aimed at redressing the masculine presumptions within marriage that positioned women as secondary to the man. The article provides two examples of marriage contracts; one from a couple who married in Los Angeles in 1972 and another from a couple married in Birmingham (UK) in 1973, and explores the benefits of making explicit the sort of marriage that might be pursued 'after the wedding'. The Los Angeles example is explicitly feminist in its orientation: for instance, the clauses on the issue of their careers are as follows:

> It is our intent that we shall each have our own careers and we agree to support each other in achieving this goal.
>
> a. We acknowledge that there will be many subtle social and psychological pressures tending to emphasise Benjamin's career and devaluating Virginia's, and we commit ourselves to be conscious of these at all times.
> b. We further acknowledge that due to the sexual biases of the society, Virginia may need more time and effort to develop her career.
> c. We value the work of childrearing and housekeeping equally with work that commands cash wages or furthers a career.
> d. We reject the idea that the person who makes more money is a more valuable human being.[26]

It also treated marriage as a something that required a degree of vigilance: 'We agree that we shall devote a minimum of one hour per week to communication of our feelings towards each other, to work through our problems, and to raise our consciousness

4.5 *Spare Rib*, issue 1, July 1972

about social and internal pressures enforcing traditional sexual roles'.[27] The example from Birmingham is less explicitly feminist but also is aimed to creating more egalitarian partnerships.

The article on the marriage contract was published the year after the feminist magazine *Spare Rib* was launched in the UK – which announced itself as 'the new women's magazine' (figure 4.5). On the face of it the two magazines couldn't be more dissimilar: *Nova* was large-format, glossy, advertising-heavy, and often featured sexually provocative fashion spreads; *Spare Rib* was a campaigning magazine that prioritised feminist-socialist politics and often had a DIY aesthetic. And yet they both covered similar issues. For instance, the first issue of *Spare Rib* included an article on the women's prison Holloway, which had been a main feature article in *Nova* in July 1968.[28] Both articles were campaigning for the closure of the prison, yet the shorter *Spare Rib* article alerts its readers to how they can become involved in the 'Radical Alternative to Prison' movement, while the *Nova* article is a 5,000-word piece of investigative journalism by someone who spent time in the prison. *Nova*, then, was positioned between the world of lifestyle magazines and the more socially engaged world of a magazine like *Spare Rib*. It delivered a version of feminism to readers who were also interested in the latest fashions and in consumer culture. But it also resolutely refused the wholehearted embrace of the culturally up-market world of the posh glossies. As one reader put it:

> *Queen*, *Harper's*, *Tatler*, … weren't for me, I saw them as for another kind of person … they were … for people who led a different kind of life and were doing different things, probably had a house in the county and a flat in town, travelled a lot, maybe the wife didn't work, or have to work, it was not within … the society that I knew. I could actually do and be in tune with some of the stuff in *Nova* whereas stuff in *Tatler* and those magazines … were for the hunting and fishing and shooting set, having parties and looking incredible – beautiful, but not for the person who buys a £3.50 Biba dress every Friday to go out on Saturday night and gets pissed.[29]

Would you live next door to my mummy and daddy?

Nova was pioneering in its use of black models for its fashion spreads. It also often featured articles on racial themes. For instance, in the January 1966 issue, *Nova*'s cover consisted of a cute young black child on the cover. Written below the girl was the sentence: 'you may think I look cute but would you live next door to my mummy and daddy?' (figure 4.6). The article featured a quiz for testing the reader's racial prejudice, while the editorial, in campaigning mode, tried to persuade the readership of the need for a Race Relations Bill:

> It could be that on the threshold of 1966 you are still in need of a good resolution [a New Year's resolution] and the one we suggest is in fact good for all years: face the facts. The little girl on the cover is one of them. She represents a particular problem about which much has been said but little done … there is colour prejudice in Britain and it is of an order which requires a Race Relations Bill to legislate against it.[30]

4.6 *Nova*, January 1966

Other articles included November 1971's piece on 'Brixton: The Ghetto that Britain Built', which prophesised that 'by the year 2000 Britain will probably have a black helot class unless the educational system is radically altered'.[31]

The racial expression of lifestyle magazines has to be understood aside from their explicit racial politics. *Nova*, the colour supplements, and various lifestyle magazines usually took a liberal line on racial matters, but they all addressed the reader as white. The rhetorical question of *Nova*'s front cover directly addresses white readers. For a black reader it would make no sense to be asked if they would live next door to the child's mummy and daddy – they were the mummy and daddy, or the aunt and uncle. The racial impact of a magazine is expressed by the kinds of images and themes it concocts and by the way it implies a specific readership. The models in magazines are part of the spectacle that the magazine is selling – they aren't stand-ins for the reader. To have black models was – in the 1960s and 1970s – to give that spectacle an exotic flavour. Magazines generate a baseline of 'normalcy' which can be understood as the readership being imagined for a magazine. This normalcy isn't to be found in editorials, or for that matter in the adverts and fashion spreads, but in the regular sections on cooking and recipes, on relationship advice, in horoscopes, in features that are about leisure and hobbies, about holidays and work, about sex and relationships. It is the lack of anything *but* whiteness in these sections that sees 'lifestyle' as a white affair.[32]

The selection of 'issues' that a magazine tackles – as issues – further works to compound what it treats as the norm. Non-whiteness takes its place along with crime, homelessness, chronic illness, war, and so on, as exceptional, out-of-the-ordinary conditions. What is relatively rare in these magazines is an image showing black and brown people as part of everyday English and British life. Even when this did occur, the emphasis was usually on the spectacle of 'foreign flavours' within London, for an audience who might consume them (rather than produce them).

The colour supplements and lifestyle magazines were a crucial vehicle for disseminating all sorts of tastes in late twentieth-century Britain, and those tastes were changing how class was being experienced. They were central to those identities that were labelled 'new middle class', as they were so attentive to emerging tastes rather than established ones. The overarching whiteness of these magazines suggests that the new middle classes were also represented as white. This doesn't mean that there wasn't a 'new middle class' emerging for people of colour in the 1960s and 1970s, but it does mean that it didn't have much visibility within a medium like lifestyle magazines (that visibility would start to emerge in the 1980s, as discussed in chapter 9). This points to a difference between the UK and the US, where a black middle class was very much in evidence and where magazines like *Ebony* – a lifestyle magazine for African Americans – had been in existence since 1945.

5
Welcome to the village

Fiona MacCarthy, the design critic for the *Guardian*, recognised immediately that shops like Habitat didn't simply sell goods for domestic interiors, but a style of life that was connected to a wider environment. At the start of 1965, when she was describing the contents of the shop, she was also imagining the perfect Habitat shoppers: 'Piled high on the chests and dressers and plain scrubbed trestle tables there are stoneware kitchen crocks, apothecary jars, preserving pans, giant pestles and mortars, rural English china with pictures of cows paddling lugubriously in brooks. People lug them off to countrify their cottages in Fulham'.[1] Habitat, for MacCarthy, wasn't just about furnishing houses, but about promoting a particular way of living in those houses in relation to the cities or towns that surrounded them. It is the verb 'to countrify' that does all the work. Habitat shoppers might be living in cities but what they were doing was countrifying their homes so that they might live in cities in a rural-ish manner. She picks up on this theme almost two years later in an article announcing the opening of the second Habitat store in Tottenham Court Road. Reading the jokey catalogue descriptions for Habitat ('what a grind – pepper mills from France', 'sweetshop jars for herbs and kitchen goodies') she finds that 'the adjectives, downright and jovial, mount up to an elaborate townsmen's code for country living. Habitat merchandise is fashionably basic, a kit for farmhouse cooking, preferably French'.[2] It is this combination of rural-urbanism that MacCarthy sees as both fake and jovial. Her Habitat shoppers are pretending to live a peasant existence in amongst the most metropolitan of places:

> In any big city, on Saturdays, you find them, living like peasants, exchanging rustic jokes. While he (ham-fisted handyman) puts up his pinewood units with melamine working tops and lots of drawers for clobber, she brings back a rough rush game bag, full of shopping and donning butcher's apron, makes a weekend rural lunch: huge hearty stew with hot crusty rolls and creamy mounds of butter (made by wooden butter-pat): then the thinnest crispiest pancakes from a heavy cast-iron crepe pan and coffee drunk in red-enameled jolly workmen's mugs. These are Conran people. Or imitation Conran. They buy their lives from Habitat, the shop in Fulham Road or else they set up cheerful home from minor Habitats, bright shops on Conran principles in almost every town.[3]

For MacCarthy this scene is phony, but she also gets the sense of the glee involved: the enjoyment of hearty stew, of coffee, of the pleasures of sensual immediacy, however much of a pretense that might be.

At the same time that MacCarthy was delivering her verdict on Habitat, a young PhD student – Michael Thompson – was combining his studies with more practical work:

> Between 1966 and 1971 I was living in North London and working as a carpenter for a small (and now bankrupt) building firm. Like all my colleagues, I also 'did foreigners' (moonlighting – taking on other jobs, theoretically in one's spare time), installing a cast-iron grate and marble surround here, building a Georgian pipe-box to conceal the gas-fired central heating there. Essentially our work consisted of transforming dilapidated early-Victorian artisans' cottages into trendy residences for *Observer* journalists, and we were all piratically engaged in the early stages of a process that has since been christened 'gentrification'.[4]

While Thompson was moonlighting, he was also contemplating his PhD topic, which was eventually published in 1979 as *Rubbish Theory: The Creation and Destruction of Value*. He was trying to understand how value worked, and more precisely how something which had become viewed as disposable might get turned into something with durable value. One of his examples was Victorian terraced houses in London's Islington (figure 5.1), which in 1965 the Housing Minister, Richard Crossman, had described as 'rat-infested slums' that 'must be demolished'. They were passed their usefulness and needed to be

5.1 Terraced houses in Islington, London, 1960s, pre-gentrification

replaced. 'Old terraced houses', Crossman continued, 'may have a snob-appeal to members of the middle class but they are not suitable accommodation for working class tenants'.[5] Thompson translated Grossman's definition as: 'An old building which, occupied by members of the middle class, forms part of our glorious heritage, is, if occupied by members of the working class, a rat-infested slum'.[6] In terms of value these houses were capable of moving from being out-of-date 'rubbish' that would require knocking down, to having durable value that would only increase in worth (exponentially as it turned out). Thompson's job as a carpenter and general builder was to help in the transformation of value; to turn something urban and poor into what, with the help of *The House Book* could result in a life of 'controlled casualness': 'The leaded fanlight has been painstakingly repaired and, affixed to the brickwork at the side of the door, is a blue-and-white enamel number plate: a little touch of provincial France proclaiming that the owner drinks Hirondelle Vin Ordinaire with his Quiche Lorraine for dinner and not Light Ale with his ham-and-egg pie for his tea'.[7] These wine-drinking, quiche eaters should be becoming familiar; now we need to see how and where they were living and what this was doing to cities and towns where they were living.

The phenomenon of old, often poorly maintained, areas of housing, gradually becoming newly desirable when bought up by middle-class homebuyers is something that would affect many cities during the 1960s and 1970s. It was particularly visible in London. The process was uneven, and in a large district like Islington often piecemeal. A single crescent of houses might consist of newly gentrified houses sitting cheek-by-jowl with blocks of bedsits in various states of disrepair, houses that had been squatted, and rented flats. The area of Notting Hill, which had become infamous in 1958 when a series of attacks by fascist groups on young West Indian men had led to riots, was, in the 1970s, gradually being gentrified (figures 5.2 and 5.3). The area had also been notorious in the 1950s and early 1960s for its exploitative renting practices by 'slum' landlord Peter Rachman. An aspect of that gentrification was establishing a form of white urban rurality based on home ownership in what had been an area of mostly multicultural rentals.

'Earl Grey tea and stripped pine stereo systems'

The taste for rustic urbanism required housing that could be reconfigured as 'countrified retreats'. While *The House Book*, and other style guides, assured the reader that the eclectic, rural look could be achieved in a high-rise flat, it was also clear that there were much more accommodating settings. As Margaret Duckett explained in her 1968 account of Terence Conran's practice of moving into Georgian townhouses and degutting them: 'good architecture counts when exposing the structural shell'.[8] The phrase 'good architecture counts' is partly a reference to the potential of older houses (Georgian, Victorian, Edwardian) to add to the eclecticism of the interior through decorative 'original features' such as ceiling roses, cornices, picture rails, and the like. As we have already seen, the Habitat-Conran taste

5.2 Dilapidated housing in Notting Hill Gate in the 1960s

5.3 Notting Hill, boutique shops and restored facades

combined an eclectic mix of minimalist decoration, natural materials and surfaces, and junkshop 'finds' designed to reveal your personality, as well as a taste for Mediterranean cuisine and settings designed to amplify informality. With older houses, 'personality' could be transferred to the house itself: the eclecticism of controlled casualness could lovingly embrace old marble fireplaces and elaborate cornicing into its designs. In one of the most detailed descriptions of this taste, the journalist Jonathan Raban dissects not just the part that taste plays in the lives of people for whom shops like Habitat were aimed, but also the effects that this growing platoon of tastemakers were having on London.

Raban, the son of a rural vicar, grew up in Norfolk, attended a private boarding school, and studied for a degree in English at the University of Hull (at the time, 1959, Hull was the only university in England that accepted candidates for an honours degree in literature without a Latin GCE). He followed this with a brief stint as a lecturer; first at the University of Aberystwyth, then at the new University of East Anglia. By the end of the1960s Raban had given up his academic career and was a full-time, relatively impoverished, writer living in London.[9] In his 1974 book, *Soft City*, Raban attempts to describe London in the late 1960s and early 1970s, from 'the inside' – as a relentlessly diverse city made up of distinct but changing localities. It is an account that focuses, in part, on the psychological effects of what it feels like to live in a metropolitan city at this time, and as part of this he provides a portrait of a new class of city dwellers, who in the 1960s and 1970s were finding a footing on the property ladder by buying run-down terraced houses. For Raban, these middle-class-moderns had a consistent approach to inhabiting what had previously been poorly maintained, rented houses: 'Wallpaper is stripped and replaced by white paint. The floorboards are sanded free of varnish, then sealed and left uncarpeted, save for the odd goatskin rug. Tasselled and richly coloured lampshades are thrown out, and vast Japanese plain paper globes are hung in their stead'.[10] Large white paper lampshades (available from Habitat but from any number of other shops as well) were part and parcel of the taste that the journalist Nicholas Tomalin had named as 'conspicuous thrift' in his 1963 article for the trend-setting, and trend-analysing magazine *Town*.[11]

In 1974 Raban saw 'a future of Japanese lampshades, *House and Garden*, French baby cars, white paint, asparagus tips, Earl Grey tea and stripped pine stereo systems' slowly and unevenly colonising large areas of London and other British cities. Echoing Tomalin, Raban sees the irony in the relationship between aesthetics and what it means to 'get on': 'the reward of success is the freedom to choose a style of elegant austerity'.[12] These houses were being made over, but they were also being unmade: the wallpaper stripping and white paint, the sanding and varnishing were undoing decades of 'housekeeping'. For instance, before the era of fitted carpets, heavy tar-black paint was used on floorboards as an edge for large, unfitted carpets: hours of sanding were required to remove this thick, gunky paint. Similarly, as the houses were modernised, the original panelled doors were often covered with sheets of plywood to conform to an unfussy and minimal aesthetic. The new, 'conspicuous thrift' style required undoing these touches of modernisation: plywood panels were removed, and the old original doors, layered with decades of paint, were treated with noxious chemicals that took them back to bare wood. 'Controlled casualness' also meant 'knocking through': taking out walls of Victorian terraced houses to open-up the downstairs either into one large kitchen-diner-living room, or two rooms – a living room and a large kitchen 'hub'.

What was taking place was not simply an imposition of a new aesthetic on old houses; such transformations were altering the neighbourhood and the people who lived there. The new arrivals didn't ignore the working-class culture that was often a feature of the areas where middle-class-moderns bought; instead elements of older and newly outdated working-class culture – such as the 'well-scrubbed pine table' – were absorbed and rebranded as trendy. A kitchen table which might have accompanied a hard, practical life became something to provide authenticity to the sensual pleasures that could be found in 'elegant austerity' and 'conspicuous thrift'. The outdated, that for one class signalled neglect, became a new taste for another:

> The Victorian public lavatory, the horseshoe pub bar, the railed verandah, the Edwardian gilt shop sign, the heavy portico, even sheet-metal advertisements for cocoa and cigarettes, turn into prized antiques at the same time as they are being torn down or covered over as vulgar objects in other quarters of the city. The frontiersmen want to conserve the working class past at the very moment when the working class themselves are trying to escape it.[13]

What was taking place in those urban areas that were undergoing some form of gentrification was, in taste terms, a conflict of perception and value. What to one group was perceived as old-fashioned and run down, was to another group something to be savoured, a sign of authentic and eccentric taste.

In his succinct and scintillating account of the 'early cultures of gentrification in London' Joe Moran writes about how the newly gentrifying areas resulted in 'not so much class warfare as mutual incomprehension about vastly differing lifestyles and cultures'.[14] If 'suspicion' was aimed at new middle-class neighbours by the working-class residents, then an even greater sense of hostility was, according to a study conducted by Jeremy Bugler in 1968, directed at the West Indian tenants living in these same squares and streets.[15] Here the stark whitewashing of the exterior and interiors of these restored houses takes on a more assertive sense of racial identity. The incomprehension of what was happening in areas of gentrification meant that prospective buyers were often mistaken as local government officials who had come to start the process of demolition and 'slum clearance' in the area.[16] The juxtaposition of run-down rental housing and elegantly developed owner-occupied properties in part of the same terrace was vividly displayed at the Daily Mail Ideal Home Exhibition in 1968 (figure 5.4). It is worth noting that this mocked-up, stark white

5.4 Learning gentrification at the Daily Mail Ideal Home Exhibition in 1968. Two houses from Countrycraft Terrace

regency terrace house and its 'haunted-house' neighbour were houses in a street named 'Countrycraft Terrace' (Countrycraft Ltd. was the evocative name of a building, developing, and property firm particularly active in the 1960s and 1970s), suggesting how closely the ties of gentrification and the aesthetics of urban rurality had become by then.

Raban provides sketches of the people were who were filling their houses with Japanese lampshades while cooking quiche Lorraines. The designation 'middle class' does little to identify the newness of these incomers, nor does it convey the nuances of their specific social characteristics. To start with, they were young, and saw themselves as distinctly un-middle class in terms of taste and political allegiances:

> the young couples had never conceived of themselves as a class – they had rejected the bourgeois ethic, just as they had rejected the florid display of Chelsea – and were strenuously, idealistically individualist. They didn't see themselves in the stereotypical portraits painted by the angry correspondents in the paper [who were bemoaning the influx of middle-class newcomers]; they were not like that, they *cared* and had scruples. How could sincere socialists be accused of class-exploitation? Or acres of white paint be construed as a vulgar exhibition of financial power?[17]

As shown in later chapters, class feelings might also include a desire to be classless. This might be seen as a feeling that class itself belonged to a previous generation, to a different time. Such feelings might be a form of denial, but they were helped along by all those ingredients that seemed to speak of peasant culture, of austerity, and of unfussy living. Such a world was miles away from one populated by dark and heavy furniture, stodgy puddings and overcooked vegetables, elaborate silverware and hunting prints that belonged to those who were *really* middle class.

Individualism was a core value to this new class. This was partly associated with some of the jobs that were emblematic of the new gentrifiers: 'Their professions are vaguely, entrepreneurially "cultural"; academics, journalists of a literary turn, television directors and producers, actors, copywriters, publishers, agents, with a few lawyers, accountants and business executives'.[18] Of course, these are the ones that were easiest to spot, particularly in areas of North London (or in the Span housing that Juliet Gardiner was living in during the 1960s). In reality the jobs that the new middle classes were undertaking would include a lot less glamorous ones: technicians of all sorts, social workers, schoolteachers, chemists, engineers, lower civil servants, and so on. They might aspire to being cultural entrepreneurs, like Raban, but their reality was closer to the suburban rank and file that, for various reasons, they wanted to disassociate from. The key characteristic of their individualism was that it took a peculiarly private form. In this they were at the forefront of one of the biggest changes in the postwar period: a shift away from publicly collective sociability – drinking in pubs, belonging to social clubs – towards a more private social life that is represented most clearly by the dinner party. This suggests that while the new gentrifiers were inhabiting the cities, they were doing so in a distinctly less-than-urban manner. In Raban's words their style was 'a deliberate renunciation of almost every possibility afforded by the city'.[19]

Of course, this doesn't mean that collective sociability disappeared, just that its character changed. The cross-generational socialising of the pub and the social club was being replaced by more age-specific night life. There were outposts of resistance. The pubs and clubs in racially diverse areas of cities like Leeds and Liverpool maintained a culture of pubs and clubs where young and old would drink and dance together, and I'm sure that other towns and cities did too. Perhaps the greatest contribution to maintaining a culture of public sociability is to be found in the gay pubs and clubs that thrived in the decades following the decriminalisation of homosexuality.

The rural urbanites discussed by Raban were usually not the securely wealthy middle class, but a younger slice of the population, made up of both the children of the traditional middle class and others moving 'up' the class spectrum. Their major investment was in property, often with budgets that had been stretched to breaking point. The austere look of bare floorboards, white walls, and peasant-style food was often not just about style, but also a response to a mortgage that left little spare cash. The shabby-chic style was symptomatic of a group ethos that seemed to simultaneously reject materialism while making it the centre of their lives in the form of property ownership.

In their attempt to escape the class confines of a previous generation, these pioneers of urban rusticity fashioned a lifestyle that had geographical and social impacts. According to Raban:

> They have rejected the suburbs, and found parts near the centre of the city which had been rendered invisible to the bourgeois eye by a century of railway engineering, immigration, and progressive dilapidation. In the blackened, small-windowed brick terraces (built for better-off artisans and the shabbier members of the lower middle class in the late eighteenth and early nineteenth century), they have seen an honest unpretension which fits well their conception of themselves.[20]

A style was creeping over the city, altering patches of housing, transforming local shops and amenities. What had been junk shops re-emerged as shops selling retro knick-knacks. A delicatessen opened here; an estate agent there. It never mounted a wholesale challenge to the world of supermarkets and corner shops, it never really competed with the franchised chains that dominated the commercial world, but it made significant inroads across urban Britain.

London is, as usual, exemplary here. The cityscapes of gentrification aren't measured only in terms of house prices and white paint, but in the cavalcade of shops and services that follow in the train of these young middle-class moderns. As the Scottish journalist Neal Ascherson describes in a 1986 *Observer* article on the recent history of Stoke Newington – which in the 1980s was a scene of significant gentrification – areas such as this tell a complex story of class and ethic change:

> At the end of Victoria's century, Stoke Newington began to 'decline' as the middle class moved gradually out and left their villas to working-class families. The place became shabby, then decidedly poor. In the post-war years, West Indians arrived, Turkish and Greek Cypriots, Asians from many countries. And then, perhaps 10 years ago, came the first ripples of the London

> middle class, soon a tidal inrush of families buying Victorian villas, refurbishing Georgian façades, bringing with them their retinue of health food shops, delicatessens, 'California restaurants,' wine bars and – of course – estate agents' boutiques.[21]

Gentrification became visible partly through shops catering to the new emphasis on lifestyle. A network of shops selling tasteful domesticity sprung up to supplement a chain like Habitat: 'All over Kensington, Primrose Hill, and Islington', writes Raban 'there are small "craftsmen's" shops selling roughly identical lines in clear-varnished wood. Stereo units which, a decade ago, used to be displayed in all their technological glory of gunmetal and knurled silver knobs, now go into grainy deal cabinets; and I have seen a stripped-pine fridge, mutely humming in its mesalliance between nature and culture'. While not all middle-class moderns would be able to afford such elegant austerity, as house prices rose, and as previous 'rough areas' became desirable, the relative wealth of an area would substantially increase: 'Such gestures of simplicity come very expensive; it is only the affluent who can afford to be so loudly inconspicuous'.[22]

The gleam of affluence and the undertow of neglect

It is worth taking a closer look at gentrification as a way of understanding the postwar period and how this has altered British cities. The first use of the term 'gentrification' to name an urban situation was Ruth Glass's essay that served as an introduction to the 1964 book, *London: Aspects of Change.* Today the term 'gentrification' is used to characterise a transformation in the prosperity and class of an urban area. Gentrification assumes that higher earners are moving into an area, and that house prices are going to increase, and that the class character of the area is changing from working to middle class. It should be noted, though, that there doesn't appear to be a similar term for the relative decline of an area, though the logic of gentrification might suggest that there needs to be a period of neglect and decline before somewhere can be gentrified. The late Neil Smith's 1982 definition of gentrification benefits by being clear and concise: 'By gentrification I mean the process by which working class residential neighborhoods are rehabilitated by middle class homebuyers, landlords, and professional developers'.[23] And yet if we go back to Glass's original essay – as well as descriptions in Raban's and Ascherson's writing – we see a much more piecemeal and complex set of changes. For Glass, gentrification is part of a process that, as well as reclassifying urban space, works to make class more and more illegible within the city.

Like many people writing in the period of the late 1950s and into the 1960s, her description of London starts with the recognition that the city itself has become more and more affluent:

> There is a gleam of affluence in most of Central London and in many of the suburbs – of a much more widespread affluence than has ever been there before. [...] It shows itself in an abundance of goods and gadgets, of cars and new buildings – in an apparently mounting flow of consumption. There are more soft and hard drinking and eating places that there used to

> be (and they are open for longer hours). The shops are crammed with personal and household paraphernalia which had previously been neither in mass production nor for mass use. The wrappings and labelling of commodities – small or large, practical or ornamental, frozen or fresh, dehydrated or puffed up – have a new gloss. The luxuries of yesterday, or the imitations of yesterday's luxuries, have become the necessities of today for large sections of the population.[24]

London has, at least superficially, been remade as a consumer city. The new world of glossy commodities is apparent in the shops, restaurants, cars, and buildings. This general level of affluence has, to a degree at least, erased an older more visible sense of class differences: 'Superficially, class distinctions in looks, clothes and in domestic equipment have narrowed considerably: differences in many of these respects are now more noticeably determined by age than by social status. Conventional terms of social categorization, such as "black-coated worker" or "white collar worker", no longer have a straightforward descriptive value'.[25] The feeling of a new, relative equality based on the common availability of goods is a common refrain, but there are two elements worth hanging onto in Glass's sentence. The first is that classlessness is a feeling reflected in shop windows, rather than a reality. But just because it isn't real doesn't make it either unimportant or incidental for understanding society. Feelings count, perhaps especially when they don't quite fit with reality. The second element is her insistence on the importance of age: the young wear one set of clothes, an older generation another. When you put the two together you get a sense that the young are expressing or hiding their social class in ways that distinguish them from an older generation. What was happening in Bolton with the factory workers on weekdays and weekends was now happening to the young on a much larger scale. The mismatch between occupation and the way you looked was becoming more and more confused. The shop workers in Habitat or Biba, for instance, didn't look like the shop workers of a previous generation, they often looked 'classier' than their customers.

So far in this book, age has been a significant factor in the flourishing of new tastes: it is the 'youngish' that have been at the frontier of the Habitat-Conran tastes, and the very idea of the 'new middle classes' or indeed the 'new working classes' is based on a generational understanding that the world is very different for those coming to adulthood during a period of increasing affluence. Gentrification is also a generational activity. Glass's essay focuses on the displacement of older working-class neighbourhoods and a new younger demographic moving in bringing with them new lifestyles and often new employment. Her account of gentrification is first and foremost a story of displacement:

> One by one, many of the working class quarters of London have been invaded by the middle classes – upper and lower. Shabby, modest mews and cottages – two rooms up and two down – have been taken over, when their leases have expired, and have become elegant, expensive residences. Larger Victorian houses, downgraded in an earlier or recent period – which were used as lodging houses or were otherwise in multiple occupation – have been upgraded once again. [...] Once this process of 'gentrification' starts in a district, it goes on rapidly until all or most of the original working-class occupiers are displaced, and the whole social character of the district is changed.[26]

A working-class neighbourhood is transformed by becoming desirable to middle-class homebuyers and developers. At the same time, though, other working-class neighbourhoods are facing the opposite of gentrification – a general withdrawal of resources, and general abandonment:

> As standards of living rise and land values even more so, as old working class districts are reconstructed, and others are increasingly hemmed in, the remaining pockets of blight become denser. Some of these quarters, off the beaten track – which are low on the list of municipal development and not 'ripe' for private investment – are left to decay. They have been neglected for so long that they are taken for granted.[27]

But if gentrification and decay signal a reciprocal process within the city, Glass is keen to show that the reality is more complex than abandonment of one area and gentrification of another. Unevenness and uncertainty are key. It might be assumed, for instance, that the middle classes might have a higher standard of living than working-class households. Yet in terms of having the latest conveniences and the most technologically advanced housing, those at the forefront of housing technology were often households being rehoused in the massive programme of council house building. 'Some of the conventional distinctions have been reversed', claims Glass writing about distinctions between the classes; 'the new homes of working-class and lower-middle-class people, who are municipal tenants, are frequently superior in design and appearance to the older "luxury flats" and expensive houses of private tenants or owner-occupiers'.[28] The new council houses were often fitted with luxuries that few but the most prosperous would think of installing in their homes, for instance underfloor heating and automatic disposal systems. If you wanted the latest built-in domestic gizmos in the 1960s and 1970s then you put your name down for a council tenancy.

Four years before her 'Aspects of Change' essay, Glass had published a book on the themes of migration and urbanism, called *Newcomers: The West Indians in London*,[29] where she and a team of researchers studied the housing and working life of West Indians in the late 1950s. What she found in areas like Notting Hill and Brixton was a housing situation where black tenants were forced to take expensive and decrepit housing because of the refusal of many landlords and landladies to rent to (in the language of the time) 'coloured' tenants. Due to the extortionate rents, these rooms would be overcrowded with several men sharing a single room. For Glass the world of simple class distinctions (working and middle – both seen at the time as inevitably white) was only one layer of the postwar urban world. Alongside that world was another inhabited by those who lived in appalling conditions: not just 'newcomers' but also those white people who had fallen out of the world of class altogether. In this world, not only was extreme poverty an everyday reality, but so too was racial violence, psychiatric illness, and social ills associated with desperation. What Glass is pointing to is an urban world that, for the most part, remains invisible and only becomes seen when a race riot requires policing, or when social workers need to act:

> We get an inkling of the existence of other remote and yet nearby worlds through migration statistics; through fascist newssheets and 'ni**er-baiting' scrawls on the wall of back alleys; through unsavoury court cases or complaints before rent tribunals; in reading Press items about witch rites, ghost hunts, visits from Martians, and take-over bids. And then again we hear of the 'hidden' societies through reports of hospital almoners, N.S.P.C.C. inspectors who deal with cases of child-battering, or through the records of social workers who bring 'meals on wheels' to lonely old people. It is an amazing, still largely obscured, panorama that thus begins to be visible – a conglomeration of groups who move, so to speak, on separate tracks, even if they do meet occasionally at a station.[30]

The city is not simply a complex of changing values along class lines, it exists on multiple planes that are often invisible to each other (figure 5.5). A single square in London might, at any one time, be home to any number of different worlds.

This sense of complexity that includes layers of the built environment – from dilapidated and restored Georgian terraces to the most recent state housing – is captured at the start of Michael Young and Peter Willmott's 1973 book, *The Symmetrical Family*:

> On the Hyde Park side of Sussex Gardens most of the cars parked at night were new. One minute and many years away, adjoining the street named by a property man of the past, Mr Praed, they were mostly of mid-century design, standing outside cheap hotels and houses

5.5 Notting Hill in the 1960s

> so shabby they might not have been painted since Hitler fell. Not far away, near Marylebone Station, run-down homes were being pulled down for redevelopment, a notion as much in vogue as a hundred or two hundred years before. In between the extremes were the large municipal complexes of the welfare state. The one at Churchill Gardens, opposite Battersea power station, actually adorned the river. Others, like those along the Edgware Road or in Lisson Grove, were the standardized tower block which were less obviously the symbols of collective life which have inspired architecture in the past than boxes for storage of the living.[31]

Gentrification by a 'new middle class' is a haphazard process within this general chaos. For Glass, even though she recognises that some areas are witnessing the complete displacement of a traditional working class, the result is not a city that is easily legible in terms of class: 'It seems', she writes, 'that what is happening is neither an obliteration nor an accentuation of long-established class cleavages, but the superimposition of a criss-cross web of social divisions, which has as yet been hardly recognized'.[32] This is perhaps the main lesson we can take from her work. Gentrification, and the tastes that accompany it, is not making the old class divisions newly visible, it is making class harder to see. And part of this is that class itself, in an affluent, home-centred society, is also changing.

The home-centred society

In 1959 Mark Abrams, a pioneer of market research, published an article in *The Listener* (a weekly magazine established by the BBC), on 'The home-centred society'. In it he charts how the growing affluence in income across the classes (at this point wages were increasing at the same rate across the middle and working classes) was affecting perceptions of class: 'More and more frequently', writes Abrams, 'in these surveys we find manual workers ready to describe themselves as middle-class because they already own or soon will own a car, a house with a garden, a refrigerator, a washing machine, a vacuum cleaner, and, of course, a television set'.[33] His team of market researchers had found that between 1948 and 1958 a huge sea change in spending patterns was taking place which emphasised the role of the home as a space of consumption, leisure, and identity:

> Today, as compared with ten years ago, we are spending far more on one-time luxuries – such as meat, fruit, confectionery, wines and spirits, housing, electricity, durable household goods, furniture, women's clothes, and motor-cars. In 1948 consumers spent only 30 per cent. of their money on these goods; by 1958 the proportion had jumped to over 40 per cent., and in 'real' terms, consumption of these, as a whole, had increased by 60 per cent.[34]

The 60 per cent rise 'in real terms' is Abrams taking account of the 20 per cent rise in household income during the same period.

This sea change was altering not just class identities but gender identities as well: 'The good husband is now the domesticated husband – the man who, when he has finished his work at the factory or the office spends his evenings and his weekends not with his workmates but at home with his family, enjoying common fireside relaxations with them, or else "pottering" round the house maintaining or improving its comfort and appearance'.[35] For Abrams, women, who – from this account at least – were already tied to the home and likely to remain there, changed from being basic housekeepers to interior designers. Even the car, which might suggest a higher degree of mobility and a move away from the home-centred society, was implicated in the general social change:

> It might be argued that the widening ownership of motor-cars constitutes a check to the growing British appetite for home-centred privacy, since it takes people away from their own immediate neighbourhood. In fact, the opposite seems to be true. Most owners treat their car as a detachable extra room to their house. They use it on week-days to travel to and from work in privacy – that is, without recourse to public transport where they would be thrown into contact with other people. And they use it at the weekend as a small mobile room that can be taken to the seaside or the country, and in which they can sit in isolation when they have arrived at their destination.[36]

It is a vision of a family-oriented, home-owning, heterosexual, patriarchal society, and clearly brackets out many other kinds of households, but the increasingly central role of the home across British society through the 1950s and onwards was a widespread phenomenon.

Home ownership – and the aspiration towards ownership – lies near the heart of this. But so too do all the consumer goods that seem to conjure up a sense of a home brim full of convenience, entertainment, and ease. Robert Millar's frenetic listing of what affluence entails (quoted in chapter 1) itemises a litany of goods and services, the majority of which pertain to the home. But while spin driers and electric toothbrushes, not to mention tranquillisers (all on Miller's list of modern essentials), can as easily furnish a rented home as one that is owner-occupied, the home-centred society as imagined by Abrams is at its core an owned rather than rented property. Or if it isn't owned, then – according to an overriding postwar ideal – the household aspires to home ownership. Certainly, the accumulation of gadgets and appliances encourages a sense of home as a site of consumption (figure 5.6).

The commitment to home ownership was something promoted by various British governments since the 1930s; indeed council houses were often built with the proviso that they should be sold after ten years at the best possible price, with the money going towards the building of further council houses. The belief that home ownership is a 'natural' desire for autonomy and independence is a belief shared by both Labour and Conservative governments. Michael Heseltine, Environment Minister in Margaret Thatcher's first government, was talking in a cross-party manner when in 1980 he claimed:

> There is in this country a deeply ingrained desire for home ownership. The Government believe that this spirit should be fostered. It reflects the wishes of the people, ensures the wide spread of wealth through society, encourages a personal desire to improve and modernise one's home, enables people to accrue wealth for their children, and stimulates the attitudes of independence and self reliance that are the bedrock of a free society.[37]

The Labour government's 1977 *Housing Policy Review* similarly argued that the 'trend towards home ownership is the sense of greater personal independence that it brings. For most

5.6 Currys advert from 1977

people owning one's home is a basic and natural desire'.[38] And such beliefs were, in many ways, a simple reflection of what had been happening in England and Wales, where home ownership had been regularly increasing since the early years of the twentieth century. Fred Gray claims that:

> The expansion of owner-occupation has been the single most important change – at least in quantitative terms – in the British housing system during the twentieth century. Before the First

> World War less than one in ten of dwellings in England and Wales were owner-occupied. By 1950, the figure had increased to 29 per cent, and to 49 per cent by 1970. In 1976 more than half (55 per cent) of households in the UK were home-owners.[39]

This isn't just a change in terms of housing, it is a massive transformation in a population's relationship with property and to its sense of 'home'. To move from a 'renter' (particularly of council-owned housing) to an 'owner' is to alter your relationship with the state and society. But it also brings with it a more practical incentive. The rise in home ownership is the catalyst that drives the growth in DIY home decoration, the installation of fitted kitchens and central heating, as well as various sundry improvements.

The movement towards home ownership was not, of course, limited to those who were colonising the working-class enclaves of North London. Working-class home ownership had been growing since the First World War. A survey of Bristol in 1940 found that '39 per cent of working-class families with per capita income above 30 shillings owned their own homes, and that even among those living below this standard 21 per cent were home owners'.[40] Nor would it be primarily white people who would participate in the move towards owner-occupation: for cultural and social reasons – the primary one being the racism of the rental sector and state provision – black and Asian households were a significant element in the decisive shift towards ownership. By the 1970s, black and Asian home ownership was outstripping white households with a similar income:

> the Political and Economic Planning 1974 survey indicated that 50 per cent of West Indian households and 76 per cent of Asian households were home-owners. Since black people are more than proportionately represented amongst manual socio-economic groups, these percentages are much higher than would be expected if the association between tenure and socio-economic group applying to white people also held true for black people.[41]

But the study also showed that West Indian owner-occupied households continued, to some degree, aspects of the racist dimensions of the rental sector: houses were more likely to be of inferior quality to white equivalents and were more likely to include larger number of householders per bedroom.

It is impossible to fully map the complex of class, race, and taste onto housing districts or housing types. The image that we have of the first-wave gentrifiers is usually the one that is most often satirised. It is the 'cultural entrepreneur' living in a 'stripped-pine wilderness' in North-West London (NW1).[42] Less visible are the social workers, teachers, nurses, technicians, and so on, some of whom belong to the bohemian arm of the new middle classes, and favour 'conspicuous thrift' as much out of necessity as for aesthetic preferences. These less-heralded and less-satirised members of the new middle classes would also include black and Asian Britons, who often go unregistered in descriptions of class (see chapter 9). The new middle classes are not a homogenous group. The Conran-Habitat taste is to some degree an extreme example of how class was being remade through taste. Few, probably, fully signed-up to a life circumscribed by Provençal cooking, stripped-pine, and junkshop finds. Many more, though, would enjoy elements of the controlled casualness and spontaneous sociability that was a way of distancing yourself from older class characterisations. As shown in later chapters, this was often a subject of satire, as if the new classes – who weren't the cultural entrepreneurs of NW1 – couldn't quite pull off the affable ease of the seasoned quiche maker.

The new middle classes weren't, in the main, gentrifiers but the style that accompanied gentrification was a key aspect of their tastes. The new middle classes also bought houses in the suburbs, in new developments, and in affordable districts of cities. Being at the forefront of gentrification was something that required a mix of confidence (both cultural and practical) and resources (either financial or manual, or a mixture of the two). You either needed to be someone like Michael Thompson (carpenter and theorist of rubbish) or able to hire someone like him. Buying a property in a new development (a Span house, or one of the thousands of modern houses advertised in the Daily Mail Ideal Home catalogues) was an option for those with steady incomes who didn't desire 'original features' and the bother of remodelling a house. The benefits of the sort of new building developments being built in vast numbers by developers and builders such as Taylor Woodrow, Percy Bilton, Laing, Barratt, Plandwell, Cottagecraft, and others, is that they were built very much with the idea of 'controlled casualness' in mind. Many of these houses, some of which were bungalows, were built with a sense of openness, light, and warmth at the forefront. Open-plan living was often standard. The idea of a separate kitchen was jettisoned, with most houses being built on the basis of a kitchen-diner, and some with a kitchen-diner-living room plan that would take up most of the ground floor. Central heating, which only really became ubiquitous in British housing in the 1980s, was much more likely in a new-build than in older homes, and all came with a large number of electrical outlets for all the modern conveniences and devices that a modern household could use (though this was quickly outstripped by even more and newer conveniences).[43]

These houses ranged in design, in quality, and in price – from the mass estates of identical properties, often terraced, to detached properties luxuriously laid out as part of a cul-de-sac development. Often the houses would incorporate features that suggested a European and Scandinavian idea of relaxed living. Just as there was a growing enthusiasm for goods that were distinctly un-British (but also un-American) in food and furniture, this was mimicked in housing (see figures 5.7 and 5.8). The quiches, yoghurts, and Ryvita crispbreads, which suggested health, modernity, and informality (while blocking older class associations), were ideally eaten in a chalet style home. And where better to put your Danish furniture, and your duvet bedding than in a Scandinavian house. This is the advertising copy for a new line of Barratt housing being showcased in 1976:

> The 'Stavanger' is a chalet style house, clad externally in stone to the first floor level with attractive timber gables above, and a full length balcony to the front elevation, access to which is from the main bedroom. The roof is carried over the balcony, providing protection from the weather in winter and a place to sun-bathe in the summer. The design includes a lounge/

5.7 'Trent', three-bedroom detached chalet house, Ideal Home Exhibition, 1976, p. 83

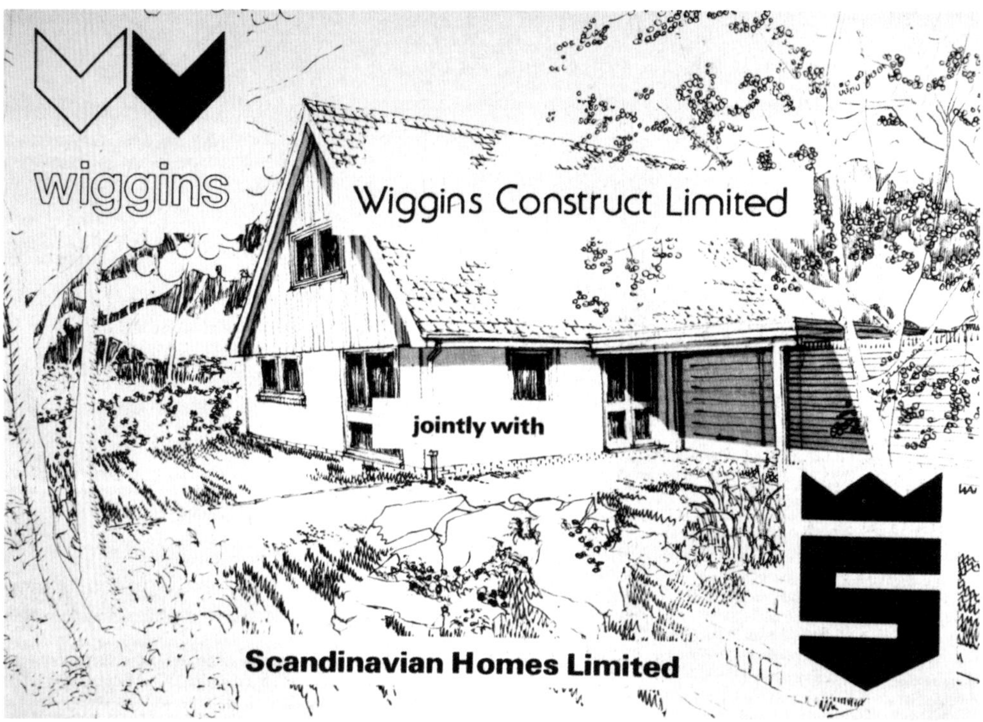

5.8 Wiggins Construct Limited, Ideal Home Exhibition 1977, p. 42

5.9 Barratt's 'Stavanger' house, Ideal Home Exhibition, 1976, p. 38

> dining room, kitchen, utility room and one bedroom on the ground floor, plus a W.C. and two large storage cupboards. The staircase is built of pine, with open treads, reflecting the natural beauty of timber. The landing, which has a pine ceiling, gives access to three good sized bedrooms and a bathroom.[44]

No doubt the 'Stavanger' (figure 5.9) was not going to be the first house a young middle-class modern would buy, but the idea of open tread staircases, some form of wooden facia, and garages were also there in the smallest and cheapest of the terrace-style housing.

These developments were often on the outskirts of towns and cities, or within a commuter distance of a metropolitan centre like London. These were the other form of urban ruralism, connected to cities by umbilical cords made up of rail networks or roads. Living rustic-urbanism could be achieved, perhaps with more conviction, on the edge of town, surrounded by woodland (figure 5.10). As we shall see, it is often these suburban new-builds that are used to parody the new middle classes. It is a Barratt home that stars in the show *Whatever Happened to the Likely Lads?*, as social mobility is sympathetically parodied with an aspirational couple taking possession of their 'executive home' (see chapter 7). But before we go there, we need to look at another semi-urban phenomenon that generated taste: the 1960s' new university and the social scientists that populated them.

5.10 Laing Homes Ltd, Ideal Home Exhibition, 1982, p. 65

6
Through the plateglass window

The fact that the *Sunday Times* launched its colour supplement in 1962 with a clutch of six people 'who represent today', and amongst that batch was a sociologist, tells us something about the new standing afforded to the social sciences in the 1960s. The sociologist in question was Alan Little, who built a career moving between academic posts (he was at the London School of Economics at the time of the article) and governmental roles (he later became director of Research and Statistics at the Inner London Education Authority, and later still, worked for the Community Relations Commission). When he died in 1986 (at the age of fifty-two) his obituary in *The British Journal of Sociology* reflected on the way that his career exemplified broader patterns of change:

> In a curious way he symbolized a whole cohort who came up to the university in the late 50s and early 60s at a time when not only were universities as a whole expanding from their miniscule traditional base, but the social sciences were held in esteem as relevant to the management of an expanding economy and an increasingly affluent society. It was a group that was not simply heir to the consequences of that growth, but also to the social optimism of the immediate post-war period which saw a bright and practical future for the social sciences.[1]

Social scientists were part of a new world of postwar planned development, who might be able to bring a more systematic approach to fields such as urban planning, housing, health, consumerism and family life.

One of the things this chapter explains is how sociology and the social sciences impacted on taste. So far, I have been using snippets of contemporary sociology (or sociological journalism) to discuss issues around the growing consumer society and how this was altering the experience of class and affecting cities. Here I want to make a stronger case about the role of popular sociology (and a writer like Jonathan Raban could be seen as an example of popular sociology) on the experience of taste. One result of the massive growth in the social sciences and the way that it spilled over into popular culture was that it became part of a mainstream conversation. People could reflect on their tastes, their habits, their situation and ask themselves if they too were 'affluent workers' or 'status seekers', and where they stood in the growing complexity of class divisions. Popular sociology provided a whole vocabulary for thinking about taste, class, and social status. But the role of sociology and sociologists also became part of a world of taste. If you were going to carry on studying after school, then nothing was more fashionable than choosing sociology. The male sociologist (and in most of the representations he is a man), decked-out in tank-top, leather jacket, and flared trousers is seen as someone offering mordant commentaries on contemporary society. A sort of DVD extra on modern life. Yet this commentary (so well-informed, so objective, so knowing) was often satirised as being at odds with a personal life of incompetence and hypocrisy. This unlikely subject of popular culture offers a way of thinking about taste and consumer society, not as an objective reality, but as a set of feelings, where taste is mixed with a new self-consciousness about the social meaning of our choices, our tastes.

Britain came late to sociology but in the 1960s and 1970s it was a vastly expanding field that had impacts far beyond the university.[2] For instance, the sociologist and doyen of Labour Party policy, Michael Young, didn't simply analyse and write about the manners and tastes of London's working class, he was also involved in the establishment of the Consumer's Association and, in 1957, the association's magazine, *Which?*, aimed at improving the consumer practices of the population, but especially the newly affluent.[3] In the 1960s, sociologists started to have a greater public prominence through magazines like *New Society* but also through the massive expansion of higher education and the way sociology was thought of as a particularly modernising discipline that fitted with the ethos of the new universities and with the general enthusiasm for all things technological that were coming to characterise the new polytechnics as they drew together the disparate elements of British post-school education.

As an aspect of national taste, the social sciences were not just there to interpret and explain, they were also there shaping tastes: offering charts and evidence as a way of imagining and recognising social change; providing an image of the expert as casually dressed and generally distrustful of the establishment. It isn't overstretching the word to say that the British developed a taste for the social sciences in the 1960s, and while this is a taste that is different in kind to a taste for Habitat furniture it isn't incompatible with it. As we will see, the image of the sociologist is the epitome of 'controlled casualness' and it is not hard to imagine him or her as favouring mayonnaise over salad cream, sleeping under a duvet, and eating quiche around a well-scrubbed pine kitchen table. The sociologist as an entrepreneur of modern tastes and manners, and as a figure of fun is most fully explored in Malcolm Bradbury's novel *The History Man* and in Posy Simmonds' weekly cartoon strip in the *Guardian*, featuring George Weber. Perhaps one of the defining qualities of new middle-class taste is that it comes already accompanied by a sociological assessment. This internalised sociological voice doesn't empty taste of its pleasures, but it does make taste self-conscious to a considerable degree, adding a flavour of irony to the 'good life'. It is this mocking, satirical edge that is attached to the popular promotion of sociology which allows it to flavour the experience of taste, so that new enthusiasms – for Mediterranean food and improvised sociability – can be simultaneously enjoyed and ironised. How often do you hear the rhetorical phrase 'How middle class am I?', sung, not as a boast, but as a self-deprecating qualification accompanying accounts of holidays, leisure pursuits, and food and drink preferences?

Universities in resort locations

Before we meet the likes of George Weber, it is worth first laying out some context for the new visibility of the social sciences in Britain. The growth of sociology in the UK is tied to the expanding world of polytechnics and new universities in the 1960s. It was part of the affluent society, part of a democratising ethos that seemed to be able to imagine a limitless growth of the economy, of leisure, of technology, and of goods. The expansion of higher education in the UK during the 1960s is rightly seen as extending the opportunities for social mobility, albeit mobility on what was still a tiny scale. But what happens if we see this expansion not just in terms of access to advanced education, but as involved in the promotion of taste? In some senses this might just seem like an obvious point to make: the one thing that is clear from the sociology of taste is that educated people tend to have 'educated' tastes! But rather than thinking of taste in terms of a liking for Molière and Mozart rather than Alistair MacLean and Fairport Convention (or as well as), I'm more interested in the way that the new furnishings and foods that were also part of an expanding university sector can induce new feelings about the world. The new, so-called, 'plateglass universities' of the 1960s were all active in promoting the flavours of the middle-class moderns in a variety of ways. Sociology doesn't come to the UK 'naked', so to say, but wrapped in images of informality and 'controlled casualness'. This has, I think, as much to do with denim-clad lecturers and the easy chairs that were used to furnish tutorial rooms and common rooms (and were the same as those being sold in Habitat), as it does to the content of any sociology syllabus. Sociology comes draped in some of the same cultural tastes that are at the centre of this book.

The expansion of British universities in this period is described succinctly by Harold Perkin in his 1969 publication for the OECD (the Organisation for Economic Co-operation and Development):

> The 1960's have been the most prolific period for the founding of universities in the United Kingdom since the Middle Ages, if not indeed in history. In1960 there were twenty-two universities and four university colleges in Britain and Northern Ireland. Since 1961, including those which have been raised to university status from amongst already existing colleges of higher education, no fewer than twenty-four new universities and a university college have come into existence. Thus between 1961 and 1968 the number of university institutions has been nearly doubled.[4]

Perkin (along with most other commentators) singled out nine or ten universities (depending on if the list included the older University of Keele) which were the direct result of state-led expansion. For Perkin what was important was that 'the ten New Universities have enjoyed the right from their foundation of granting their own degrees and therefore of planning and controlling from the start their own curricula and methods of assessment, and, indeed, their own structure and organisation.'[5] To differentiate them from the older redbrick universities such as Manchester and Birmingham, or the civic universities like Reading and Nottingham, commentators like Michael Beloff referred to them as plateglass universities on account of the preponderance of an architectural modernism that used expanses of glass and concrete to create a light, breezy ambiance.

Universities such as the University of East Anglia (figure 6.1) and the University of Sussex (figure 6.4 and 6.5) had a number of things in common. First of all, unlike most previous universities, they didn't go through a period of being overseen by a 'parent' institution before becoming autonomous institutions. Secondly, and as part of this, they were entirely new campus universities. As Perkins has it: 'In the New Universities [...] it is not only the buildings which are new. The whole man-made environment – roads, footpaths, lawns, newly-planted trees and shrubs, playing fields and car-parks – is new, and freshly risen from the rural landscape'.[6] The nearest equivalence would be the building of New Towns, which these campuses often resembled as totally planned environments. Thirdly they weren't located within the heartland of industrial Britain, as were nearly all the redbrick and civic universities of the nineteenth and early twentieth century. 'The new ones',

6.1 University of East Anglia, architect Denys Lasdun, opened in 1963

writes Perkin, 'are all on the outskirts of small or medium-sized towns, usually with little or only light industry'.[7] Fourthly the plateglass university was notable 'for its emancipation of women. On no campus is the ratio of male to female students higher than 6–4, and, at East Anglia for example, in the first year there were more women on campus than men [...]. This proportion contrasts with Oxford's of 8–1 in favour of men'.[8] Every element of the new universities was designed, from the landscape architecture to the canteen cutlery. Add to this a relatively even distribution of men and women, and the new university looked a lot like a small modern town dedicated to youth.

The North American sociologist David Riesman, famous for his bestselling book *The Lonely Crowd: A Study of the Changing American Character* (1950), spent six months at the University of Sussex in 1965 and during his stay made a point of visiting as many universities in the UK as possible. Recounting his experience he claimed (in prose that has a distinct 1960s' feel): 'It is impossible to visit the older civic universities without hearing bitter, sometimes envious, criticisms of Sussex in terms of its spread-out resort location (as well as its supposedly unsound experiments, its undeniably attractive young women, and its all-too favourable publicity)'.[9] That 'all-too favourable' publicity wouldn't last the decade as Sussex and other universities would be pilloried as hot-beds of revolution, pot-smoking, and sexual licentiousness. The 'resort location' was a feature that was commented on by others: 'For anyone who enjoys leisured strolls and the open-air life with, except for Warwick, the coast not far distant, the Plateglass universities can be described in the lush prose of the holiday brochure'.[10] The shift from industrial heartland to somewhere that might feature in a 'holiday brochure' chimes with an aspect of social change that was becoming more and more central to both sociology and politics: namely that Britain was moving from a country dominated by manufacturing to one that was becoming oriented to consumption and service provision.

Unlike in many other countries, higher education in the UK usually involved young adults living away from 'home', in residential halls or in shared private rentals. University education often involved not simply learning about different lifestyles but living them. While the newspapers in the 1960s and 1970s focused on the radical politics, the drugs, and communal living, the reality was, of course, often much more banal, but no less important. And it is this soft, modest, and often domestic revolution of taste that is worth focusing on. For instance, in Ann Eatwell's oral histories of the food memories of the first cohorts of students at the University of Sussex, it is the experience of first eating a Ski yoghurt that stands out:

> James Earney described the food service: 'one a no-choice queue where you got meat and two veg plus a desert for 2s 6d (12 ½ p) and a multi-choice queue. Actually there was a choice of dessert, either fruit pie and custard or Ski yoghurt in a conical pot'. The Ski yoghurt was a novelty remembered by a large number of alumni for whom it was a revelation in line with the modernity of the new University. In 1965 for Pauline Hughes Plummer, 'It was in the Refectory that I saw and ate my first yoghurt. I didn't know what it was.'[11]

6.2 Ski yogurt in conical pot

Prior to the 1960s yoghurt was seen in the UK as a relatively obscure health-food product that only those dedicated to an alternative, 'hippy', lifestyle would seek out. With the introduction of the 'Swiss recipe' Ski yoghurts in the early 1960s, what had been decidedly leftfield took on mainstream appeal. But that appeal was tied up with a different kind of life: one associated with a less-British, healthier and more European way of living. The iconic Ski yoghurt (figure 6.2) was part of a modern aesthetic way of living, because it was seen as part of a light, healthy diet associated with continental Europe and Scandinavia. Like the architecture that was such a significant part of the plateglass university (figure 6.3), the Ski yoghurt embodied a new way of living.

At the Plateglass universities an unadulterated diet of modern design was everywhere. It was inescapable. This doesn't mean that it was loved: at Essex, staff and students were asked to name the monumental residential towers after famous writers: their top choice was 'Kafka'.[12] But if the architecture didn't always delight, other aspects of the new environment were experienced as part of everyday life, designed for informality and sociability. At the University of Sussex, for instance, the architect Sir Basil Spence (or 'Sir Basil Expense' as he was called by those watching the costs of the construction skyrocket)

6.3 Stamp of the University of Essex and others. Part of a range of stamps representing university buildings released in 1971

6.4 and 6.5 University of Sussex library. The library was designed by Sir Basil Spence and the London branch of the architectural firm Spence, Bonnington and Collins. Work began on the building in 1962 and it was opened in 1964

designed not just the buildings but many of the furnishings. The tables and chairs in the main dining hall were designed by Terence Conran and even the cutlery was a commissioned design for the university rather than bought wholesale. Across all the new universities, as well as in some of the older universities, a lightweight comfortable chair was introduced that became synonymous with universities and later with institutional life more generally. It was the embodiment of controlled casualness: it wasn't an armchair, and it wasn't an upright chair that you would use to sit at a table. It was a 'tamed' version of the sort of chairs that had once been at the forefront of the avant-garde in the shape of chairs made by Le Corbusier and by the designers working at the Bauhaus. It embodied thoughtful informality. When you sat on it you were low to the ground and supported by a fitted foam cushion on a stretched rubber base or on elasticated strapping. The back of the chair was often solid or had similar elasticated strapping. They were placed in halls of residences, in offices and studies, in common rooms and bars. Versions of them were everywhere (figures 6.4 and 6.5) and they suggested a casual sociability, an ambience of light modernity.

One version of this chair was produced by the furniture company Lupton Morton (which, as already mentioned, became part of Habitat in 1969). The well-named Campus chair was designed by John Morton who:

> initiated the Living and Learning exhibition, touring towns where new universities were planned. The outcome was Campus, a range of flat-pack self-assembly furniture. By 1967, 18 universities had purchased Campus, and it was also sold to the public through a number of innovative schemes. One direct marketing campaign, through the Sunday Times' colour supplement, accepted payment by Visa credit card, then a novel idea; at weekends it was sold directly from the factory in Wallingford, on the Thames in Oxfordshire.[13]

Such chairs didn't require their occupants to 'believe' in a different lifestyle. Simply by sitting in them you became part of the new taste, the new world of easy informality. What could be more natural than to eat your Ski yoghurt sitting at a table designed by Terence Conran, then go for a walk along Basil Spence's modernist cloisters and end up relaxing in a Campus chair. Perhaps to top it off you could read the latest edition of *New Society*.

New Society

What the environment of the new university offered was a mixture of social informality and a loose feeling for modernism as part of everyday life. This is what made them such fitting sites for the social sciences with their shared sense of shining the light of reason on everyday life. Alongside the new universities, the social sciences had other vehicles for communicating their approach to modern life. Eight months after the *Sunday Times Colour Section* was launched, a new weekly magazine hit the newsagents. Billed as 'the social science weekly', *New Society* was a magazine that promoted a broad and inclusive idea of social science but also supported non-academic writers who might seem a world away from Alan Little's idea of sociology. Writers like the novelist and essayist Colin MacInnes, who had published a sequence of novels (*City of Spades*, 1957; *Absolute Beginners*, 1959; *Mr Love and Justice*, 1960) centred on West Indian life in London and the new 'affluent' teenager, found a home in *New Society*.[14] In 1962 he had recently published a collection of his essays where he is described as 'England's most sensitive recorder of the contemporary scene'.[15] MacInnes was given a weekly column for discussing a topic of his choosing and he started in characteristic fashion by describing his bankruptcy proceedings. Elsewhere the magazine delved into psychology, anthropology, popular culture, political and social policy, as well as a variety of sociological studies.

The first issue (figure 6.6) set out some of the terrain that the magazine would investigate. The featured article is on 'teenage marriage' and is a good indication of the approach the magazine adopted.[16] The long article is accompanied by four detailed tables that are the result of research with over 500 young marrieds undertaken by the Population Investigation Committee in collaboration with Gallup Poll. The article seeks to dispel the myth that teenage marriages are nearly always forced because of pregnancy, and it works statistically to show the 'facts' of teenage married life. The article brings a scientific approach to an area of life that was still shrouded in shame, myth, and innuendo. The magazine's ethos was most clearly associated with the article by Barbara Wootton (who had made a name for herself

6.6 *New Society*, first issue, 4 October 1962

in 1950 with her book *Testament for Social Science: An Essay in the Application of Scientific Method to Human Problems*[17]) titled 'Socrates, science and social problems'.[18] For Wootton, the social sciences were valuable precisely because of their 'scientific' approach, and because of this they were in a position to inform state policies with the sort of proof that had recently shown how cancer was connected to smoking. The social sciences, in Wootton's view, were able to improve life by advising committees and institutions on the proven facts, and to do this with techniques that were truly democratic. 'Ordinary people' writes Wootton, 'have reason to applaud the invention of contemporary polling techniques inasmuch as these make it possible for every shade of opinion on any topic to be accurately measured and assessed. Incidentally this is, no doubt, one reason why these techniques are unpopular with politicians'.[19]

New Society exhibited strong links with the expansion of social sciences at the plateglass universities. In the third issue Asa Briggs, who was Dean of Social Studies at the University of Sussex, announced how social studies at Sussex was 'designed to bridge the conventional gaps between various university departments'.[20] This third issue also introduced *New Society* readers to one of the most important sociological studies of the 1960s: John Goldthorpe and David Lockwood's 'affluent worker' study. In their announcement of some of their initial findings, revealed in the actual title of the piece – 'Not so Bourgeois After All' – they emphasised that the financial affluence of Luton car workers, didn't simply translate into a change in their class identity. Relatively wealthy car workers don't suddenly become middle class because of economics, but nor do they simply remain the same. Their study was one of a number of investigations looking at how elements of the middle classes were taking on cultural aspects associated with the working classes and vice versa. Their speculative conclusion was that: 'what we may be witnessing is not a working class increasingly adapting its attitudes to those of a relatively static and homogenous middle class, but rather the formation of a large new potential social stratum which is neither middle class nor working class'.[21] It is this sense of a large number of people whose class was 'neither middle class nor working class' that was of exceptional interest to *New Society*.

In another study, this time conducted in Swansea, the social scientist C. C. Harris investigated, in the spirit of Mass-Observation, the way that class experience negotiated the discrepancies between economic class and what could be called 'cultural class'. For instance, the very categories of class didn't simply point to the kind of work that might be a source of income, but to a set of values, beliefs, and practices: 'To be called working class', Harris writes, 'is from one point of view to be disapproved of: to be thought rough, not nice; to be called middle class is from the other standpoint to be accused of being stuck up, standoffish, a snob'.[22]

The discrepancy between class as a category that could be numerically measured (in terms of earnings, rental costs, house values, etc.) and class as a world of social judgements (the feeling that so-and-so is looking down on you, or that a neighbour is bringing the tone of the neighbourhood down) spoke to the broad field of the social sciences that *New Society* was concerned with. It allowed C. C. Harris to see class as often being ambivalent. This was particularly the case for those who either through affluence or through new categories of employment could be seen as in-betweeners: 'this group by its cultural ambivalence – expressed in its members' confusion over class terms and reluctance to accept class ascriptions – provides a sort of no-man's land between the classes [and] permits the recruitment by the middle class of new members, and offers it a wider range of marriage partners than could be found within its own ranks'.[23] The new middle classes (which was what this intermediate class was starting to be called) was going to be as much identified by its cultural tastes and habits as it was by its earnings and employment.

Investigations like Harris's were often speculative, trying to capture something emerging rather than something that had settled:

> What will happen to the people in between? Will the culturally mobile be absorbed in the middle class by becoming occupationally mobile, will they form a new stable and truly intermediate group, or will they constitute a new, non-traditional class of their own, whose standard of life is near to that of the traditional middle but whose way of life is different from both the traditional classes?[24]

This was a key concern: how do you describe groups of people and their experiences when they don't fit older categories of class? Clearly these are people who don't exist outside of class. Sometimes the best that could be done was to name them as 'new' or 'intermediate'. It wasn't much of a description, but it would have to do.

The sense of exploring emerging class culture by looking at taste and leisure was also pursued in various other ways in *New Society*. For instance, the magazine was pioneering in its attention to popular culture from a social science perspective. The various writings on pop music, which were scattered through the pages of *New Society*,[25] were one of the few sources in English that treated it seriously. For students at the University of Sussex studying the social sciences alongside humanities subjects like English Literature or History, *New Society* would be essential reading for answering a question like: 'Do the forms and contents of pop music help us to understand contemporary Britain?'[26] This was one of the questions that was included as a final exam paper and taken by most undergraduates in the Schools of Social Studies and English and American Studies for the exam on 'Contemporary Britain' in 1964.[27] Similarly, work on advertising, such as Stephen Aris' article on an advertising campaign for central heating, suggests that *New Society* was one of the places where the new field of Cultural Studies was being fashioned.[28] Aris's article explores an advertising campaign that produced an image of an ideal consumer, 'Mrs. 1970', who is carefully constructed so as not to demonstrate 'stuffy' middle-class tastes while also not being specifically working class. Through such analysis, *New Society* show us a world where 'the new middle class' wasn't simply a fact of changing employment but was being culturally produced by the new techniques of consumer society (advertising, mass culture, media, and so on) as well as by the techniques of the social sciences (polls, surveys, statistics, and the ethnographic 'sound bite').

Malcolm Bradbury and the Kirks

I'm certain that Malcolm Bradbury read *New Society*, and there can be little doubt that the anti-hero of his 1975 novel *The History Man*, Dr Howard Kirk, would have read the magazine and mercilessly critiqued its 'bourgeois' claims to be politically non-aligned. *The History Man* is a novel about a youngish couple in their mid-thirties with a shared working-class background growing up in Northern England. After a grammar school education, they meet at the University of Leeds and get married. Initially they conduct their lives in a similar way to their parents: they have children, a dull sex-life, and a dutiful approach to work and parenting. While Barbara gives up her academic career to raise children, Howard pursues a doctorate and becomes a young sociology lecturer. The story is about how the 'old Kirks' reinvent themselves as the 'new Kirks'. After Barbara has casual sex with a university friend, they start having an open marriage, but what fully allows the Kirks to become 'new' is when Howard gets a job at a new university on the south coast of England. Howard Kirk is the *history* man because he imagines that he is making history, and because he believes that history is an unfolding liberation with him at its centre.

The setting is the invented plateglass university of Watermouth. When we first meet Howard, we are told that: 'he lectures at the local new university, a still expanding dream in white concrete, glass, and architectural free form, spreading on a hillside just to the west of, and just outside, the south-western sea-coast town in which they live. The university, having aspirations to relevance, has made much of sociology; and it would be hard to find anyone in the field with a greater sense of relevance than Howard'.[29] (Malcolm Bradbury took up a position at the University of East Anglia when it was only two years old; he also had a northern working-class upbringing.) At Watermouth (the town and the university) the Kirks support every radical cause and participate in every radical lifestyle.

Like other plateglass universities, Howard Kirk's workplace lies on the edge of a town associated less with industrial manufacture than with consumption: 'Leeds was working class' writes Bradbury and 'was built on work; Watermouth was bourgeois, built on tourism, property, retirement pensions, French chefs'.[30] We don't find out much about Watermouth, but we do get a sense of how its civic centre exemplifies a mix of modernist planning and consumerism:

> The precinct has straight angles; it has won an architectural award. There are long glass façades, the fronts of supermarkets, delicatessens, boutiques, the familiar multiple stores, displaying the economy of abundance; there is a symmetry of tins and toilet rolls in the windows of Sainsbury's; spotlights and shade permute the colour range of sweaters and shirts, dresses and skirts, in the Life Again Boutique. In the open space in the middle are multicoloured paving stones; amid the stones, in some complex yet deducible code, are tiny new trees, fresh-planted, propped by wooden supports. A waterless fountain contains much litter.[31]

In trying to find a place to live in Watermouth appropriate to their radical lives, the couple (with their children, who are almost entirely absent in both the novel and televised adaptation) studiously avoid the sorts of places that might be associated with traditional middle-class existence (the suburbs, the surrounding villages) and opt instead for a large derelict Georgian townhouse that has been slated for demolition and which they are renting from the council.

The plot of the novel is played out across a single university term and involves the intricate politics of Howard Kirk's department as well as the sexual exploits of the couple. The story centres on Howard's various campaigns, both large and small. One is an attempt to expel an undergraduate student who he wants to fail for not being sufficiently Marxist. Another is a plot to get his department to invite a geneticist to lecture, in the belief that this will unite the student radicals and some staff to protest the visit (today it would be called 'de-platforming'). Howard, of course, will lead the protests even if he does so behind the scenes. *The History Man* is a book that today reads like the fever dream of those who are obsessed with the idea that 'wokeness' is wrecking higher education. But the plot need not concern us too much here.

What makes the book, and the televised mini-series, relevant is the way that it draws together a world of taste through the new universities and the social sciences. The tone of the book is satire: Howard is a monstrous figure who writes ill-researched popular sociology in pursuit of the latest trendy topic and the most radical political position. The book ruthlessly derides, not so much sociology as the pretension of sociology to be the only discipline for understanding society. The satire, however, is not aimed at the content of Howard's scholarship but at the couple's way of life and the way that they live-out their sociological knowledge. Yet the way that the satire is achieved is itself sociological: the couple are ridiculed as a product of various social trends, most of which are seen in terms of taste and lifestyle.

Their house is – in their eyes – a sort of free space unencumbered with bourgeois ideas of privacy and property. It is the discord between their perception and the reality that fires the satire. So, while 'they believed they had almost no possessions, being free-floating people', the more literal truth was that they had amassed a household's worth of consumer goods: 'the cooker, the stereo system, the television set (for by now they had bought one), the blender, the wickerwork rocking chair, the Habitat crockery, the toys, the two filing cabinets and the door that Howard laid across them in order to construct his desk'.[32] The Kirks' belief that they are not amassing commodities is due to the nature of the things that they are buying. This is a lifestyle made up of objects that appear to be 'finds', furniture that has a lightness and disposability to it that is as free-floating as the lifestyle that it tries to promote. Bradbury might be telling us that this family is deluded, but it is a delusion that was being carefully promoted by magazines and retailers: a consumer culture selling freedom as a lifestyle.

According to Phillip Simpson, who interviewed Bradbury when the TV version was being aired, the novelist drew on Biba catalogues and copies of the *Guardian* to describe the clothing and the environment of the characters.[33] No doubt he also had a few Habitat catalogues by his side. The domestic world that Bradbury describes is kitted-out with the tastes that this book has been focusing on. It is controlled casualness writ large. The legal squat that they had rented from the council (for almost nothing) has been turned into a home that we might find in Conran's *The House Book*:

> At first the main furniture was the mattresses and the cushions that lay on the floor, but gradually the Kirks got around to going and buying things, mostly on trips up to London; what they bought was transient furniture, the kind that inflated, or folded up, or fitted into this into that. They built desks with filing cabinets and doors, as they had in Leeds, and bookcases out of boards and bricks. What had started as a simple attempt to make space liveable in gradually turned into something stylish, attractive, but that was all right; it still remained for them an informal camp site, a pleasant but also a completely uncommitting and unshaped environment through which they could move and do their thing.[34]

In their old, condemned house (figure 6.7), they had restored its 'period features' and fashioned the rooms into the 'controlled casualness' that was the ethos of the Habitat and Conran style. They had enlisted students to sand the floorboards: 'Four of them with a rented sander exposed, and then waxed yellow with a rented waxer, the good old wood of the floors'.[35] The kitchen featured a well-scrubbed stripped pine kitchen table with bentwood chairs (figure 6.8). Their concerted political refusal to participate in capitalist society is cloaked in commodities from the bohemian wing of consumer culture: 'Barbara is already standing, waiting for him to come. She wears a white, pinch-waist, full-length raincoat; she carries two red canvas bags, Swiss, from Habitat'.[36] Even her trips to London to visit a lover are framed in the language of consumerism: 'These she calls her shopping trips, for she shops too: she makes avaricious love to Leon over the weekend, and then moves on to Biba, coming back home on the mid-morning train on Monday with a brighter look on her face and several dresses, each in their elegant, dark-brown bags'.[37] At the university, Howard, like the rest of the faculty, works at 'black-topped

6.7 The Kirks as played by Antony Sher and Geraldine James in the 1981 BBC adaptation of *The History Man*, outside their 'legal squat'

6.8 The Kirks with their well-scrubbed, pine kitchen table and bentwood chairs, preparing for a day of 'controlled casualness' in the 1981 BBC adaptation of *The History Man*

Conran desks', and when the university awards degrees the recipients and faculty wear 'Mary Quant robes'.[38]

The press coverage of the novel immediately understood that the book was staging an encounter between ideology and taste. *The Daily Telegraph*, for instance, in describing the couple explained that 'the Kirks give deliberately "unstructured" parties in their condemned Regency house where they are legally squatting and which they fill with sealed pine units, wall spotlights and Habitat dishes'.[39] While the book received praise and prizes, criticism was levelled at the insistence by which Bradbury repeated his litany of tastes: 'It is lazy to keep using "Habitat" and "boutique" as snide adjectives: we know the connotations all right; it is not effective constantly to invoke them'.[40] The novel relies on the repetitious naming of Habitat, Biba, Conran as well as on the inclusion of more 'personality-based' items like 'junkshop chest of drawers', for instance, not to achieve psychological depth but to give it a sociological feel. *The History Man* is itself a contradiction: a novel that seems to critique and deflate the power of the social sciences, while being absolutely reliant on a sociological perspective to make its points.

The emergence of consumer society in Britain had been Bradbury's theme since the 1960s. In two small humorous books written in 1960 and 1962 he ironically describes how British society had been altered by consumerism and how it had obscured class identities. These little books look at the existential effects of consumerism and how it had unmoored people from a sense of a common class belonging. In the books, class, within consumer capitalism, is something that you fashion in the same way (and requiring the same resources) as you might fashion the interior look of your home. When these books were republished as a single volume in 1982, Bradbury remembered observing the symptoms of a new society emerging in the early 1960s:

> In London this uncharacteristic taste for the modern and the new was even more apparent [...]. Shops in Marks and Spencer's international style were going up apace. In the streets, there was a lot of youthiness. In the shops, Swedish glass and Danish furniture indicated that the British were acceding to what the experts in these things – and now, suddenly, Britain was filled with experts in such things, calling them sociologists – called cultural drag. Commercial television had started, and the jingle-writers were showing off their wares, the pop stars screeching in mid-atlantic accents.[41]

The suggestion is that sociology, far from being a way of understanding these changes, is a symptom of them. Bradbury's position is tinged with a vague conservative nostalgia which often makes his critique of the social sciences feel part of a taste war in which he decries the inauthenticity of the new tastes in comparison to a world that produced George Eliot and clear class categories.

But *The History Man* and the earlier humour books also make some precise sociological points. One of the implicit points which the book argues is that there is little class difference between the old friends of the Kirks, the Beamishes – who live 'in an architect-converted farmhouse where they were deep into a world of Tolstoyan pastoral, scything grass and raising organic onions'[42] – and the much more radical inner-city style of the Kirks. While the Kirks might see the Beamishes as bourgeois, the primary difference is that although the Kirks are in their mid-thirties, they dress the same way as the students at the university who come to their parties, while the Beamishes dress in a similar way to their parents' generation. This is the consistent point of the novel (and one of its major limitations): the Kirks are revealed over and over as hypocrites; for instance, they believe in gender equality but casually exploit female students for babysitting and housework. No one else in the novel is similarly exposed. The big set piece joke is that Howard is writing a book called *The Defeat of Privacy* (a follow up to *The Coming of the New Sex* which detailed his and Barbara's sex life, but without asking her permission) and when one of his students starts reading the manuscript his response is apoplectic: 'You'd no business to do that [...] It's private'.[43]

Howard Kirk was a monstrous figure: self-absorbed, hypocritical, simultaneously pious and narcissistic. He was frighteningly affective in wrecking the lives of those around him. The fact that he was strongly left-wing seemed to count against him. The novel seemed to suggest that living progressive politics is as much a pose as imagining you are eating an authentic cassoulet in your rural retreat in inner-city Birmingham. Or as authentic as imagining you could understand the world through sociology. The novel and the 1981 TV adaptation coincided with a fall in the fortunes of sociology as a subject within British universities. How much this was down to Bradbury's depiction of Howard is anyone's guess.

Posy Simmonds and the Webers

At about the same time that Howard Kirk was stalking the Watermouth campus, a much more genial social scientist was working at a less prestigious institution – a polytechnic. His name was George Weber, and he was the brainchild of the cartoonist Posy Simmonds. After a period producing cartoons for *The Sun*, Posy Simmonds began working for the *Guardian* in 1972. Initially she provided the illustrations to accompany one-off articles, but in May 1977 she started a regular cartoon strip that revolved around three female school friends and what had become of them twenty years after leaving school. All of them had married: one to a polytechnic lecturer, another to an advertising copywriter (his second marriage), another to a whisky salesman. After a few months the strip began to take on a distinctive character, particularly around the Weber family. As Simmonds recalls, the newspaper ran the strip before it was ready:

> Although I'd created a lot of characters, I didn't know who they were. [...] Then I drew the family. Especially George Weber and Wendy Weber. I took them to Cornwall, to Tresoddit, and I knew who they were on holiday and I thought, 'Actually, I know you. [...] You'd really like to be at Cambridge but there you are at this Polytechnic.' And that was George. And Wendy had lots of children, was a nurse and also wrote children's books, and a feminist.[44]

The Weber family were at the epicentre of a strip that ran for a decade from 1977–87 under different headings but was most consistently titled simply 'Posy'. The Webers have been described as 'ludicrous middle-class, middle-aged leftists trapped by an impossible ideology'.[45] When Simmonds won the award for the best humorous strip in a national newspaper in 1978, the *Guardian* let the fictional polytechnic lecturer George Weber explain the strip's appeal: 'My peer group of Stanhope and Trish Wright and Edmund and Joanna Heep, though a privileged sector, are organically structured to create a subtle send-up of late capitalist society and stress subliminally the values of the countervailing culture'.[46]

The fault-lines of the Webers' 'impossible ideology' became clearer as they tried to square their deep-seated belief in liberal individualism with their commitment to feminism and socialism. The Webers became adults in the 1960s and were part of the hippy movement, supported CND, protested the war in Vietnam, smoked dope, and wore frayed denim. But as they hit middle age in the late 1970s, on the crest of second wave feminism, they are often caught on the horns of a dilemma. For instance, throughout the early strips the Weber's seventeen-year-old daughter Belinda (the Webers have six children) wears clothes that the parents feel demean women; she goes out with guys who clearly objectify her sexually; and she aggressively rejects her mother's feminism. What the strip shows is the mismatch between Wendy and George's internal feelings (they hate their daughter's choices) and their external actions, where they refuse to tell her what to do. They explain their liberal approach to their friends: 'We don't want her to have any of the hang-ups we had about work and sex. When I think of how my parents were! "Your hair! Those awful clothes! You think the world owes you a living!'"[47] But we also see the scene from Belinda's perspective who sees her parents' liberalism as irresponsible parenting. When Wendy and George do intervene however, they are unmasked as total hypocrites with Victorian attitudes. As every parent knows – you can't win that one. The cartoon strip gently exposes the Weber's impossible quandaries and their diffident approach to dealing with them.

As readers of the cartoon, we usually see the world from Wendy Weber's perspective, and the first book-length collection of strips was titled *Mrs Weber's Diary* (published in 1979). In her Monsoon skirt, baggy jumpers, and saggy boots[48] Wendy Weber's feminism is often stress-tested by her children, by neighbours, and by friends and acquaintances. Her husband George provides a sardonic commentary to what is going on. We are told that George Weber is a lecturer in Liberal Studies – a vague enough name to cover everything from philosophy to media studies, with a broad commitment to the social sciences.[49] In the May section of the diary we see George working on an essay titled 'The Meta-Megalith: A Structuralist Interpretation of the Career of Buckminster Fuller' (figure 6.9), and in the same spread we see that his collection of critical essays entitled *Weimar, Chicago & the Cultural Squash Ball* has been rejected by a Canadian University Press. His commentaries on what his family, colleagues, and friends are up to often refer to the anthropologist Claude Lévi-Strauss on the role of taboo and the structuring importance of ritual, and he

6.9 George Weber in his garden writing

also uses insights drawn from sociology.[50] He is a keen admirer of Roland Barthes and imagines writing a book called *Boring the Barthesian Well.*[51] Given that George's academic interests stretch across design and architecture, anthropology, sociology, and cultural history, his field 'Liberal Studies' would correspond to the relatively new and expanding field of Cultural Studies, which was finding a home primarily in Polytechnics in the 1970s and 1980s.

The importance of Posy Simmonds' strip is the way she shows how a sociological attitude was becoming available to a growing section of the population by the 1970s, and how a sociological approach to taste often resulted in self-consciousness and anxiety. The pleasures of the good life came with a veneer of reflexivity, and a knowingness that provided its own pleasure. George and Wendy know that they are middle-class liberals who like wine and worry about poverty, and they know that their behaviour is often stereotypical. They also enjoy knowing that they are self-critical rather than deluded! This is especially evident in two themes where the sociology of taste is particularly important: housing and socialising.

Early in the strip we see that the Webers are part of a wave of middle-class incomers in a street mainly consisting of skilled manual workers (plumbers, builders, etc.). The Webers are part of a gentrifying force and are seen by the local residents as 'nobs' and are genially and regularly teased by them. As middle-class families like the Webers become more prevalent in the street we see their influence having a disproportionate impact. When the Webers and others establish an annual street party, the rift between the classes is revealed not in terms of economic differences, but in terms of cultural differences. But these differences are presented as a reverse image of an older class hierarchy. The Webers' idea of sociability entails casual dress, wholesome and Mediterranean-styled food, and wine and 'ye-olde-worlde' drinks like mead. The scene has the look of a rural festival enjoyed by mediaeval peasants (preferably Italian or French) – undermined by the Coca-Cola-loving, olive-hating children. The blue-collar neighbours, with their more sophisticated drinks and dressier clothes, look on in amused disdain as they consider joining the 'peasants.'

The involvement of the Webers in gentrification isn't limited to suburban streets. The Webers also go on holidays to the fictional Cornish village of Tresoddit (figure 6.10) to stay with one of George's ex-polytechnic colleagues – Kevin Penwallet – who has moved to Cornwall and opened what in the 1970s was called a 'health food shop'. As part of an influx of metropolitan migrants Kevin not only pushes up the prices of local properties, he also inflicts his (crazily expensive) food preferences on the locals. His shop offers lentils, brown rice, and organic tomatoes, while the locals ask for 'cake mix, salad cream, cola and frozen chips'. The incomers believe that they are saving the local area by modernising decaying cottages and by bringing the 'good life' (in the shape of brown rice) to the local population. The locals are neither interested in Kevin's version of the 'good life', nor can they afford his prices.

6.10 On holiday in the fictional Cornish village of Tresoddit

The sociological self-consciousness of the new middle classes is most vivid when they are either planning or attending dinner parties. As middle-class moderns, advertising executive, Stanhope Wright, and 'former art gallery assistant', Trish Wright, can't be seen to mimic the traditional formalities of the traditional middle-class dinner party. Nothing too formal. They carefully prepare for something much more improvised and spontaneous, where the 'controlled casualness' can be given full expression. Stanhope's daughter from his first marriage – Jocasta, currently at art school – looks on and provides the sort of commentary that wouldn't look too out of place in the sociological critiques of the time (figure 6.11). But what adds to the archness of the scene is that while Jocasta's insights might well be fuelled by the sort of Cultural Studies that she is learning at art school, Stanhope and Trish aren't the sort of cultural dupes caught in the grip of an ideology that they don't see or understand. Far from it, the Wrights are stage-managing the dinner party with exactly the same sociological precision and knowingness that a sociologist might bring to the event. They know they are carefully constructing an atmosphere of carelessness, that their orchestrated informality is manicured spontaneity. And it is an ambience that they want, that they enjoy, and presumably, will result in the sort of socialising that they find pleasing. They know what controlled casualness requires: you can't be nonchalant when it comes to nonchalance.

Jocasta's amiable commentary on what journalists have called 'conspicuous thrift', as well as her observations on the complex negotiations that are required to produce simple spontaneity, are offered not to decry middle-class hypocrisy, but to relativise taste. If a traditional middle-class dinner party could be seen as an arduous preparation of formal observance, then the middle-class moderns' theatre of spontaneity is neither without work, nor without anxiety. But that doesn't mean that the results are equivalent: no doubt

6.11 Jocasta Wright's commentary on her father and stepmother's party preparations

that studied informality of the Wrights' party isn't quite as informal as it might appear, but neither is it as uptight and mannered as its more traditional predecessor. Today that sociological voice can be heard like a Greek chorus accompanying every purchase of hummus, every child's meal of 'pasta and pesto', every hipster's delight in a small-batch ale. What the middle-class moderns needed wasn't simply the material means to stage the 'controlled casualness' and 'planned spontaneity' of their everyday life, but a style of performance that could simultaneously internalise the sociological critique while also revelling in the pleasures their tastes afforded.

7

Status striving and other myths we live by

In J. B. Priestley's 1968 novel, *Out of Town* (the first volume of his two-volume novel *The Image Men*), two down-at-heel academics, one a professor of philosophy, the other a lecturer in literature, see their fortunes dramatically change when they rebrand themselves as sociologists. Coming across a British-born American heiress, Mrs Drake, who is determined to spend her late husband's fortune establishing a sociological research institute in England, the two itinerant scholars who had previously been teaching in Latin America and 'out East' propose to set up the *Institute for Social Imagistics*. The literary scholar describes 'social imagistics' as 'the selection, creation, projection … of suitable and helpful images' adding that 'you must know, Mrs Drake, how immensely important the image is now in politics, advertising, business'.[1] The project of 'social imagistics' was dreamed up by the two men one whisky-drenched evening, and copied some of the interests and language that could be found in a magazine like *New Society*:

> We live in a world increasingly dominated by the Image' argues the philosophy professor, 'There are so many of us now. Our urban industrial societies are so highly organized, so complicated. And we depend more and more upon mass media, which in their turn are compelled by their very nature to deal in images.'[2]

In an attempt to gain some academic credibility for the Institute they contact one of the new universities – the half-built and fictitious University of Brockshire – as somewhere that might provide a suitable home. The sociologists already ensconced there veer from being deeply sceptical to enthusiastic about the new venture. In setting up the Institute of Social Imagistics the two professors recruit a young lecturer, a new undergraduate student who is also an ex-model (today she'd be called a celebrity model), and a PhD researcher. It is down to them to undertake fieldwork: '*Social Imagistics* demand an immense amount of up-to-date information – for example, about where and how people live, about clothes and shops, restaurants and amusements'.[3] They have to scour London's West End, talk to their friends and acquaintances, and record what they already know, to describe what is 'in', what is 'fashionable', what is part of the group image. One of the university's sociologists, Dr Hazel Honeyfield, who isn't currently aligned to the Institute but is keen on its aims, is an expert in the sociology of 'status'. As Dr Honeyfield explains to Dr Owen Tuby (the literary scholar and deputy director of the Institute), 'I've been reading Kuhn's *Study of Society* – and considering his point about the choice of coffee, tea or milk in a restaurant being part of a hierarchy, and about the behaviour selections of having cream or sugar and tilting the cup, and I think I'll have a special restaurant-and-teashop section in my Status Enquiry'.[4] As well as studying the 'status' embedded in tearoom behaviour, and other phenomena, she studies 'pot plants as status symbols'.[5] For the Institute and for Dr Honeyfield, anything, it seems, can be 'status-conferring'.[6]

The choice of treating 'pot plants as status symbols' in a satirical novel about sociology is not accidental. George Orwell's 1936 novel *Keep the Aspidistra Flying* saw this hardy pot plant as a sign of Victorian middle-class respectability, as did many other social commentators. He had introduced the phrase 'keep the aspidistra flying' the year before in his novel *A Clergyman's Daughter*. In that novel a group of hop-pickers sit down to some well-earned refreshments, and one of them bemoans that she was used to a more refined way of taking tea: 'not having no nice clean table-cloth like I've been accustomed to, and the beautiful china tea service as our mother used to have; and always, of course, the very best tea as money could buy'.[7] In response, another of the group sings 'keep the aspidistra flying' to the tune of 'Deutschland, Deutschland über alles': he is mocking her pretensions to middle-class values. A year later the group of amateur social researchers who were setting up the Mass-Observation project wrote that one of the first things that they intended to study was the 'aspidistra cult'.[8]

Reading Orwell's novels and Priestley's *The Image Men* you get a sense that, satirically at least, everything is a possible status symbol, and that the marketing industry, consumer society, lifestyle magazines, travelling salesmen, and sociologists have all conspired to make everything understandable primarily in terms of status. In an essay looking back on his book *The History Man*, Malcolm Bradbury noted that the huge explosion of sociology in the 1960s and 1970s is itself a sociological event and needs to be explained sociologically.[9] The seeds of that explanation would be found in the rise of consumerism and advertising. Faced with a massive variety of home furnishings or an extensive choice of what to eat, choice or taste would become something to be studied. In the 1960s, the difference between the sort of market research undertaken on behalf of a commercial client and that devised by academic and journalistic sociology, is mainly an issue of tone. Market research has, as one might expect, a more gleeful, more upbeat tone, whereas sociology is often tinged with a note of moral disapproval towards consumerism. What happened in the 1960s and 1970s is that a version of sociology (one that was often mediated through journalism) became a form of popular culture that could be a subject for satire, for Priestley and for others too. We might also want to speculate about the effects of all this. Do the fine nuances of social superiority that sociologists (both imagined and actual) find in the choice of pot plants become part of a general experience? Does it generate a sea of anxiety around setting up home? Or something less noticeable: a degree of self-consciousness that might make taste in the postwar period more self-reflexive? It is worth exploring further the sociological presumptions around the sort of 'status enquiry' that Dr Honeyfield was involved in, where it came from, and how it took on a particular form in the postwar period.

Keeping up with the Joneses

In the age of affluence there was a substantial growth in writing which started out from a sociological presumption that people's choices weren't simply likes or dislikes, but complex ways of negotiating social hierarchy, of getting a leg up, of keeping up with the Joneses. In Priestley's novel this is a presumption that is both derided and capitalised on. When Dr Tuby hears Dr Honeyfield describe her 'Status Enquiry' project he can't help but laugh. She thinks she is being mocked because she is woman (which to a large extent is true – the novel is marinated in misogyny): Dr Tuby, in a moment of candour, tries to put her mind at rest, 'I was laughing – now, take it easy – *at sociology*'.[10] But of course Dr Tuby is also trying to turn that sociological approach towards taste into something that can make money.

In 1955 the sociologist, Dennis Chapman, published one of the first sociological studies of domestic tastes and behaviours carried out in Britain. Chapman, who had in the 1930s been part of the Mass-Observation project, drew primarily on the work of American sociologists like Thorstein Veblen and F. Stuart Chapin for his approach, with the primary goal of trying to improve the living conditions within working-class housing. His approach tells us something about the basic premise of mid-century 'Status Enquiries':

> the possession of taste is an important in-group characteristic and one which is subtly differentiating. It may derive from education or culture, and be based on demonstrable standards, or it may merely be the accepted mode of a clique [...]. In our society such values are created by 'society', by intellectuals, and by the press, magazine literature and by the advertising of manufacturers and traders, all agencies to which the middle-status groups are particularly susceptible.[11]

The crucial presumption here is that it is the middle-status groups (or the middle classes in general) that are most vulnerable to the cultural techniques of consumerism. It is a position that is often reiterated and is based on a belief that by being poised between an aristocracy that sees taste as a birth right, and a working class who are seen as having more communal tastes, the middle classes have a precarious relationship to taste. For Chapman the proof of their susceptibility is based on a readership survey from 1950 which 'shows that the proportion of the "well-to-do", the "middle class" and the "lower middle-class" who read magazines directed to the cultivation of the home is about twice as high as that of the "working class"'.[12] The sense of susceptibility suggests a peculiar weakness to be swayed by the direction of others and to develop 'status anxiety', and to be prone to peer-pressure.

Chapman's book is much more sophisticated than I have suggested but its basic assumptions connect it to a barrage of literature around taste in the postwar period: people, and some people more than others, make their choices with the intention of impressing others, or shoring-up their position in society, and of gaining status. It is this intention that I want to question. For a start, and as I have mentioned before, this is an intention that is nearly always described from the outside. Other people have status symbols and status anxiety; authors who write about status are themselves miraculously immune from status striving and choose things because they like them and value them. In the various accounts from the postwar period of people describing their interiors or their taste choices, I couldn't find anyone who describes their choices in terms of intentionally seeking status. Status seeking is an activity that other people are engaged in as they chose their wallpaper, flooring, furniture, and curtains. But, of course, a host of other intentions are just as likely and often much more plausible – practicality and comfort being obvious contenders. As demonstrated throughout this book, taste is probably best understood as multiple, and of course it is possible to like something on its own terms and because it shows that you in a good light (as modern, as switched on, as tasteful). Developing a taste for yogurt in the 1960s while at university might involve several kinds of enjoyment: you can enjoy the yogurt as a new kind of non-British taste you hadn't experienced before; you can enjoy it because you feel it connects you to a new sophisticated world of continental tastes; and you might also enjoy going back to your parental home and showing off the new foods that you now enjoy! Emphasising how different you were from your parents was, and probably still is, a popular pastime for young people.

As outlined in chapter 1, this book takes the attitude that taste exists across various layers: it is about personal preferences, while also being about social feelings, and about historical change. Each layer is powerful, and I don't think that new tastes ever really take off unless a combination of all three layers are in play. Status striving relates to the layer of social feelings but is often an impoverished way of understanding that layer. If they weren't actually enjoyed, Ski yogurts would have had little chance of success. Their popularity was amplified by advertising and by associations that linked them to healthy lifestyles, casual sociability (and probably casual sex), and continental Europe. One minor aspect of this might be that this could be used as a way of exhibiting social status amongst non-Ski-yogurt-consuming friends! How cool am I with my yogurt! And as a taste it has historical force as part of the general internationalising of food consumption in Britain after the 1960s. (Today, it can also be seen as part of an early wave of what would soon become a tsunami of getting food in plastic packaging.) Choosing Habitat was probably a surer way of participating in status positioning, but there again, to reduce that to a jockeying of social standing misses much of the way that it promised a life that was less uptight and more informal. It strikes me that this layering of taste can be both fraught with anxiety (your choices might be greeted with disdain by those whose opinions you value or who you 'look up to') and an occasion for delight. And sometimes both at the same time. But while I don't subscribe to the idea that taste is most productively thought about as a form of status striving, this was a hugely popular way of treating taste in the late twentieth century and is therefore an important part of my story.

The real turning point in the popularisation of sociological approaches to taste was from a more journalistic source than Chapman. In 1960 the UK publication of American journalist Vance Packard's *The Status Seekers: An Exploration of Class Behaviour in America*[13] paved the way for similar accounts that combined 'status enquiry' with new attempts to elaborate class differences: in Packard's case it was the rejection of the duality of white-collar and blue-collar workers, to a more intricate five-tier system that took much more account of education. When it was published in the UK it was described as a 'runaway No. 1 bestseller' and widely reviewed.[14] The reviews in the national daily newspapers range from a quick précis of the book to more considered analyses.[15] Peter Willmott in his review in *New Left Review*, like many with a more academic investment in sociology, bemoaned the book's impressionistic approach and lack of scientific rigour, but took the opportunity of discussing the relevance of its finding for a British context. He noted, for example, that Packard's assessment that in the United States education was becoming the main route to class advancement was being mirrored in Britain: 'All the evidence suggests that there has been little change in the *extent* of mobility in both countries; the difference is almost certainly in the *means* of achieving mobility, which was formerly via the shop floor and now characteristically through the Eleven Plus, Grammar School and University'.[16] Willmott, who had just finished writing *Family and Class in a London Suburb*,[17] with Michael Young also recognised that: 'In Britain, as in the United States, the bulk of new housing since the war has been outside existing towns and cities. Whether public or private, New Towns or housing estates, these new communities are essentially one-class, essentially one-age, essentially suburban'.[18] He goes on to explain what he means by 'essentially suburban': 'low density, two-storey three-bedroom housing, with wire-fenced gardens back and front, wide green verges, empty concrete roads [...]. These kind[s] of places, where everybody is new and seeking to "place" their neighbours and themselves, seem to be great generators of status striving and class awareness'.[19] Willmott and Young's research of the London suburb of Woodford doesn't entirely bear out this opinion, but it is one that, as we shall see, has certainly had a powerful influence in the postwar period. The next chapter comes back to *Family and Class in a London Suburb* because the contradictory representation it gives of the 'new classes' is a useful way of challenging the idea of the new suburbs as cauldrons of bubbling class resentment played-out through taste.

The new suburban estates and the new middle classes in Britain were often at the centre of the popular sociology that emerged in the wake of Packard's *Status Seekers*. For instance, the Scottish journalist Robert Millar followed his 1963 book, *The Affluent Sheep*, a study of consumerism in Britain, with a book that in various ways echoes Packard's, *The New Classes: The New Pattern of British Life*, published in 1966.[20] The second book develops some of the ideas of the first book but draws out the implications of consumerism for the British class 'system'. One of its presumptions is that consumer goods are symbols. So rather than being goods that help clean clothes or pick up dirt or get you about the place, these goods are primarily 'status-conferring devices'.[21] He even has a chapter named 'Status Symbol Society'.

In the chapter on the home, he describes the 'technicists' (his name for what others were calling the new middle class) and their taste in floor coverings:

> A fitted, wall-to-wall carpet has also become an important status symbol in the Technicist class. Indeed, some families told me that they considered this the most important, and most expensive, acquisition when moving into their new homes. The development of broadloom carpets, often with rubber backing, which can be cut to fit a room by the owner, has brought fitted carpets within the means of most people. This type of floor covering is certainly no longer a middle-class status symbol. In most technicist homes, however, the floor is still polished hardwood blocks, covered with one or two Axminster rugs.[22]

Fitted carpets (figure 7.1) were becoming relatively cheap in the 1960s and added warmth and comfort to rooms.

A carpet, fitted or not, is not first and foremost a sign or symbol, it's a material object that is soft or rough, deep or thin, and so on. Treating such objects as symbols puts them into competition with other symbols, while often ignoring how they might provide comfort, warmth, quietness, and so on. The historical sense of how whole swathes of a country become more comfortable, quieter, and softer gets lost. The image of this Axminster fitted carpet doesn't immediately suggest that the carpet's main role is as a symbol of status; it suggests a world of controlled casualness, of new forms of ease and relaxation, of listening to music and drinking wine. As the magazine copy reveals, the carpet is being joined by a 'Modern Magistretti table in glass fibre, from Habitat in London and Manchester' which 'proves the carpet's versatility. Stereo Cassette Recorder is by Philips'.[23] Part of that enjoyment might entail a sense of social status, but in addition to, rather than instead of its material characteristics.

In his review of *The Status Seekers*, the anthropologist Geoffrey Gorer made that point that sociology in the UK had much to learn from US sociology. For Gorer, British sociologists were too concerned with social extremes: with the extremely poor and disadvantaged or the super wealthy and ultra-privileged, and didn't pay enough attention to the vast swathes of people who lived between these poles: 'It seems probable that English sociology will continue to be preoccupied with Our Betters and with the "under-privileged", at least in the books addressed to the general reader, and that Americans will continue to study themselves. From their self-consciousness we may be able to profit'.[24] What followed *The Status Seekers* in the UK, both in terms of popular sociology and in terms of the fictional worlds that used a sociological perspective, proved Gorer wrong, at least to some degree. American sociological 'self-consciousness', though, was not something that just found its way into professional sociology in Britain. In many respects it invades popular culture as a loss of innocence. Taste self-consciousness means recognising that different tastes have different social values, and that your enjoyment is somebody else's cultural cringe. Of course, this is something everyone has always known: the earthy laughter of one class is the epitome of tastelessness for another. But in consumer culture this becomes part of the general experience of consumption: a self-conscious layer that sits on top of our likes and dislikes.

7.1 Axminster fitted carpet, *Good Housekeeping*, October 1967, p. 55

At times it might even add to our enjoyment with the spice of irony. The use of self-conscious kitsch is an aspect of this.

Having it so good?

One of the most famous representations from the 1970s of a household who treated their home as a symbolic display of status, as well as a space for festering class resentment, was Mike Leigh's play *Abigail's Party*. It was broadcast on 1 November 1977, on the BBC's 'Play for Today' slot. Previously the play had been running in the Hampstead Theatre during 1977 and the televised adaptation is a lightly edited version of the play transferred to a television studio. The TV version is staged in an open-plan lounge-dining-room-kitchen and we only leave this space on rare occasions to go into the hallway to the front door and the downstairs toilet. From the doorway the audience can see that the house is part of a new development of houses, with another new house only a few yards in front.

The play takes place one evening when Beverly and Laurence invite their neighbours Sue (a divorcee who lives next door with her two children), and another young couple, Angie and Tony (who have just arrived in the neighbourhood), to come round for a drink. The two young couples are childless, and both live in new houses as part of the same development, whereas the older neighbour, Sue, lives in a more established property. The reason for the evening, which also gives the name to the play, is that Sue's daughter Abigail is having a party and Sue has been ordered to leave her house. Abigail, who we never see, has a pink streak in her hair and safety pins in her jeans. We find out quite quickly that Beverly doesn't work but used to be a beautician in a department store and that Laurence is an estate agent. We don't know what Sue does or did, but we know that her ex-husband is an architect. Angie is a nurse, while Tony is a computer operator, though he used to be a professional footballer.

It is Beverly, who *The Sunday Telegraph* described as 'a reptilian predator of sex and social pretensions', who dominates the proceedings.[25] And yet it is her husband, described by the same paper as 'a craven and grasping little Jewish estate agent', who is presented as having greater snobbery.[26] Beverly is a bossy grotesque: in the name of socialising she forces people to drink, to dance, to smoke – usually against their will. And she seems to take endless pleasure in pushing her husband around (and pushing his buttons, as they say). At the start of the play, when he returns from work, he is already explosively tense, and from then on, he just gets worse. In one exchange, Laurence and Beverly argue directly about taste. Laurence has just accused Beverly of being ignorant because she prefers pop music to classical:

LAURENCE: D'you know something, Beverly? You're ignorant!
BEVERLY: Oh, so I'm ignorant, now, am I?
LAURENCE: Now? You always have been!
BEVERLY: It's not a question of ignorance Laurence, it's a question of taste!
LAURENCE: Taste! And what would you know about taste?
BEVERLY: The trouble with you Laurence is that if somebody doesn't happen to like what you like, then you say that they've got no taste!
LAURENCE: That's rubbish!
BEVERLY: Oh, is it rubbish?
LAURENCE: Yes!
BEVERLY: Then what about that picture I've got upstairs in the bedroom, then?
LAURENCE: That is cheap, pornographic trash!
BEVERLY: Laurence, just because a picture happens to be erotic, it doesn't mean it's pornographic.
LAURENCE: Oh, shut up, Beverly!![27]

The play ends with Laurence having a fatal heart attack as Beverly goes to fetch the 'cheap, pornographic trash' that Laurence had consigned to the bedroom. What provokes Beverly to get the print is Laurence pointing out to their guests the pictures that they have on their downstairs walls, most notably a copy of Van Gogh's 1888 painting of a chair (figure 7.2). The print that Beverly fetches, and much prefers, is a much more recent painting by Stephen Pearson, *Wings of Love* (figure 7.3), that was sold in its thousands in the 1970s by the poster manufacturer Athena.[28]

7.2 Vincent Van Gogh, *Chair*, 1888

7.3 Stephen Pearson, *Wings of Love*, *c.* 1972

In relation to the cultural tastes operating at the time, both the print of the Van Gogh and the Pearson would have seemed distinctly un-sophisticated to the one securely middle-class person in the room, Sue. She, however, is too polite to join in such arguments and is preoccupied by worrying about what is happening in her house while Abigail's party continues (the audience hears muffled rock music coming from the party throughout most of the play). For a 1970s' theatre audience, and for the critics who wrote about theatre and TV drama, it was clear that the viewer was being invited not to consider questions of taste, but to laugh at both of these choices, and to laugh particularly at Laurence for imagining that he had 'good taste' by having a reproduction Van Gogh. But there are other tastes that presumably both Beverly and Laurence agree on, that aren't contentious, and that don't come in for discussion, which are working to set the play in amongst the new middle classes. This is the taste of the room itself: its furnishings, its ambience.

The open-plan arrangement of the downstairs is divided by a shelving unit that allows the kitchen to be partly screened from the lounge area (figure 7.4 right hand corner). The freestanding shelving unit, used as a room divider, was a popular way of portioning space in the sort of open-plan layout that was often a feature of the new houses being put up by housebuilders such as Barratt, Taylor Wilson, and the countless other speculative builders. These shelving units were produced by companies like Ladderax, Interflex, and Furni-Kit (figure 7.5). They were flexible systems which could fit into any number of spaces, and

7.4 Mike Leigh, *Abigail's Party*, 1977, BBC. From left to right: Angie (Janine Duvitski), Beverly (Alison Steadman), Laurence (Tim Stern), Sue (Harriet Reynolds), Tony (John Salthouse)

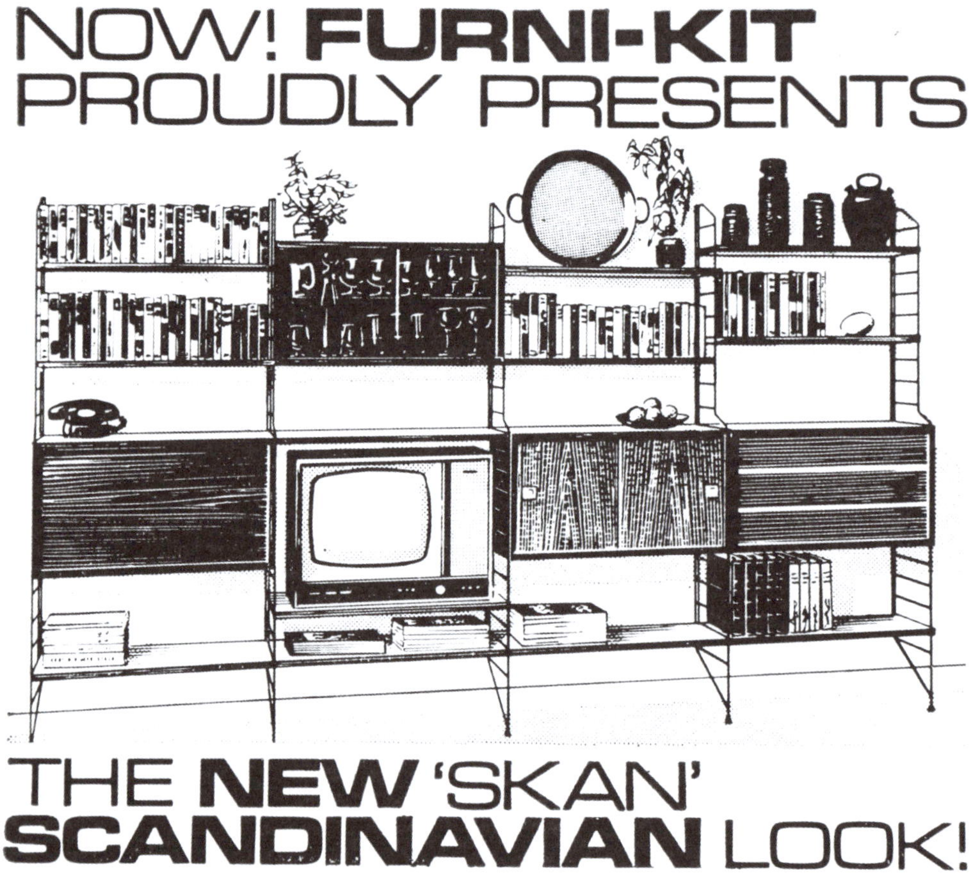

7.5 Furni-Kit, *Homes and Gardens*, February 1968, p. 132

which could be altered through new additions, and which came with choices of shelves, cabinets, and so on. The Interflex systems was advertised as 'the system that fits ANY space' and 'includes cupboards, drawer units, desks, cocktail cabinets' as well as a space for 'Hi-Fi units'.[29] Beverly and Laurence's shelving unit is their centrepiece, and the play revolves around the drinks cabinet and the Hi-Fi system which are part of it. The shelving unit is where the endless rounds of drinks are dispatched and where the ceaseless war of musical tastes are enacted (Tom Jones and Demis Roussos, for Beverly, versus Beethoven and James Galway, for Laurence). It is also where the leather-bound, unread, and gold-embossed complete works of Shakespeare lives, which Laurence proudly displays to the group: 'it is part of our heritage', he declares, while adding 'not something you can actually read, of course'. The unread books and the paintings are of course symbols, and clearly for Laurence and Beverly they are tied up with status. But the shelving unit is not a symbol, or at least it is not primarily symbolic.

The shelf-divide allows Laurence and Beverly to organise their room around 'controlled casualness'. Spontaneous sociability is encouraged by such furniture, as someone in the kitchen can pass food through the shelves. The shelves allow occupants to move from the space of the dining room or the kitchen into the space of the lounge while continuing to chat to anyone else in this large space. It allows the stereo and the drinks cabinet to have a central position, which means that they can be easily and constantly accessed without anyone having to leave the 'action'. But in the play, casualness (controlled or not) is the opposite of the mood in the room. The easy sociability imagined by the designers of such shelving systems fails in Laurence and Beverly's house and becomes instead a site of tensions and animosity. Mike Leigh and his ensemble cast (who devised the play collectively through seven weeks of rehearsal) are enacting what they see as a sociological perspective: 'what we're trying here is a form of social documentary', claimed Leigh.[30] The sociological presumption, which is the foundation of the play, is here based on the idea of 'status striving' (with the emphasis on the striving). And with such striving comes the 'inevitability' of failure. Of course, there is no reason why Beverly or Laurence should inevitably fail to achieve the sort of lifestyle promised by the housing estate and by its furnishings. The failure is treated as a class position, a class defect.

The reviews, even the most favourable ones, had a sense that what they were watching was often a form of gross 'condescension',[31] with the *Daily Mail* critic titling his review 'I'm ashamed to say that I laughed'.[32] For the *Daily Telegraph* the criticism was more decisive: 'there was a residual impression that the production was made from the outside; that the director and his players were commenting on those behind them on the ladder from a position of comparatively secure middle-classness'.[33] But it was the playwright, Denis Potter, who skewered the play:

> This play was based on nothing more edifying than rancid disdain, for it was a prolonged jeer, twitching with genuine hatred, about the dreadful suburban tastes of the dreadful lower middle classes … it sank under its immense condescension. The force of the yelping derision became

> a single note of contempt, amplified into a relentless screech. As so often in the minefields of English class-consciousness, more was revealed of the snobbery of the observers rather than of the observed.[34]

Abigail's Party took some of the sociological presumptions that had been circulating in the 1960s and 1970s – the idea that the new middle classes or lower middle classes were the ones most infected with acquisitive greed and status envy – and blew it up into a tragic farce. Taste was weaponised to the point where it killed Laurence.

A much more nuanced and sympathetic portrayal of the new middle classes had been provided a few years earlier by the television sitcom *Whatever Happened to the Likely Lads?* (1973–74). The context of the drama is the return of Terry Collier back to Tyneside after some years in the Army. He returns to his hometown and catches up with his friend Bob, who is on the verge of marrying Thelma. Bob and Thelma have bought a semi-detached Barratt house on a new estate (the Barratt Highfields development in Killingworth, North Tyneside, was used for all exterior shots of the house and the estate). Bob and Terry had been childhood friends and had both grown up in working-class terraced houses (figure 7.6), where Terry's parents still live. The comedy revolves around Terry's sentimental attachment to an older way of life, and the working-class culture he associates with it, and his attempts to derail what he sees as the social climbing of his friend and his friend's fiancée.

7.6 Terry and Bob, *Whatever Happened to the Likely Lads?* (BBC, 1973–74) in Terry Collier's working-class childhood home

The Tyneside that Terry comes back to has been modernised to a degree that makes him both nostalgic and a little lost. The sitcom uses various markers of class, sexuality, and gender to show how much life has changed. The local barbers, for instance, has become 'Michelle, Gents Hair Styling', and when Terry and Bob visit so that Terry can get a more up-to-date haircut (which to Terry's alarm involves hair-washing and blow-drying), Terry is terrified that the male hairdressers are homosexual. When Bob reprimands him he does so, not so much for his homophobia, but for holding old-fashioned, aggressively masculine views. To reassure the audience that Terry is just not up with current tastes, the hairdressers are revealed to be football-loving-beer-drinking-heterosexuals. Terry's sister, Audrey, who also lives on a new estate, has changed too. She has a new baby who is called Fleur, and practices yoga (on a dining room table). In *Whatever Happened to the Likely Lads?* Bob's world of long, salon-styled hair, of new housing estates and office work, is seen as modern, light, with much softer forms of masculinity, though still resolutely heterosexual. To Terry, Bob is being seduced into an unfamiliar world, primarily by his fiancée Thelma (figure 7.7). And this world is one dominated by female class aspiration.

In its depiction of Thelma, and Thelma's mother, the sitcom ends up replaying a central gendered stereotype around taste and the new middle classes – namely that it is women who are most responsible for status striving, and social climbing. For Terry, Bob's imminent marriage to Thelma is going to take Bob into a world where his 'lad' masculinity, and working-class roots are going to be fundamentally altered. Terry has his own idea of tastes associated with middle-class life. When Bob mentions that Thelma is knitting him

7.7 Thelma and Bob, *Whatever Happened to the Likely Lads?* (BBC, 1973–74) in Thelma and Bob's Barratt house with shelf dividers

a cardigan, he replies that he hates cardigans. And when Bob responds that Terry's dad wears a cardigan, he clarifies that it isn't *that* sort of cardigan that he objects to but the ones that are 'all wiggly, chunky wool, and beige and faun and rugby clubs, and Sunday morning open air drinks, and Cocker Spaniels, and barbeques, and gin and tonics, and Cross and Blackwell's'. For Terry there is an inevitable path that would take you from a chunky-knit cardigan or a Barratt's home to becoming a member of the Golf Club and Sunday morning drinks with the company director. To take one step into that world is to surrender to the whole ensemble of assertively aspirational middle-class culture. One minute you're wearing a chunky-knit cardigan, and then before you know it, you're discussing share options and holidays in Bermuda while teeing off on the fourteenth hole. For Bob and Audrey, Terry's view is ten years out of date: while Terry has been away the nature of class itself has changed.

The link between gender and status striving is made most evident when Terry and Bob are being fitted for their morning suits for Bob's wedding. Terry is complaining to someone else in the shop that the groom's parents are 'jumped up from nothing' and that Bob's mother-in-law 'sees herself as the Jackie Onassis of the Tudor Estate Set'. Of course, this being a sitcom, it quickly turns out that he is talking to Bob's soon-to-be father-in-law who admits that he had indeed come 'from nothing':

> I'm a builder. I did very well in the postwar boom. We managed to survive that bad patch and I'm doing alright now. I was a brickie before that and I'm still a brickie at heart. It's Thelma's mother what's got all these fancy ideas. […] We only take the *Telegraph* to impress the newsagent's wife. It's all airs and graces. It's daft but it's harmless enough, mostly.

The status striving of the newly wealthy is put firmly in the hands of the mother and daughter. Yet despite such misogyny, *Whatever Happened to the Likely Lads?* has a warmth entirely absent in *Abigail's Party*: the new world of consumer goods and changing manners is given a chance, and the tastes of Audrey, Bob and, to some degree, Thelma, don't receive the disdain that Mike Leigh serves out.

In his article on the opportunities of modern British sociology in the wake of *The Status Seekers*, Geoffrey Gorer praises the work of writers like Richard Hoggart, with their depiction of working-class culture which, he argues, 'differs from those of earlier decades by stressing the "warm human" values which illumine the lives of the poor and compensate for the greater material possessions of the "cold and materialistic" middle classes'. But he also warns that 'these books are implicitly nostalgic and retrospective, as are explicitly the number of autobiographies of working-class childhood which, although not directly sociological themselves, are the raw material from which sociological generalisations can be drawn'.[35] In the 1960s and 1970s the new middle classes (both their bohemian wing, and the lives of 'salaried workers' like Thelma, Bob and Audrey) never quite found a sociological perspective that could describe their 'warm human values'. Perhaps if there had been it would have had something of the tone of *Whatever Happened to the Likely Lads?*

TV dinners

If the tastes of the new middle classes were going to have a life beyond status anxiety, then they needed a platform where they could be seen as a normal part of everyday life. While television's portrayal of taste in its comedy dramas concentrated on taste as status, a more varied picture was offered in TV cookery shows.[36] Television, like shops and magazines, is part of a modern infrastructure of taste, and like them it supplies resources. TV cookery programmes offer resources for developing tastes: recipes, demonstrations of cooking skills, explanation of ingredients and cooking processes, and so on, which help TV watchers to expand their cooking repertoires. But alongside this there are other resources that are crucial to understanding changing tastes in the postwar period. TV shows us different ways of performing: attitudes and ambiances that are also expressive of taste. The 'flair' and 'controlled casualness' that might be needed to pull-off a new style of cooking is part of what we consume when we watch cooking shows. We might want to cook the food that we see being produced by TV chefs, but we don't want to do it in a state of mounting panic, we want to do it with the cavalier ease and *joie de vivre* of Keith Floyd, the nonchalant elegance of Nigella Lawson, or the ordinary care of Delia Smith. Today's food programmes are sold as much on the idea of the chef's personality as the skills and quality of the cookery: what would the early Jamie Oliver be without the tousled hair, and little-boy glee, and his bish-bash-bosh style of cooking? Or Ainsley Harriott without the ebullient, explosive enthusiasm?

Delia Smith was a major cookery presence on television from the mid-1970s onwards and Keith Floyd first started presenting food programmes on the BBC from 1984, pioneering a more relaxed and sensuous approach to cooking and to how cooking was going to be presented on television. In terms of tone and attitude they could be seen as polar opposites, yet both offered resources for the new middle classes. Delia's approach (her celebrity status is confirmed by the fact that her first name is all she needs to be identified) was fundamentally educational: she took the viewer through the various stages of preparation and cooking, explaining what was happening, offering handy hints, and noting the various things that might go wrong and how you could put them right. Floyd's approach was much more anarchic. It was a performance that was often liberally dowsed in alcohol, with an irreverent attitude to the conventions of television presentation.

Delia Smith left school at sixteen without any qualifications and initially trained as a hairdresser. Her interest in food was sparked by visiting restaurants in London that were cooking modern Mediterranean food. She supplemented this by becoming an avid reader and collector of cookery books. Her inquisitiveness about all things culinary eventually led to her becoming a recipe writer and food journalist, first for the *Daily Mirror* and then with the *Evening Standard*. It was her almost evangelical attitude to teaching culinary basics, and to providing a style of cooking that could be accomplished by anyone following her step-by-step instructions, that led to her great success. In 1978 she presented *Delia Smith's Cookery Course* on the BBC and the accompanying books cemented her reputation as the preeminent TV presenter of home-cooking.

You only really get a sense of what made Delia such a phenomenon when you view her in contrast to the world of TV cookery before she hit the screen. Since the mid-1950s, British TV cooking had been dominated by Fanny Craddock (figure 7.8), who would often present her shows wearing elaborate ballgowns, as if she were preparing to enter an aristocratic cocktail party at any moment. With her cut-glass accent, and deep resonant voice, she came across as if she were lecturing at a Swiss finishing school. Against such a landscape, Delia Smith (figure 7.9) was presented as someone with 'a totally regionless accent; it's not quite Estuary English, it's slightly London suburbia affected. It's an almost unidentifiable classless voice which appeals across the board'.[37] While Craddock's performance was often aristocratic and intimidating, Delia, according to Egon Ronay, 'inspires confidence because she is so much like any ordinary member of the public. There are no airs about her or gimmicks. She talks very plainly, like one person to another, and that in itself is an unconscious art'.[38] That unconscious art of appearing ordinary also included her dress sense: 'They used to take me to the Wardrobe Department and show me the kind of clothes you would see people wearing at a Buckingham Palace garden party. They tried to get me into those, but they didn't have much success'.[39]

7.8 Fanny Cradock, 1972

7.9 Delia Smith, *Cookery Course*

Delia Smith on TV was a performance of ordinariness that epitomises one aspect of the new middle classes: a refusal of traditional signs of class. Here ordinariness becomes something of a neutralising agent, emptying out the sort of high-charisma performance that you might associate either with the upper-middle-class world of Fanny Craddock or the sensuous pleasures of the televised working classes as they were represented in 'kitchen-sink' dramas, or on the soap operas that have been crucial to the television schedules since *Coronation Street* began at the end of 1960. Delia's *Cookery Course* felt like a technical demonstration that could be easily copied at home, and the sense of 'technician' attitude was also conveyed by the guests that she brought on to explain cuts of meat or the world of spices. In the episode on spices and flavourings she brings on one Michael Adler, a marketing manager for a company 'that exports spices all over the world'. 'In the past ten years', declares Adler in conversation with Delia, 'spices have grown fantastically, they have become very, very popular, as people have travelled to Spain, to Italy and France and have had new flavours that have made their mouths water'. It is hard to get much of a sense of 'mouths watering' or the sensuous properties of spice, as Adler and Delia show us the various options available and encourage us to use fresh ginger rather than the powdered version. But if we aren't blown away by their charisma and by their ability to evoke tastes and flavours, we are confident in their technical knowledge and their technical skills, and it is this that the programmes provide. It is a technical performance of ordinary expertise that can be passed on through the wonders of television and the well-thumbed, multi-million selling cookbooks emblazoned with the name Delia Smith.

If Delia has a down-to-earth, functionalist approach, Keith Floyd's (figure 7.10) ambiance was positively bacchanalian. Delia spoke to her audience as if to a room of diligent, note-taking, self-improving cooks; Floyd spoke to his audience as fellow sensualists. The studio setting of Delia's cookery located it firmly in the home; Floyd took cooking outside. What characterised Floyd's approach was an evident enjoyment in the sensual properties of food. He beckoned you as a viewer into the screen, wanting you to taste and smell the food, wanting you to share his excitement. It was his performance as an enthusiastic exponent of quick, seemingly improvised cooking that became his trademark. He first came to a television audience in his 1984 series *Floyd on Fish*. The improvisational aspect of his performance seems to have emerged due to the relative inexperience of the production team. This is Floyd remembering one of the early shoots of cooking a hake dish:

> I glanced up while the onions were frying in the pan and realised the camera was fixed on me, not on the food. What possessed me to say it I will never know, but I did. I said quite curtly, 'If this is meant to be a cookery programme, we ought to be looking at the food not me. Point the camera down there, please.' I suddenly realised that Clive was now staying on the onions for too long and I didn't know what to do next, because those onions had to soften before I could add wine. In desperation I said, 'Hey, Clive, back up to me for a sec … I want to say something to the viewer.' I said, 'Ah thank you. Look, while those onions are sweating down, which will take about five minutes, I think I will just have a quick slurp of wine'.[40]

7.10 Keith Floyd, *Floyd on France*

The improvisational performance, with constant instructions to Clive the camera operator, asides to the audience, and liberal libations, brought together sensuous delight and a form of spontaneous sociability. This was casualness, but it was barely controlled casualness.

In his 1987 series *Floyd on France* he combined cooking and travel television in a weekly tour of the gastronomic regions of France. Driving through Provence, wearing sunglasses and a white safari suit, he spoke directly to his audience: 'yes, I know, I'm posing, but it's my show, and anyway it's only rock and roll, and if you don't get a buzz out of being in this dramatic land, then, my dear faded gastronaut you must be on the way out. You can't help being carried away by the sense and the colours, the atmosphere is heady, it's magical'. The mixture of easy cosmopolitanism, self-reflexiveness, and unalloyed delight in being in the French countryside made the programme a multi-sensory experience. Floyd's performance, with his signature bowtie, was very much the upper-crust, eccentric, bon vivant. His actual family background was working class, and he grew up in a council house, but through his parents' financial sacrifices and 'grant assistance' from the local authorities he was privately educated. The result was a presenter who combined arrogance and affability and seemed to produce television 'off the cuff'. In one scene from the episode focusing on the Périgord region, he is shown cooking an omelette with a filling of sauteed cèpes (forest mushrooms), according to a Frenchwoman's recipe, who is also watching him cook. As he cooks and talks to the camera, she is giving him directions and criticising his manner of cooking. At this point he takes the pan off the stove: 'we'll start again – I've already had a row with the crew this morning, the lighting man isn't feeling very well, I'm trying to speak in two languages, to five people who don't understand any damn thing, and the fat's getting too hot'. He remakes the dish and while the Frenchwoman, whose kitchen it is, is more approving of the finished result, it is still not quite up to the standard she requires. In response Floyd asks her to take over, and she produces a much firmer omelette. The cramped, hectic, but amiable exchange embodies the idea of cooking as a form of sensuous sociability, where cooking is not just a necessary supplement to living but lies at the centre of living a good life, living *the* good life.

Delia and Floyd had different ways of performing the art of cooking. Her careful, matter-of-fact approach to cooking brought a large repertoire of dishes to her large audience of eager learners. (Her recipe for minestrone soup is still a favourite in our house.) Floyd, on the other hand offered a squiffy version of the sort of performance cookery that was evident in chains like PizzaExpress and showed how 'controlled casualness' could be extended to the enjoyment of cooking as well as eating. Bob and Thelma would probably have got more out of Delia than they did out of Floyd, but if their tastes also embraced the sort of improvised sensuousness being promoted by Habitat and others, they might have been devotees of Floyd as well. It is hard to imagine Beverly and Laurence cooking at all, let alone enjoying it.

8

But isn't that a class thing?

In September 1983, at the University of Sussex, the anthropologist David Pocock invited a recently recruited team of Mass-Observers to describe their domestic circumstances for a 'historian of the future'.[1] The invitation was framed in a way that would encourage detailed description and was 'inspired by a visit from a curator in Scunthorpe who regretted that our wartime material is so thin in detailed description of house interiors. If you have seen historical reconstructions of ordinary rooms in museums, you will know how much they tell us about life in those times. I would like our written reconstructions to be as faithful an account for the 1980s as we can manage'. It led to one correspondent's response: 'I am interested in this project but do not see how any house is "typical" of the period. Well some are I suppose. Perhaps the 1970s and 1980s when reconstructed in museums will be pure HABITAT? But isn't that a class thing?'[2] This response rightly points out the impossibility of typifying domestic taste across a period while also raising the question of the relationship between class and taste. But it leaves other questions hanging: what is this 'thing' called class; is it a 'thing' at all; and what is the relationship between things (carpets, quiches, and clothes) and class?

In the postwar period, class is often presented as a dichotomy: you are either middle class or working class (often with the remains of an aristocracy, or upper class absorbed into the indistinct middle). Already we have hit a confusion: the terms don't logically connect. Middle seems to point to a spot somewhere between 'upper' and 'lower' in a hierarchy, whereas 'working' suggests another logic is in use where the opposite term should either be 'non-working' or 'leisure'.[3] Throughout most of the twentieth century and on into the present, the terms 'middle' and 'working' have been the dominant names for class. This rough duality bears the echo of probably the most famous account of class. This is Karl Marx and Frederick Engels in the *Manifesto of the Communist Party*: 'Our epoch [...] possesses, however, this distinctive feature: it has simplified the class antagonisms. Society as a whole is more and more splitting up into two great hostile camps, into two great classes directly facing each other: Bourgeoisie and Proletariat'.[4] It feels so nineteenth century, don't you think? The image that springs to mind is of an industrial landscape where a tiny number of factory owners face the growing army of workers that they are trying to exploit. Could there have been much doubt about who was going to win that struggle? From that vantage point the dictatorship over the proletariat must have seemed inevitable.

Marx and Engels, of course, were theorising and as much as my caricature image of bosses and workers confronting each other is decidedly shop-worn, it would, I think, be unwise to dismiss the gist of their argument: isn't today's talk of the global 1 per cent of the super-rich who own the multinationals a sign that they were on the right track and that ownership and wealth has been concentrated in fewer and fewer hands? Such an argument would suggest that terms like working class and middle class are a mere smokescreen to obscure the reality of a shared set of interests amongst the 99 per cent. Taste, it would be fair to say, has had a prominent role in obscuring that reality. Why would a doctor and a plumber feel that they had the same interests when one drove a new Mercedes and the other a second-hand Skoda? But terms like 'bourgeoisie' and 'proletarian' never really caught on in a country that was much more at ease in turning class into a matter of manners and breeding.

A very different account of class is given by an anonymous female Mass-Observer in response to a question from June 1939 asking the volunteers about their thoughts and attitudes regarding class. She claims that there are twenty-eight classes on a social scale, with royalty at the top, while at the bottom are 'people who are crude, dirty and irresponsible. Have no community feelings outside their own grade and 27. Quite content to live and produce children on the dole. Of their circumstances they would say "It's good enough for the likes of us". It seems they know their own value'.[5] It is an eccentric scale with grades four through to nine left blank apart from the proviso that 'I know nothing about these except from books'.[6] The writer describes her own class in the following terms: 'I really don't know to which "class" I belong. I was born in grade 28 with relatives in grade 27. My husband was born in grade 10 with relatives and ancestry in a higher stratum. We both live in grade 19. This is the grade to which we belong if it is income that counts'.[7] Here class is both a reality of income and an amalgam of heritage: we can see her moving up the social scale as her husband is moving down.

The terms 'working class' and 'middle class' often only vaguely connect to the complexity of people's experience of class. Often writers seem to describe their own class as though trying to hit a particularly tricky target. George Orwell, for instance, describes his class as 'shabby-genteel', and writes that he 'was born into what you might describe as the lower-upper-middle class'.[8] It is a contradiction of culture and income, a recognition that you could be both poor and posh. Jonathan Raban hits roughly the same target describing his childhood in Norfolk, growing up as the son of a vicar: 'At about £700 a year, a vicar's stipend in the 1950s was roughly the same as the wage of a skilled labourer living on the council estate [...]. We had the money of one lot, the voices of another – and we had an unearthly godliness which removed us from the social map altogether'.[9]

Even trying to describe life securely within the middle class involved some qualification. This is the sociologist Ann Oakley describing her childhood as the daughter of a social worker and the social researcher Richard Titmuss:

> The house was composed of matt white surfaces, dull carpets that wouldn't show the dirt and such an economy of decorative items that the eye was mildly shocked to chance on any of them. There were a few highly polished dark wood tables and chests inherited from my mother's respectable South East London family, and later some blonde wood constructions, my mother's pride and joy, acquired in the 1960s from new furniture stores such as Habitat. It was a house bought by my father and made by my mother in a formula rife among the English middle-middle-class in the 1950s.[10]

'Middle-middle-class' might seem a redundant phrase, but Oakley is navigating (albeit differently) through the same thickets of qualifications as Orwell and Raban.

Perhaps the most fraught term for locating yourself on a spectrum of class is the phrase 'lower middle class' or petit bourgeois. It seems to suggest a precarious positioning, of doing well but not quite 'making it'. And yet as the historian Frank Mort and others have shown, the lower middle classes at the start of the twentieth century were often characterised by strong religious orthodoxy and a commitment to respectability that on the face of it suggested the very opposite of social precariousness. Mort's own family came from a tradition of small, successful builders. His father departed from the family tradition to become an accountant for ICI. Becoming an accountant, unlike becoming a doctor or a lawyer, didn't require a university degree. Accountancy, and somewhat later, social work, were growing professions in the postwar period (in 1958 there were three times as many accountants as there were lawyers).[11] To be an accountant you might study for a two-year diploma at a commercial college either full-time or as an evening class while working.[12] (Like education colleges, art and design colleges, and technical colleges, commercial colleges would get swept up into the new polytechnics by the end of the 1960s.) Mort describes his father as a modernist making a 'transition from the old to the new petty bourgeoisie'.[13] His story, like any story that wants to get under the hood of class experience, reveals numerous tensions.

Mort's family were living a 'new' lower middle-class life (something recognisable within the terms of the new middle classes), while bound to 'old' lower middle-class family and emotional conventions. Mort's father participated outwardly in the world of the middle-class moderns, but like many, refused the new opportunities for relaxed social attitudes and new forms of familial intimacy:

> Our move to the new house coincided with my father's transmutation into a stern and emotionally absent figure. With the new house came a Triumph Herald car. There were holidays in Cornwall, weekends at the motor show in London, experiments in eating out at Chinese Restaurants in Chester and Liverpool. My father joined a wine society and brought home bottles of Pouilly Fuissé to try at Christmas and Easter, when my mother began to cook guinea fowl rather than turkey. After 1964, when we moved again, this time to Buxton, there were more overt trappings of modernity. The new home was a chalet-style bungalow with central heating, parquet floors, and large picture windows: 'A home of your own! We at Buntings specialise in homes for people with a limited budget and a thirst for perfection. We build (and we mean BUILD) with one thing in mind from foundations to fittings-QUALITY.' This was the house builder's brochure. But quality came at a price. As a child I remember that the objects of

> affluence were fraught with a sense of insecurity. Part of this sense had to do with my father's tightly managed domestic economy and his fear of living beyond his means. But it also had to do with the awkward position these goods occupied in my parents' lives.[14]

These are the houses featured in Ideal Home Exhibitions in the 1960s that we saw at the end of chapter 5.

Outwardly the chalet-style bungalow suggests social ease, 'controlled casualness' and a general enthusiasm for new tastes. But class and taste come together in complex ways that are social but also tempered by elements that seem so particular and personal – emotional temperament, personality, and confidence. The world of the new middle-class moderns – with its focus on relaxed informality – was often inhabited uneasily. Older beliefs, such as insisting on strict good manners, for instance, or 'knowing your place', might be played-out in a setting that looks, to all the world, like the model of progressive living. Others, though, may grasp the loose bohemianism that was made newly permissible, with a confidence that belies their class origins. If it hadn't already been clear before the Second World War, the postwar world demonstrated that the British class system was more confused and more contradictory than Marx and Engels could have ever imagined. The finely calibrated hierarchies of work culture with their associated pay grades never quite match up to a world of flat pack furniture, television, and supermarket abundance. How you experience class at work or at school might not be how you experience it at home, or in the pub, or the nightclub. This confusion is partly amplified and partly side-stepped by taste.

Middle-class manual workers

In 1965, writing on the twentieth anniversary of the end of the war in Europe, *The Times*' editorial claimed that:

> Historians of the future will surely marvel at the speed with which the British nation [...] finally shed so much of its pre-war thinking and way of life. Large areas of national activity were transformed. Much former privilege was destroyed. A new middle class began to arise. A welfare state was created. And all this done by a nation which was supposed to be completely exhausted by two world wars, in each of which the British people had fought from the first day to the last.[15]

We might want to snigger a bit at the jingoism of that final sentence, but that sense of a new class or classes emerging alongside other social and cultural phenomena is, I think, undeniable. *The Times* only mentions the welfare state, but we could add other developments to this: the massive rise of home ownership across the classes; the presence of 'modern conveniences' in most homes (washing machines, refrigerators, electric irons etc.); the almost ubiquitous take-up of television; the endless expansion of clerical work; the rise in women's employment; the growth of new industries with technical operators (plastics, chemicals, electronics). It would seem hardly surprising if this didn't have a confusing impact on class experience. If class for Marx and Engels was partly explained in relation to ownership, then, as I asked in the introduction, could you still 'feel' proletarian *and* own your own home and car, and take an annual holiday in Spain? And just as importantly, could you feel properly bourgeois just by being a pen-pusher, wearing 'business-style' clothes, and drinking wine rather than beer?

It is class *feeling* that became increasingly at issue in the postwar period. The contradiction between class position and class feeling had already been discussed before the war: journalists like George Orwell in Britain and Siegfried Kracauer in Germany were particularly interested in the class that Kracauer termed *die Angestellten* (the employee as opposed to the labourer – *der Arbeiter*).[16] These were people who sometimes had a salary rather than a wage, sat behind a desk rather than stood with machines and tools: they were non-manual workers. These employees were clearly workers, with no more 'ownership' of the business where they worked than the riveters in a shipyard or the bricklayers on a building site. The large insurance companies, for instance, employed thousands of clerical workers to process claims, and these were workers who routinely earned less than the manual workers involved in industry. What drew Orwell's and Kracauer's attention was the way that, culturally, they 'felt' distinct, as if they were of a different class than manual workers. And, inevitably, their political and cultural affiliations were sometimes not aligned with those of the manual workers.

This sense of class confusion was even more intense by the late 1950s and into the 1960s when higher wages, the expansion of property ownership, and the seemingly ubiquitous bounty of consumerism led to a situation where the designation 'middle class' wasn't simply reserved for non-manual jobs. When Peter Willmott and Michael Young undertook their sociological study of the London suburb of Woodford, they found that:

> Many manual workers have so improved their standard of life that it is increasingly 'middle class'. To them class depends not so much upon occupation or education as on income, not so much on the world of production as that of consumption. It is therefore not surprising that many of them did not consider themselves as 'working-class' at all. We asked what class people thought they belonged to and found that nearly half (48%) of the 355 manual workers in the general sample considered themselves middle class – 3% said upper middle, 35% middle and 10% lower middle.[17]

Willmott and Young's first thoughts were that in calling themselves middle class, some of the skilled manual workers were keen to distinguishing themselves from other manual workers. They thought it might be the equivalent of identifying yourself as an electrician rather than an unskilled factory worker:

> Of course, by and large, the skilled workers are better paid and, therefore, one would think, more able to afford to buy a house, a car and other consumption goods. But 'middle-class' identification is hardly less frequent among the unskilled and semi-skilled than the skilled. Of the 257 skilled manual workers in the general sample, 49% said they were 'upper middle', 'middle', or 'lower middle'; of the 98 semi-skilled or unskilled 43%.[18]

It might seem odd, then, that Willmott and Young use the category of 'manual work' and 'non-manual work' as the ultimate marker of class. Their account simply defines working class as manual workers and middle class as non-manual.

What Willmott and Young find in Woodford amongst the manual and non-manual classes are similar levels of material comfort:

> On their way to work electricians and bank clerks wear the same sort of clothes, and, what is more, so do their wives. They sometimes drive the same sort of cars, and sometimes the interiors of their houses are indistinguishable too. In each you can watch the same television set from the same mass-produced sofa. In the homes of the young couples there are plenty of signs of the post-war redistribution of incomes which can be viewed instead as the general adoption of middle-class standards.[19]

But alongside the similarities in taste (clothes, cars, sofas), there is a recognition of class differences and signs of both contentment and resentment. When their interviewees talk about money the primary view is not that the working classes have too little money, but that they have (from the perspective of the non-manual workers) too much. 'I think the richest class today', this is according to a works manager 'is the working class'.[20] Of course, this widespread belief that the working class were the 'new wealthy' was often based on exceptional cases of skilled workers working extensive amounts of overtime and comparing this with a teacher or a newly recruited trainee manager. What it never accounted for was the opportunities for career advancement that a middle-class 'professional' career offered, nor the significant amounts of overtime necessary to have middle-class standards of comfort when your job involved working in a factory.

In the 1950s and through into the 1970s many sociologists and journalists, as shown in chapter 6, treated the topic of class as their main concern. They were often concerned with the borderlands of class. They were interested in the way that various white-collar workers were increasingly forming unions, and the way that blue-collar workers (skilled, semi-skilled, and non-skilled manual workers) were taking on some of the social and cultural traits of the middle-classes.[21] Two general phenomena were often commented on. The big headline was, of course, that improvement in the material circumstances of many manual workers meant their lifestyles were now often indistinguishable from many non-manual workers. The other, less heralded, issue was the feeling amongst some middle-class households that the closing of income gaps was also joined by a general decline in the social esteem of some middle-class professions. A teacher reflecting on their class would tell Willmott and Young: 'I suppose before the war I'd be middle class. Teachers had a high social standing then, but now professional people are the lowest. At least that's in money. Actually, we're pretty high class'.[22] Class, in this one instance, seems an experience of contradiction. Here is one person seeing themselves as simultaneously 'low class' in terms of income and status, but somehow also 'high' in terms of innate or cultivated class.

The level of class confusion within a single household suggests that the experience of gender was also a significant element in differentiating class feelings. The 'affluent worker' studies overseen by David Lockwood and John Goldthorpe looked at the relatively well-paid car workers in Luton. Many of the interviews that the team of researchers conducted were amongst couples in their home. The different perceptions between husband and wife add to the sense of class confusion. The following is taken from one of the original interview transcripts where the sociologist's questions are in italics, and the wife is in parenthesis (as was the custom within all these interviews):

> Well, there are different classes.
> *What are they?*
> Well, you've got people who're financially in a safe and secure position – business and professional people. I mean they do tend to form classes of their own, don't they.
> *Are there other classes?*
> You've got people with the money and people without – they form their own classes.
> *What do you call these people?*
> The upper class and the lower class – I think the middle class is nearly extinct (wife – I think we're all middle class unless we're very rich or very poor). Umm (wife – well, what do you call us then?) Working class – what do you say? (wife – well, we're all middle class now)
> *What about this middle class?*
> (Wife – I think there's a poor, rich and middle class …) but take the so called working class people earning good money in factories, they're really working class people, even though they may call themselves middle class.[23]

For the man, the 'middle' of the class system is 'nearly extinct', obliterated by a definite splitting into 'upper' and 'lower'; for the woman, it is the middle which has absorbed all but the 'very rich or very poor'. Such different perceptions within a single household give us a glimpse of a situation where cultural background, future hopes, and economic factors are all vying for recognition.

The classlessness debate

As mentioned in the introduction, the confusion about class, and the emergence of new class identities, raised an explicit political issue in the 1950s and early 1960s. After the success of Clement Attlee's Labour government in the 1945 General Election, the Labour Party were in power only until 1951; between 1951 and 1964 the Conservatives were the party of government. The issue facing the political left was framed in class and taste terms: if the Labour Party was established to protect the interests of the working class, then what happens when people no longer perceive themselves as part of the traditional working class, or else continue to identify as working class but no longer see their politics primarily in terms of class interests? The worry was that the working class had – through higher wages, the protection of the welfare state, home ownership, and the abundance of material goods – simply become middle class.

The relationship between class and taste during this period of affluence became a central political issue. For the political right, the golden age of affluence was a sure sign that class distinctions were a thing of the past, and that market economics had worked to overcome such old-fashioned identities. For the left, the question was how to safeguard traditional working-class institutions (the unions, primarily) while also maintaining the great modernising impulse of the immediate postwar years. One theme that crossed the political divide – though in quite different ways – was the idea of 'classlessness'.

Stuart Hall, in an essay from 1958 titled: 'A Sense of Classlessness', set out some of the key arguments for thinking about the relationship of class, taste, and politics for the forthcoming decades. Hall, a stalwart of the new left, wasn't buying the triumphalist rhetoric that became increasingly popular within the Conservative Party, namely that because of affluence and the welfare state, 'class' no longer existed. What was key to Hall's argument (and has been key to this book) was that in the postwar period, class society was simultaneously continuing, while at the same time it was being *felt* in a confused and confusing manner. Hall wasn't arguing that 'classlessness' actually existed, but he was insisting that the left needed to take the feeling of 'classlessness' seriously and to see it as part of the new world. The title was carefully worded – this wasn't about classless society – but about the *sense* and *feel* of classlessness.

A good deal of Hall's essay remains firmly within the 'status enquiry' school of social thinking, and he sees the situation of the late 1950s as one where 'status' had taken over from 'class' as the overarching feeling within society 'where there is no sharp sense of class, but where there are "exquisite" distinctions of status'.[24] Hall sees modern society as governed by a form of 'people's capitalism', where old solidarities have given way to an endless striving for status, for keeping up with the Joneses. But while his emphasis on status was very much the attitude of left-leaning social thinking by the end of the 1950s, Hall makes a series of points that are important for understanding how the world of taste, work, and class collide in the 1960s and 1970s. He notes, for instance, that the 'line between the skilled worker and the minor technologist is breaking down, particularly in industries based on chemical processes'.[25] But instead of seeing this blurring of class differences as ending up with a huge middle class that is endlessly engaged in exquisite distinction, he sees something else taking place. He calls this 'the proletarianisation of the middle class'.[26] This, he notes, is the opposite of what Marxism had predicted: 'This "mass" has been, if you like "proletarianised" – not as Marx thought *downwards* towards minimum wage levels, but *upwards* towards roughly middle-class styles of living'.[27]

This idea of 'upward proletarianisation' is Hall's name for the simultaneous improvement of living standards amongst manual workers *alongside* the depletion of 'esteem' amongst a variety of professions (such as teachers). It is, in other words, exactly what Willmott and Young were finding in the 1960s in suburbs like Woodford: a general sense that most people (manual and non-manual alike) had achieved a 'middle-class' lifestyle while inherited forms of esteem were disintegrating. And it wasn't just esteem that was being erased from many middle-class jobs. Part of 'upward proletarianisation' was the growth of all sorts of jobs which on the surface seemed to be middle class but offered little of the autonomy, prestige, and power which was once a hallmark of a middle-class occupation. One symptom of this is the increased bureaucracy in many professions, another is the inflated titles that people are given when their job is really one of obedience to a boss. The professions of the two men in *Abigail's Party* – Tony and Laurence – are interesting examples of what Hall is describing. Tony is a computer operator (and for Laurence the stress is on the word 'operator'), while Laurence is an estate agent. Both are doing well financially, but it is clear that Tony has a boring job and Laurence has to pander to the whims of his clients to achieve sales. Neither of them is, as you might say, the captain of their ship.

To disguise this upward proletarianisation the modern workplace has increasingly implemented what Hall calls 'personalisation'. The massive growth of what was called 'personnel departments' in the 1960s and 1970s (and is now called hauntingly 'human resources') are part of the creation of new work feelings where white-collar workers are constantly set individual targets, given regular appraisals, sent on training courses, and made to feel that their employers are keen to foster their personal development and personal advancement. To stop you feeling like an office drone, you are being given the opportunity to advance to the role of deputy assistant to the assistant deputy. The sense of being a worker who might have solidarity with other workers on different wages or salary scales is disguised by an invitation to take part in *personal* development and *personal* advancement. 'But whereas Marx saw the "humanisation" of work coming through direct participation and control, including control over ownership, from below' writes Hall, 'the development in capitalism is towards the "personalisation" of work, through guided participation, excluding ownership, from above'.[28]

If we translate Hall's understanding into what we have been looking at in relation to taste, we might want to note several connections. The first is that there is no better forum for producing 'exquisite' differences than the world of taste. We might all like yogurt now, but while your yogurt is manufactured in a factory, my yogurt comes from the small deli and is made by authentic Greek peasants! We might also want to note that Hall's sense of workplace 'personalisation' can feel similar to the way we were encouraged to add personality to our homes through junk shop finds and the like. But the bigger political point that Hall is making is that the postwar period of affluence can be seen as the emergence of a new class (a new working class, or a new middle class, which might amount to the same thing) that can't see itself as a class of shared interests because consumerism and taste works to disguise it. Affluence, the welfare state, and bureaucracy mean that a Luton car worker and a national health dentist might now belong to a single class in terms of employment, but this might well be disguised by the exquisite differences where one has fitted carpets and the other sanded and varnished floorboards.

Hall's essay was quickly picked up by the historians Ralph Samuel (who became better known as Raphael Samuel) and E. P. Thompson. Samuel notes that within Hall's assessment we should also note 'the decline in status of the black-coated aristocracy – bank and insurance clerks'.[29] E. P. Thompson's response was characteristically spikier and wasn't directly aimed at Hall's essay. His article was a broad attack on socialist writers who are 'angrier about ugly architecture than they are about the ugly poverty of old-age pensioners, angrier about the "materialism" of the Labour Movement than about the rapacity of financiers' and where 'the thousands of young men and women who flock every night into the Technical Colleges at Batley, Stoke-on-Trent, or Darlington, do not come into the picture at all, except as exemplars of the ethos of *Room at the Top*'.[30] Where Thompson's article does differ from Hall is in its refusal to stay loyal to the idea that affluence is dominated by a competitive 'status striving'. For Thompson, the washing-machine

> is not a symbol of 'status' but a machine to wash clothes with. I do not know what moral and cultural values are attached to the kitchen sink, a washboard, and the week's wash for a family of five. But if we are getting more washing machines, we should recognise in that fact at least the *potential* of greater emancipation for working women.[31]

This simple move, to take the washing-machine at face value, is Thompson asking his comrades to stop being so sanctimonious about consumer culture (in this he was in agreement with Hall). The general availability of domestic appliances not only alters daily life for everyone, it has the potential to alter the gendered labour of the home. For Thompson and for Hall the anti-consumerism of the left can look like nostalgia for a time when working-class solidarity was accompanied by poverty. What the left needed to be able to imagine was a form of progressive solidarity amongst all sorts of workers (including doctors and teachers) where everybody has a washing machine!

Thompson's general position (as later became clear in his 1963 volume *The Making of the English Working Class*) was that class was not something that passively happened to people, but was an activity that we were all involved in. As he clarified in his 1968 postscript to that book: 'class itself is not a thing, it is a happening'.[32] As a happening it would include the making of new classes, new forms of consciousness and new feelings. For Thompson, the fixation on 'status striving' was part of a way of obscuring the reality of class and played into the hands of an 'Establishment' keen as ever to divide and conquer:

> I hope we may become a little less self-conscious ourselves about status and class, and cease to play the game of the Establishment by drawing an abstract line between the 'real working-class' of heavy industry, and the teachers, the technicians, the draughtsmen, the white-coated workers and the rest. We do not want the jealous neighbourhood community which erects barriers; we want the socialist community which includes all.[33]

When Hall responded to Thompson it was clear that they had much in common. Both recognised that the divide between manual and non-manual workers wasn't a class divide in any meaningful political sense: 'Of course the "class" interests of the secondary modern teacher and the shop steward at Morris Motors are the same. But it is very difficult, and a matter of socialist tactics, to make them seem the same in a society where skills are highly differentiated'.[34] They both recognised the strategic need for the left to be able to speak across a population that is being separated by the fragmenting and individualising of class.

Thompson imagines new coalitions of trade unionists, middle-class radicals, and various subcultures. Writing about the ability of the Campaign for Nuclear Disarmament (CND) movement to make new collectives, Thompson writes: 'Next year the banners of Trades Councils must move from Aldermaston to Trafalgar Square: but the skiffle groups and the jeans-and-pony-tails must still be there'.[35] Taste, of course, is caught up in this. It has the power to unite but it also has a way of separating us out.

The rise and fall of the technicians

Looking back on the class debates from the 1950s and 1960s you can't help but notice that often there is a marked hostility towards the lower middle class (often taken as the main culprits of 'status striving'), an antipathy that Thompson, partly through his commitment to CND (which he shares with Hall), is trying to purge.[36] Terms like 'lower middle class' and the 'new middle class' were baggy categories at best and seemed to be able to name everyone, from the bohemian culture of the new cultural entrepreneurs (often metropolitan), who might be CND campaigners, to the more expansive range of intermediate classes (clerks, technicians, social workers, etc.) who were simultaneously escaping the frameworks of the traditional working-class and middle-class culture. The novelist Malcolm Bradbury is clearly referring to the more affluent end of what was covered by the term 'new middle class' when he wrote in 1960:

> You can see them on their patios in their sun-loungers drinking drinks with ice in, or sitting in red sports cars with foulard scarves tucked in the necks of their open shirts, before returning to their modernized cottage in the Kentish village where the thatched shop specializes in antiques. In their living room, the Danish furniture gleams as he works the Sodastream while she prepares the lasagne and courgettes. The new middle class is the slightly-better-than-average viewer, the just-above-typical housewife, the up-market consumer; all you need is a red setter and a Volvo, and you are as good as there.[37]

Alongside satires like Bradbury's were attempts to define more clearly the various threads of the new middle classes, and to give names to the various factions. The most famous of these was the attempt to name a 'technician' and 'administrator' class. But while these attempts were well-publicised, they had, in the end, little popular acceptance. The dichotomy of working class versus middle class not only structured sociological studies of the postwar period, but also structured most people's experience of class and taste even if they led, as we have seen, to a general confusion for many.

The oddest example of trying to name a new class without simply sticking the word 'new' in front of an old class category, was Michael Young's 1958 *The Rise of the Meritocracy 1870–2033*, where he imagines a Technician Party (superseding the Labour Party) that will represent the interests of the technician class, who emerge partly through changes in the mechanisation of work, and partly through a new educational system based on the persistent measuring of children's I.Q.[38] Young called his work 'speculative sociology' and used the genres of science fiction and satire to imagine how a new class might form a political party. He also warns about the dangers of a metrics approach to education. It is, in the end, a dystopia written after the narrator has died in an uprising. Things don't work out so well for the Technicians in the 2030s! The book imagines that the dominance of the Technicians produces a new subaltern class, who didn't quite get the grades at school, and who in the end rise up to overthrow the Technicians.

The idea of naming a class (or classes) that are neither working class nor middle class is regularly returned to in the 1960s and 1970s. For instance, the journalist Robert Millar, writing in the mid-1960s, divided British social classes into four main categories: Elite, Administrators, Technicists, and Artisans.[39] His four class categories were fleshed-out in terms of profession and finance: the artisans included 'some skilled, semi-skilled and unskilled workers, pensioners'; the technicists were 'highly-paid manual workers, white-collar employees, small businessmen, poorly-paid professional men'; the administrators were 'professional and businessmen, top managers and salesman, industrial executives'; while the elite were 'aristocracy, top men in industry and the professions'.[40] Clearly these categories were, to some degree at least, fairly porous: it would have been relatively easy to move from technicists to administrators if you were a successful professional person, say a solicitor or a surveyor, by getting a more lucrative position within their profession. A career like teaching would, according to Millar's schema, move from 'artisan' to 'technicist' solely based on the pay increases that would accrue due to work experience.

What drove Millar's work was that, in his estimation, by the mid-1960s most of the working population in Britain were now a hybrid class, neither working class nor middle class. According to Millar:

> The hybrids have been assimilated by, or have merged with, the lower-middle class. And so we have a new class in Britain which probably embraces a majority of the population. And it is revolutionary because it represents something quite new and dynamic. This new class, the Technicists, incorporates the spirit of the new Britain. For the force which binds its members together is their economic power.[41]

Not only do the Technicists wield the most economic power; they have also shaken off the lack of confidence that might have characterised pre-war representations of the lower middle class, and have become those that now set the standards of the 1960s:

> It is the managers and technicians in the new consumer goods industries, and not the lawyers and retired proconsuls, who now lay down the standards of behaviour of the class. Those who run the mass media, sales and export organizations are demanding, and getting, a status comparable to doctors, clergymen, and the landed gentry'.[42]

But, and in an echo of Stuart Hall's argument, this is a 'class' without political allegiances: 'one of their characteristics is that they have no strong political loyalties'.[43]

The term 'technicists' never really caught on. But the term 'new middle class' certainly did, for a while at least, and seemed to mainly define the area covered by the 'technicists' with some elements of the 'administrators' (particularly where it came to the new cultural entrepreneurs working in the media). In its vague usage 'the new middle class' often referred to new patterns of taste and behaviour. For instance, in an article from *The Times* on wine drinking, the socio-economic category of class gives way almost completely to a taste category:

> The new middle class are leaving behind them what was the old working class pattern of drinking; the husband who stopped at the pub for a pint on the way home from work; the home that contained drinks only on celebratory occasions. In the new pattern the wife may accompany her husband for a drink at the local on the weekend evening. And, for the first time, drink may be kept in the home to offer to visiting relatives or friends.[44]

In this view it is not clear who the drinker is at all. Are they the same person who once behaved towards drink in a working-class manner but have now adopted the new pattern? Or is this someone who, through social changes and educational opportunities, has left one class to become part of another?

The political relationship between class and taste is, to my mind, described most brilliantly and bitingly in an article by Raphael Samuel writing in *New Society* in 1982. The article examined the recent founding of the Social Democratic Party (SDP), a party formed in 1981 by disgruntled members of the Labour Party who were unhappy with its direction under Michael Foot: the radical left-wing of the party wanted to leave the European Union, and the party's manifesto included a commitment to unilateral nuclear disarmament. The SDP were moderates. Instead of treating the SDP as a symptom of a crisis in the Labour Party, Samuel saw it instead as the political representation of the new middle class. And rather than analysing their policies, he described the party in terms of the tastes and manners they seemed to promote. Samuel's article could almost be seen as a social analysis of the taste for 'controlled casualness' that I've been mapping in this book. He starts with an emphasis on the notion of *instant* good taste: 'The new middle class have a different emotional economy than that of their prewar predecessors. They go in for instant rather than deferred gratification, making positive virtue of their expenditure, and treating the self-indulgent as an ostentatious display of good taste'.[45] They are, of course, lapping up Habitat's 'can't-wait-to-get-it-home-feeling'.

What is particularly useful about Samuel's argument is the way he treats taste less as a way of gaining status, and more as a means of producing what an anthropologist might call a 'whole way of life'. Rather than a set of symbols aimed at securing a social position, clothes, kitchens, and furniture all contribute to a way of life, to a lifestyle:

> They [the new middle class] dress down rather than up, for parties, in tight trousers rather than dinner jackets, pinafores rather than gowns. They go hatless to work and spend long and expensive hours at the hairdresser's, to cultivate a windswept look. They make a show of peasant pots in their kitchens. Their homes are imitation farmhouses rather than miniature stately homes, with stripped pine rather than period furniture, linens rather than chintz, and concealed lighting rather than cut-glass chandeliers.[46]

This is a world I've been describing throughout the book, a world of well-rehearsed improvisations that, in its desire to shrug off the formalities of the past, embraced a world of scrubbed pine kitchen tables, quiches, and Japanese lampshades. It is a world that would include the Webers and the Kirks, though neither would have voted for the SDP.

The article describes a world of a luxurious informality that revels in openness (open-plan living) and transparency:

> The new middle class are outward-looking rather than inward-looking. They have opened up their homes to visitors, and exposed them to the public gaze. They have removed the net curtains from their windows, and taken down the shutters from their shops. They work in open-plan offices and establishments, with plate-glass windows and see through partitions and doors. In their houses they make a fetish of light and space, replacing rooms with open-access living areas and exposing the dark corners to view. They turn servants' attics into penthouses and make basements into garden flats. Back yards blossom out as patios; kitchens are aestheticized; even the lavatory is turned into a miniature folly.[47]

Samuel's account goes far beyond the one-dimensional description of class caught in the grip of status-hunger. Instead, he links domestic tastes to new kinds of work environments. You can almost see the middle-managers in pastel chinos – 'call me Dave' – at some brainstorming session organised by personnel. Dave has no need to change clothes when he gets home, he seamlessly moves from a world of offices that look homely (all those potted plants) to a home that looks officey (knick-knack-free surfaces and industrial looking cookers).

Samuel suggests that the taste for a free-and-easy life so dear to the new middle classes is never quite what it seems: older forms of inequality and power operate just below the surface of this new informality. He describes a world of taste that is essentially contradictory, not because those who practice it are being hypocritical or purposefully deceptive, but because taste can't overcome the social reality of class society. In this Samuel sees the SDP as political gentrifiers:

> You could interpret the rise of the SDP as a political counterpart to the phenomenon of gentrification, with the SDP as the imaginative 'modernizers', taking on the national equivalent of a rundown street. On this view, its rise could be seen as a movement of home colonization by a newly self-confident class (or of a distinct cultural stratum within it) taking on the role of society's natural leaders, and transposing into the field of politics some of those innovative capacities which, in the 1960s, made them leaders in national taste.[48]

In the end the SDP only had a short life span. They quickly formed an alliance with the Liberal Party, and by 1988 they had fully merged to form the Social and Liberal Democrats which then became the Liberal Democrats. By the mid-1990s, the Labour Party under Tony Blair had become a very similar party to that imagined by the original members of the SDP. There is a danger, of course, in equating taste and politics too neatly. Eating quiche Lorraine, drinking wine, stripping your floorboards, and painting your walls white is no guarantee of political allegiances. It is perhaps not surprising, for instance, that when we try and eke out a cultural politics from the new middle-class world of taste we are left with very vague associations: an attraction towards European culture and an aversion to 'Little England'; a feel for individualism, informality, and a home-centred society; an unease with many forms of collectivism. Such tastes are, of course, no guarantee that in your everyday politics you might not also hold racist views. These tastes may well have laid the groundwork for a general neoliberalism. E. P. Thompson's late 1950s' dream of a world where the Trades Union Congress and skiffle-groups could come together in a politics of anti-nuclear struggle is not made any less possible through the wide availability of quiche and washing machines.

Pretentious? Moi?

When I was fifteen or sixteen, in about 1976, I read Dostoyevsky's *Crime and Punishment.*[49] I remember that before I read the novel, I wanted to be someone who *had read* Dostoyevsky. I'm not at all sure I was particularly looking forward to the actual *reading* bit. My taste had intentions. I wanted it to achieve something. I wasn't simply reading a 'great work' but a 'great work' of *Russian* literature, with various associations to existentialism and other exotic ideas. The intention of my taste was complex. Perhaps taste always is. I wanted to be an intellectual, or to seem to be an intellectual. It was a way of identifying with a way of life that I had no idea about, but more crucially, as a way of distancing myself from a way of life that I had far too much knowledge of. Reading *Crime and Punishment*, and a whole host of other books that no doubt appeared pretentious and ostentatious, was a way of going beyond the stifling culture of a provincial boarding school, and the snobbery that was marked out in accents, manners, houses, and clothes. It was important to me that it was 'difficult literature', of course, but more important that it wasn't Dickens or Hardy or any number of novels that could have filled the criteria of 'great works'.

But taste doesn't end at the moment of intention. Books have their intentions too. The novel drew me into mid-nineteenth-century St Petersburg and to the dilemma of the student Raskolnikov as he tries to come to terms with his grim actions of murdering a greedy pawnbroker. I remember being more fascinated with the details of being both an adult and a student (who knew?), than the moral questions the book raised. It took me into dank bedsits and unrealisable love. I followed in its wake (but without murdering anyone). Books do things to you. They transport you emotionally and intellectually to other places, other times.

Is a book, as a taste, essentially so different from a piece of furniture, a recipe, a drink, or a holiday? We might decide we want to be the kind of person who drinks wine, who holidays in Brittany, who cooks quiche Lorraine, and we might do these things for a complex number of reasons. We might want to show off at work (or not), we might be driven by a sense of curiosity or because we want to escape the insularity of our upbringing. We might be imitating our parents or purposefully snubbing our noses at them. We might want to drink wine *and* beer, to holiday in Brittany *and* Britain. Scandinavian furniture doesn't take us on a journey in the same way that a Dostoyevsky novel (or a Knut Hamsun novel) does, but it changes our material environment and the physical worlds we inhabit. Tastes form connections, dispositions, ways of living. Eating Ski yogurts while sitting in a campus chair aims you at the world in a particular way.

Taste is a world of feeling and it is this which most connects it to class. How we inhabit taste is not a simple matter. You may come to a new taste hesitatingly, with trepidation, and feel fraudulent as you feel your way to becoming someone who likes mayonnaise and vinaigrettes rather than salad cream. Taste doesn't make class all on its own of course, but conversely, it is not standing there on the side-lines either. If taste is fundamental to how identity is experienced and felt, and I think it is, then we need to think more broadly about identities, particularly those identities that appear to be implicitly excluded from a representation within British class culture.

9

From the West Indian front room to *Root*

The tastes that I've been charting in this book grew in the late 1950s and through the 1960s and 1970s and beyond, echoing into the present. At the same time, Britain was becoming a society with a much more diverse population. The period that this book covers saw a sustained influx of new arrivals, often coming to the UK as British Colonial Citizens: 'In 1945 Britain's non-white population stood at 30,000. By 1973 this figure was over 1 million and grew close to 5 million by 2001'.[1] From 1948 to 1962 the so-called *Windrush* generation arriving from the Caribbean to the British Isles were travelling on British passports with the same rights of movement as someone moving from Scotland to England, or Doncaster to London. The 1962 Commonwealth Immigrants Act and subsequent immigration legislation aimed at Commonwealth countries sought to racialise what it meant to be a British subject within the new 'empire' of the Commonwealth.

What does this mean for the tastes I've been tracking? Is this a landscape of taste that was perceived and inhabited as an exclusively white culture? And how does the racial framing of taste relate to the question of how class and taste are linked? Is the term 'class', within the context of British postwar history, something that is experienced as a predominantly white phenomenon and experience? In a recent study of British black middle-class experience, Ali Meghji finds a degree of resistance to the very idea that middle-class identity and black identity can be articulated together. For one of his interviewees – a doctor living and working in Oxford – her racial identity as a black or a non-white person precludes her thinking of herself as middle class, and she instead identifies as part of a professional class: 'when you think of middle class I think of middle-class England. And the thing that pops up, or pops into my mind is that well-spoken, southern, *white* individual, who normally have a nuclear family and shop at Waitrose. That, to me, is what middle class *says*'.[2] Here the term 'England' becomes a name for whiteness, as it did in much of the postwar literature. Another interviewee, an academic art historian, whose parents also had middle-class jobs, recounts her experience of undertaking a class survey run by the BBC which situates her as 'firmly working class': 'I'm just wondering what middle class really means. Does it really *work* for Black people?'[3] And yet, whatever your racial and ethnic identity, class, as an economic and cultural position is unavoidable. The feeling of class, though, doesn't always fit with an experience of living in a society where various forms of inequality exist in disharmony.

As we will see, class was central to how non-white migration was experienced in the postwar period, but that experience was often impossible to disentangle from the racism that was also part of arriving in Britain from both colonies and former colonies. I'm using the term 'non-white' uneasily to name people who today might chose to identify as 'People of Colour', or 'Black, Indigenous, and People of Colour', or 'Black and Asian Minority Ethnic', or 'Visible Minority Ethnic' and who might also identify as 'British Caribbean', 'British Bangladeshi', and so on. Umbrella terms often fail to register the significant differences between the opportunities and lack of them that relate to different ethnic groups. For instance, in Vaughan Robinson's 1980s' study of 'the new Indian middle class in Britain', British Indians not only account for a much higher proportion of male white-collar employees than other British Asian groups or those with Caribbean heritage, they also outstrip the class ratios of the white population: 'there are now more Indian men working in non-manual employment than there are Pakistani, West Indian or East African Asian men [... and] the proportion of non-manual employment for Indians now even exceeds that of the indigenous white population'.[4] At the same time, the experience of class demotion was often an experience common to all non-white migrants when they first came to the UK.

In this chapter my claim is that while a taste for 'controlled casualness' as part of a domestic lifestyle was not something that was consciously adopted by first-generation migrants, it did become a taste that was available to the children and grandchildren of migrants, to those who were born in the UK or came to Britain as children, and who adopted a 'new middle-class' lifestyle. At the same time, the class pattern for non-white people in Britain suggests that the growth of Black and Asian new middle classes followed very different trajectories: 'in 1971, quantitative sociologists claim that 0 per cent of Black women and 1 per cent of Black men were in professional occupations', with 'the emergence of a distinctive Black middle class' only really establishing itself 'in the 1990s'.[5] Taste, race, class, and generation are threads that have been scattered throughout this book: here I'm attempting to weave them together.

Boutique cosmopolitanism

The popularity of the tastes mapped in this book suggests a gradual transformation of what it meant to be British. After all, many of the elements of this taste – Mediterranean foods, duvets, yogurts, modern Scandinavian-style furniture, open-plan interiors – were cultural imports rather than home-grown developments. The tastes that have been at the centre of the book have held out new promises and feelings: of a lighter way of living; of a way of life less hedged in by a past tied to traditional ideas of nationality, of class, of manners; and more immediate sensual enjoyment in food, social life, sex, and leisure. No doubt many of these promises remained either unfulfilled or only partially realised. One promise that was fulfilled was a more routine connection to mainland Europe for a large proportion of British people: cheap holidays in France and Spain; the increased availability of 'continental' food and drink; German and Dutch domestic technologies (alongside those from Japan and Taiwan), and so on.

One name that could be attached to these tastes would be 'cosmopolitan'. It is a taste that placed emphasis on the aesthetics of Japan, the food of the Mediterranean, the 'ethnic' decorations of India and the subcontinent, the furniture of Scandinavia, and 'peasant' cultures from around the world. On the face of it, it might seem that such tastes would likely be much more accommodating to people from other countries than an insistence on traditional British taste. Yet the cosmopolitanism of this taste was a particular sort of cosmopolitanism that might be termed 'boutique cosmopolitanism'. I'm adapting a phrase that the writer Stanley Fish once used to describe a particularly superficial kind of multiculturalism. For him 'boutique multiculturalism' named a 'multiculturalism of ethnic restaurants, weekend festivals, and high-profile flirtations with the other'.[6] It suggested a surface enjoyment of the sensual exotica of multiculturalism, minus a more everyday engagement with a diverse population. In the same way, we could say that this taste's 'boutique cosmopolitanism' was cosmopolitanism without the cosmopolitans: without much contact with actual Japanese or Scandinavian people, with a mythologised and idealised concept of a general European peasant culture that could be 'borrowed' as a way of accessing a looser, more informal lifestyle. It was, in many ways, a form of borrowed authenticity that could be put to work to fashion a more spontaneous, less uptight version of social life, a life of yoga and bamboo, of natural woods and impromptu salads, of sandalwood and sanded floorboards. If Indian fabrics were valued for their authentic spirituality, Indian people were invisible when it came to representing them as part of a world of taste circulating in Britain.

This 'boutique cosmopolitanism' becomes more visible when it is contrasted with a political idea of internationalism, or with the material realities of the cosmopolitan lives that were physically shaping Britain in the postwar period. For this it is worth returning to Mike Leigh's play discussed in chapter 7. At one point in *Abigail's Party*, Laurence, the splenetic estate agent, is trying to provoke a discussion about changes in the character of the neighbourhood. He asks the older neighbour, Sue, who within the small group has lived there the longest, about the changes she's seen: 'the class of people, now don't you think that's changed' he enquires. Sue says that she doesn't think it has changed. Laurence continues to insist that things have changed, and finally Sue gives her verdict:

> SUSAN: It's more mixed, that's all.
> LAURENCE: Mixed? Yes, I suppose you could say it was more mixed! – More cosmopolitan.
> SUSAN: There's nothing wrong with that.
> LAURENCE: Oh, you don't think there's anything wrong with that?[7]

The discussion has shifted from class to something else. Here 'cosmopolitan' acts as a euphemism for the changing ethnic and racial make-up of the expanding London suburb where they live. 'Cosmopolitanism' suggests, without explicitly stating it, that some of the new residents are not white.[8]

The discussion is not pursued any further and we are left none the wiser as to who Laurence is referring to. Is he upset (and he clearly is upset) by the presence of Afro-Caribbean families, of Pakistani or Bangladeshi households, or is his complaint vaguer, aimed at a general non-white, non-British culture?[9] One of the themes of *Abigail's Party* is its representation of new middle classes as emotionally volatile. It is class on the edge of a nervous breakdown. Laurence inhabits a world of material abundance and new opportunities, but he does so uneasily, and certainly not with the nonchalance of someone who has made it. The play doesn't develop the racial aspect of class, but it exists as a subtext. The play can't quite reveal that here is a suburb where new class identities are not simply being fashioned for white residents but are now being shared by 'cosmopolitans' in a way that for Laurence was deeply troubling.

Race alters the experience of class in Britain. The idea of a 'white working class', who, some commentators claim, are being systematically ignored by policy makers, is a symptom of an inability to think of the working class as multicultural. The withholding of resources and opportunities from working-class communities occurs in areas deemed white-British as well as those classified as mixed. The very idea that there is a white working class undergoing extra forms of hardship only makes sense if there is an expectation that whiteness is going to protect you from class divisions. It is a strategy of division. But as we will see in the next section, a degree of upward mobility amongst employees required another workforce over which a sense of superiority could be exercised.

There is a sense that the 'real' cosmopolitans (those who learn new languages, or uproot their home, to live in Britain) reveal the sort of boutique cosmopolitanism of the new middle-class taste as a thin veneer attached to national identity: Englishness without Colonel Blimp moustaches, but still with a strong national sense of belonging. The real cosmopolitans are not those dabbling in Indian spirituality and Mediterranean cooking, but those who've been blown hither and thither by the winds of history. The tastes associated with the new middle classes are both a vague nod to a form of multiculturalism and to a rebranding of national identity. And yet we could make too much of the exclusionary whiteness of this taste. One of the aspects of it that I've been keen to stress is its looseness. Rather than being a dogmatic taste, the taste culture of the new middle class left wiggle room for eclecticism, for idiosyncrasies. Open-plan living and bare floorboards might be accompanied by décor for a nostalgic Britain (enamel Oxo signs, for instance), but it could also, potentially at least, accommodate other ethnic experiences. But to get to that possibility we need to look more carefully at what class means in the context of what in the postwar years was called *Colour in Britain*.

A frosty reception

In 1959, during the brief existence of the West Indies Federation (1958–62), the BBC Caribbean Service published a pamphlet titled *Going to Britain?* It was aimed at the populations of West Indian countries who since 1948 had become 'citizens of the UK and Colonies' and 'enjoyed identical citizenship, on equal terms, to Winston Churchill'.[10] The pamphlet told these British subjects what to expect if they came to Britain. It was based on a series of radio broadcasts by various writers (such as the Trinidadian novelist Samuel Selvon) offering information about what to pack for the journey, what to wear when you got to the UK, how to find accommodation, and how to keep yourself warm and well. It had hints about how to have a party in your digs and how to conduct yourself at a dance. It was predominantly aimed at Caribbean men who might be looking to come to Britain to work and live. While the information about social life was provided by West Indian writers, the sections on employment were predominantly written by a senior civil servant (David Muirhead, Chief Community Development Officer in the Commission for the West Indies, British Guiana, and British Honduras). While the phrase 'expectation management' was yet to be coined, the pamphlet is an exercise in just that: preparing travellers for a climate of cold winters, and an even colder reception from the locals.

The information about employment is insistent that travellers to Britain who might have had middle-class and lower-middle-class employment in the Caribbean should set their sights instead on manual labour. 'There are very few clerical jobs for men' states Muirhead in the pamphlet 'and you must be prepared to take manual work'.[11] Age and perceived levels of competence, readers are told, will disqualify most if not all Caribbean applicants for white collar work:

> It is very difficult for white-collar workers over forty – Englishmen as well as West Indians – to find a job in the United Kingdom. Prospects are a little brighter if you are under forty but you must remember that competition for office jobs is tough. There are for instance large numbers of English school-leavers coming on the labour market every year. Employers like these youngsters because they can be 'brought up', so to speak, by the firm. [...] The white collar worker in the West Indies who, without any school leaving qualifications, got a job as a clerk in an office or as a salesman in a store will find that things are very different in England. Many English employers say that conditions differ so widely that the West Indian clerical worker has to be re-trained.[12]

At the same time, it is equally clear from the pamphlet that one of the main reasons for migrating from the Caribbean to the UK was to increase employment prospects through education and social mobility. Here the advice is simple: keep quiet about it: 'Many working Englishmen do not bother to study as the majority of working-class West Indians do, so don't go shouting that you are studying this or that. It may make your mates feel inferior, or that you are high-lighting their lack of ambition'.[13] Similarly, if a new arrival is looking to enter the housing market: 'Don't go telling everyone that you have saved so many hundred pounds and now want to purchase a house. These boastings will make people resentful'.[14] It is no wonder, then, that a few years later Stuart Hall could write that: 'Our cities are full of young, coloured citizens of Britain trying to tiptoe through society'.[15]

The story was both similar and different for migrants from the subcontinent. As already mentioned, by the 1980s, British Indians were the group with the highest proportion of people in professionally middle-class occupations (proportionally higher than their white counterparts). And yet class is never simply an objective position – it is also a feeling, and feelings of class are tangled up with feelings of race. For instance, the many migrants who, instead of trying to negotiate the systematic racism of large institutions and companies, set up small, autonomous businesses such as restaurants, wholesale retailing, and corner-shops, might objectively fit the class terms petit bourgeois or lower middle class.[16] Yet the relevance of class feelings was often overshadowed by the experiences of being a racial minority, and by the reality of their employment.

Some of these contradictions are mined in Hanif Kureishi's 1990 novel *The Buddha of Suburbia*. The novel revolves around the lives and families of two childhood friends – Haroon and Anwar – who came to England from India in 1950, and the story is narrated from the perspective of Karim, Haroon's son. The class background of the two friends who grew up as neighbours in Bombay (Mumbai) was distinctly middle class. Haroon's father was a doctor and had a house in the prosperous neighbourhood of Juhu: 'Dad and Anwar would sleep on the veranda and at dawn run down to the sea and swim. They went to school in a horse-drawn rickshaw. At weekends they played cricket, and after school there was tennis on the family court. The servants would be ball-boys'.[17] Arriving in London they studied for professional qualifications: Anwar in aeronautical engineering and Haroon in law. But their eventual employment in Britain never realised these ambitions: Anwar bought a lease on a shop which he runs with his wife Jeeta, and Haroon becomes an 'employee of the British Government, as a Civil Servant clerk [...] badly paid and insignificant'.[18] Haroon's prospects are slight: 'The whites will never promote us [...] not an Indian while there is a white man left on earth'.[19] Anwar and Jeeta, in contrast, have a degree of autonomy but are chained to their business, Paradise Stores:

> Paradise Stores was a dusty place with a high, ornate and flaking ceiling. There was an inconvenient and tall block of shelves in the centre of the shop, around which customers shuffled, stepping over tins and cartons. The goods seemed to be in no kind of order. [...] Outside were boxes of vegetables. Paradise opened at eight in the morning and closed at ten at night. They didn't even have Sundays off.[20]

It is hard to see the relevance of the debates about the 'new middle class' in relation to Anwar and Haroon's experiences.

The lives detailed in Kureishi's novel echo those of the Islamist scholar Ziauddin Sardar, whose father came to Britain in 1959 from Pakistan. In Britain 'his qualifications as a mechanical engineer were dismissed as worthless'[21] and after a few years he 'gave up his ambition of finding a job as an engineer and started work at the Ford factory in Dagenham'.[22] Sardar's mother worked in the Corgi factory making match-box cars. As Sardar explains:

> Asians who came to Britain in the 1950s and 60s looked up to Britain as the source of modern culture and education. Doctors and other professionals came to acquire higher qualifications that would be internationally recognised. Those seeking academic careers came to obtain their doctorates. Artists came to these shores to become part of the modern movement and to make a reputation.[23]

The fact that many or most Asians, as well as those from the Caribbean and Africa, had these expectations thwarted, and had careers stunted by institutional racism, often forced to accept the worst jobs, has indelibly stained this period of migration. The 1948 British Nationality Act which proclaimed that 'the expression "British subject" and the expression "Commonwealth citizen" shall have the same meaning', was written in law, but clearly didn't translate into practice.[24]

The difficulty of mapping non-white lives onto the British class system is perhaps most keenly felt in the work of the Jamaican sociologist Ken Pryce in his study of West Indian lifestyles in Bristol. Pryce undertook fieldwork between 1969 and 1974 as a researcher at Bristol University within the discipline of criminology. The research was published as the book *Endless Pressure: A Study of West Indian Lifestyles in Bristol* in 1979. The criminological orientation means that the focus was primarily on people with Caribbean heritage living a precarious subsistence in the St Pauls area of the city. In the book the street-corner culture of the St Pauls neighbourhood is peopled by 'Hustlers' and the area is referred to as 'Shanty Town'. Other groups that make up West Indian culture in Bristol are: 'Proletarian Respectables' (those households with skilled and semi-skilled long-term employment); 'Teenyboppers' ('a young West Indian who is either already a delinquent or in danger of becoming one'[25]); 'Saints' (those Proletarian Respectables whose main cultural attachment is to the church); 'Mainliners' (educated West Indians in white-collar employment often in fields like social work and race relations); and 'In-betweeners' (often with the same background as Mainliners, but more race-conscious and Afrocentric). The overriding emphasis is on men (nearly all the women in the book are part of the 'Proletarian Respectables and Saints' group). As should be clear, such designations mix class, politics, religion, and criminality – there is no straightforward account of class, yet class is an intrinsic ingredient in the narrative.

The group that comes closest to the idea of the new middle classes is the Mainliners, and to a lesser degree the In-betweeners. The Mainliners are those who are more concerned with 'adhering to the official line of thinking on all matters relating to immigrants than with articulating a black-oriented viewpoint of their own'.[26] The group 'comprises mostly [of] literate, middle-aged, well established West Indian residents, as well as some younger people from the law-abiding community who because of their better education as students, nurses, teachers, etc., are constantly sought out by social workers and other mainliners to assist in local community activities. Together these people form a very small but self-conscious and elitist sub-group in the community'.[27] Pryce is clear that Mainliners and In-betweeners 'represent a burgeoning, lower-middle-class orientation', but that opportunities for an emergent black middle class are constantly frustrated. His example is nursing:

> There has been a constant flow of West Indian girls into the nursing profession, where the SRN [state-registered nurse] qualification can open the way to a middle-class career. Yet a high proportion of West Indian trainees are denied the opportunity to become state-registered nurses, because they are concentrated at the bottom of the nursing hierarchy in non-teaching hospitals: here they are deliberately encouraged to pursue SEN [state-enrolled nurse] qualifications, which confine them to the ward floor in Britain and which restrict their professional mobility.[28]

If this was the situation in the mid-1970s then it is clear from the work of Meghji and others that at least by the 1990s – if not earlier – there was a 'full-blown' black and Asian middle class in Britain. What did this mean in terms of taste?

Migrant tastes

Taste is a way of creating identity, of opening oneself up to new worlds, new sensations, new experiences. It is also a way of connecting to the past, consolidating a sense of belonging, of establishing material roots and routes. And taste, perhaps most routinely, is a way of negotiating a path between the past and the future, of navigating between the old and familiar and the new and unknown. Our tastes are often a mixture, concocted out of what is nearest to hand, what seems most desirable, what we remember, what holds promise, and what sustains us (emotionally, politically, and socially). For colonial migrants in the 1950s and 1960s one of the most difficult things was maintaining the sort of social life that had been part of life 'back home'. The London-based Caribbean magazine, *Magnet*, poses the problem in both geographical and class terms:

> One of the things that takes some getting accustomed to in England is the limit to the amount of entertaining that one can do in a flat or bedsitter. Most of us women come from countries where it is quite simple to give the housemaid orders to prepare dinner for a small party, or where one has enough time in the evening after work to really come up with a Cordon Bleu meal. In London, apart from the disadvantages of most flats, the price of liquor and the fact that one cannot order a delivery of toothpicks, are deterrents enough to make the most domesticated housewife tremble with fear at the thought of preparing a meal for guests.[29]

Bedsits and small, cramped flats were the initial reality of migration, but as we saw in chapter 5, migrant households were often at the forefront of house buying. And it was here, in owner-occupied houses and council-rented properties that a lifestyle could be realised which knitted together a relationship with a place left behind and the reality of living in the UK.

One characteristic of migrant taste, particularly for first generation migrants, was the ability to maintain something of 'home'. Migration is a process as well as an event. When we leave somewhere to take up residence somewhere else, we bring with us threads of connection, not just to family and friends left behind, but to the people we were before and the lives we once led. For the London-born broadcaster and journalist Ekow Eshun, his family home in England was infused with the sensual reminder that his parents had not simply left the newly independent country of Ghana but that they had brought many aspects of it with them:

> My parents arrived in London from Ghana in 1963. They never meant to stay. And even though they have spent most of the past forty years in Britain, Ghana is still their home. When I was a child growing up in London, its sounds and smells pervaded our house. Ghana was there in the hot pepper scent of palm nut soup tickling your nostrils as you entered the house; the highlife songs from the stereo; the sound of my mother shouting down a capricious telephone line to her sister in Accra.[30]

This, then, was a different cosmopolitanism to the world of sisal flooring and improvised Mediterranean cooking. If the newly acquired tastes for controlled casualness of the white new middle classes meant disconnecting from the weight of British traditions, then the Eshun family home was brimming over with connections to a world left behind.

The same was true for Ziauddin Sardar, who came to London in 1960 from Pakistan as a nine-year-old child, and grew up in houses tethered to other places, other practices:

> Our family moved along to accommodate the consequences of migration, buffeted by change in our struggle to thrive. My sister, brother and I grew up. We were not the people we would have been had we remained in Pakistan. But Pakistan was recreated in our home. Our home was a haven of familiarity shaped by all that my parents considered valuable and enduring. Our shelves were crowded with books in Urdu: novels, poetry and works on Islam. Every other Saturday, we held a *mushaira* – a poetry recital. Friends of my father would gather to read their latest compositions and participate in poetry contests, reminiscent of the poetry gatherings I witnessed in […] Bhawalnagar.[31]

Our tastes are ways of fashioning domestic space, negotiating values and commitments, as well as the routes that we have taken. Most crucially they establish feelings and moods.

The design historian and curator, Michael McMillan, grew up in High Wycombe 'as a second-generation, black British person from an aspirant working-class family of Vincentian parentage'.[32] In 1998 he began collecting and exhibiting artefacts, as well as oral histories, that eventually became the installation 'The West Indian Front Room: Memories and Impressions of Black British Homes', which was exhibited at the Geffrye Museum in 2005–6 (figure 9.1).[33] The installation and the accompanying book is an invaluable record of what McMillan calls 'migrant aesthetics', a maximalist taste that navigates roots and routes, belongings and becomings. The instillation displays a typical front room for households that Ken Pryce would have no doubt named 'Proletarian Respectables' and includes a settee, highly patterned carpets and wallpaper, a radiogram and television,

9.1 Michael McMillan, *The West Indian Front Room*

a class cabinet, artificial flowers, a drinks trolley (featuring a plastic pineapple ice bucket), and various photographs and mementoes. In taste terms it seems like the antithesis of the 'good taste' promoted by Terence Conran, Biba, and Habitat. On the wall is a black velour scroll with a map of the island of St Vincent, titled 'Souvenir of St. Vincent':

> As reminders of 'back home', these souvenirs embodied a sense of pride and belonging. The black velour scroll was succeeded by varnished wooden clocks carved in the shape of a Caribbean island or country. Souvenirs from outings in England were also displayed. These might have originated from a trip with the church to Margate, Great Yarmouth or Brighton, for instance, or travels abroad to other places in the Caribbean, Florida or Toronto for example, and would come in the form of decorative plates, straw bags, dolls and ornaments.[34]

Souvenirs like this aren't tied to the past but show a cosmopolitan and migrant reality where friends and family are spread around the world and where new memories are being made in a new home environment.

In Stuart Hall's contribution to McMillan's project, Hall links the 'West Indian front room' to older traditions existing in both Britain and the Caribbean. The look and feel of this room originated in the very formal Victorian parlour that went on to shape working-class respectability in Britain *and* middle-class interiors amongst Caribbean households.[35] The Victorian parlour was not a place of informality and casualness, nor was it a space for children. The West Indian front room, as fashioned by first-generation migrants, was a similarly sanctified space, but now as a 'retreat' from the hostile realities of everyday life in racist Britain, as well as a physical demonstration that the social position that they were seen to hold in Britain was not a reflection of who they were. As the British-Guyanese writer Mike Philips put it:

> The internal décor of the front room represented a characteristic migrant space with mementoes of back home, ways of expressing a sense of dignity and self-respect, ways of conducting a social life and promoting a platform for moving into the society. This is why it had such an emotional impact and created such a moment of recognition and pleasure that resonates profoundly'.[36]

The front room was a triumph of hope and perseverance over hostility and disappointment, made out of limited resources:

> As a migrant you have to start again: there are no native materials from 'back home' except English and Western furniture which, if you can afford it, you source by looking for something that reminds you of the front rooms or of the homes that you had left behind. Reconstructing the front room out of these materials is trying to deal with the rupture of migration.[37]

For the children of these pioneers there is a different relationship to a Caribbean sense of home and a different relationship to taste. For those whose heritage connects them to other places, other histories but who were born in Britain, or who came to Britain as children, domestic taste didn't have to be shaped so vividly by dislocation and a Victorian sense of politeness.

Because I want to keep in touch with my roots

Gradually the tastes of migrants who settled in Britain incorporated more and more hybrid elements, as 'home' blended elements of 'over here' with 'over there'. The journalist and broadcaster Krishnan Guru-Murthy, for instance, who was born in Liverpool in 1970 and grew up in rural Lancashire in a middle-class Asian-British family, was fed traditional Indian food at home but with English twists. He and his friends' favourite after-school snacks were puri (a puffed fried bread popular across India) eaten by the dozen and always accompanied by the British staple Heinz tomato ketchup.[38] As the children of migrants set up their own households, loyalty to the first generation's lifestyle and tastes were to some degree abandoned, and domestic style moved ever closer to the almost ubiquitous taste for uncluttered informality.

McMillan's collective account of the West Indian front room traces how a second-generation has had their own impact on domestic space. For the journalist Steve Pope (born in Barbados in 1961 but growing up in Wolverhampton from the age of nine), the significant changes have been to do with the way children occupy the home. For the first generation 'the front room had to be aspirational because it represented many hours of hard graft to earn the money to buy all those nice things', but 'the second generation has almost rejected their parents' values about possessions in order to become part of the minimalist anti-clutter movement. And as the home has become a more informal space, children have now moved in and taken over the living room and the boundary between children and adults has become blurred'.[39] Echoing the Victorian parlour, the first-generation Caribbean front room was a no-go area for children. The shift between generations was most vividly demonstrated by the intermingling of adult and child spaces, producing a new atmosphere of informality and casualness. For the fashion historian Carol Tulloch (born in Doncaster in 1956 with Jamaican parents), the difference between generations is fundamental: 'We became so minimalist as the second generation that once when a friend came round and saw my bare mantelpiece they said "I'm so sorry, when were you burgled?"'[40]

But the move towards informality wasn't simply generational, it was also historical. Thus, the artist and educationalist Cyril Husbands (born in London in 1959 with Barbadian parents) saw the transformation of the front room taking place in his parents' home:

> Anything that looked vaguely antique did not cross the threshold and the nail in the coffin was the 70s fashion for the thru-lounge and I don't think it took very long for my mum to resist the tide and the front room was no more. Other things conspired against the front room such as the arrival of Argos, IKEA, Littlewoods catalogues, department stores lowering their prices and people on TV instructing you how to do DIY and decorate your home.[41]

By the 1980s, for many children of migrants, 'controlled casualness' was a taste that was widely available and could be used in a way that wasn't simply set by the dominant white culture. At the same time, the class identity of a new middle class became newly relevant as a category that could speak to livelihoods that neither fitted the idea of 'Proletarian Respectables' nor the identity of a Waitrose-shopping, white middle-England. Black and Asian social workers, teachers, lecturers, technicians, solicitors, accountants, and so on, could inhabit the taste for controlled casualness while also expressing a feeling for a 'race-conscious and Afrocentric outlook'.[42] And now there was a lifestyle magazine that could accompany it.

Root magazine, with its subheading 'Britain's biggest Black magazine', was started in late 1979 as an attempt to come up with a magazine that was partly a listings magazine (a Black *Time Out*),[43] partly a magazine of socially informed journalism, and partly something glossier and more to do with lifestyle. According to Lionel Morrison, 'In October 1979, Godfrey Hope, a wealthy young Guyanese, the financial backer, Neil Kenlock, Patrick Berry, Wayne Wilson and Hal Austin founded *Root*, a stylish monthly magazine. The idea was to produce a British *Ebony*, only more connected to the reality of how people live in Britain'.[44] The magazine began from a conversation between the photographer Neil Kenlock (who was a staff photographer for *West Indian World* – 'Britain's first West Indian weekly'[45] and had been the official photographer for the British Black Panther movement) and the arts reviewer Patrick Berry (who had previously worked for the Minority Arts Advisory Services). For Kenlock the magazine was an extension of his previous cultural work: 'When I came up with the idea of *Root* magazine, it was at a time when I felt there was a need for black people in this country to have positive images of themselves. Everything we had at that time was negative'.[46]

The magazine mixed fashion and politics, music and advice, and ran a regular advert for the magazine with a quote from Marcia Barratt of the group Boney M: 'I read *Root* magazine because I want to keep in touch with my Roots. Do you?' The magazine was clearly 'race-conscious and Afrocentric' in outlook, with features on the experience of Rastafarians in Ethiopia, the politics of Nigeria, racially motivated arson attacks on British homes, and so on.[47] It was also oriented to a new black middle class with features on wine, furniture design, and house buying: 'If the house is modern then the very large living room is likely; this brings lots of advantages in day-to-day living, but also privacy problems when, for example, children of the family do their homework and when distraction should be minimal'.[48] It promoted some of the same items that could be found in all Habitat shops:

> A terracotta Clay Baker chicken brick from Italy. An excellent piece of equipment for gourmet and health conscious cooks or for anybody interested in the art of cooking. This method of cooking really enhances the flavour and makes the chicken/meat/fish more tender. It virtually steams in its own juice taking on the aroma of onions/garlic/herbs which may be used for flavouring. Before using the Clay Baker the lid should be soaked in warm water for 15 minutes and it is advisable to soak the whole chicken brick for 30 minutes the first time it is used.[49]

This chicken brick had, by 1981, become synonymous with the Habitat style, yet here it takes on the flavour of a different ethnic orientation. Towards the end of its short, eight-year life, the magazine ran adverts for conservatories:

> Furnishing for most conservatories is plants. Either leave open spaces on the floor for direct planting or use pots. Cane or wooden blinds are often necessary to protect plants from frost and scorching. Go [...] for terracotta, tile, wood or stone flooring and cover with rugs or rush matting. Furniture must be able to withstand extremes of temperature, so opt for rattan, cane, bamboo, wicker, slatted wood, plastic or metal. You can be exotic or functional as you like, after all your conservatory is your very own place in the sun.[50]

By the time it was advertising conservatories, its commitment to politics and Afrocentric outlook was definitely in the background: hair and beauty had taken over.

Habitat had included black models in its catalogue from 1975, before there was a visible new black middle class to inhabit that world of controlled casualness. By the time that *Root* expired, some sort of black middle class was exerting a taste for a more Afrocentric version of Habitat style. Unlike the United States, Britain didn't develop a sociology interested in exploring how middle-class life was experienced by non-white Britons till the late 1980s.[51] Writing about the Black middle classes in the mid-1990s Deborah Phillips and Philip Sarre state that '"Race" is as invisible in most discussions of middle-class formation in Britain as the middle classes are invisible in most discussions of the class position of ethnic minorities'.[52] They go on to write that 'we interpret the common assumption that black people are nothing to do with the middle classes as a result of a past process of class formation that was intrinsically built on race: the middle class or classes, whatever else they might

9.2 Habitat catalogue 1975, featuring: Ny Chairs and chaise longue (top); Metro chairs (bottom)

be, were in fact and theory indubitably white'.[53] The whiteness of British middle class is evident across the tastes I've been looking at here, but it is also an issue within sociology itself, which was always keener (often, for very good reasons) to look at race from the perspective of poverty, inequality, delinquency, and drugs. The tastes I've been looking at in this book are part of the story of multicultural Britain, but not in any simple way. It is tempting to see this as a question of history, with black and Asian Britons delayed in taking up this taste, and the delay being caused by the structural racism that stymied earlier chances for non-whites to develop a middle-class culture. There is no doubt some truth in this. But it is never just a question of time. Geography was also at play. The tastes of the black new middle class allowed a loosening of what tethered the home to another home 'elsewhere' without abandoning a sense of connection to the routes of cosmopolitan migration.

10
Adrian Mole, the future of taste, and me …

If you look in my kitchen cupboards you will find rough-thrown terracotta bowls that we have brought back from Majorca. We cook vaguely Mediterranean food in them. Most of our floorboards have been sanded to within an inch of their life. Twenty or so years ago we would have done this sanding ourselves. For this house we didn't. We don't have a large, well-scrubbed pine kitchen table, but we would like one. The house we live in used to be bedsits: on the downstairs banister you can see that someone has carved 'Becki is a slag' into the wood. When we moved in about twenty years ago there was a petrol station opposite. Now there is a delicatessen and a small independent café that makes 'award winning' pizzas. A family-run pharmacy has been there forever. The local Indian take-away has just closed down. House prices have, of course, gone through the roof to the point where our children will only be able to get a foot on the housing ladder with the help of the 'bank of mum and dad'.

About forty years ago I lived in various 'legal squats' in south London which were similar to the house that the Kirks occupied in *The History Man.* Floor cushions, potted plants, and bookcases made from scaffolding planks and bricks were our furnishings and decorations. Mattresses lying on the floor or on pallets were our beds. We had house plants, lots of them. On a good day, if we'd cleaned up, one or two of the rooms wouldn't have looked that out of place in *The House Book.* No one in my group would have actually shopped at Habitat, but we managed to approximate the sort of look that it and other outlets had taught us to want. I'm not writing this book from the distance of academic objectivity, but from the centre of the storm, so to say. I have grown up in this world of taste and used it to mark my distance from a previous more up-tight world. The consumerism of the 1960s and 1970s and onwards through to today is the culture that I have swum in, and to a large extent still do.

Today, in most towns and cities in Britain you can walk into cafés, restaurants, and pubs, and be greeted by bare-brick walls and well-scrubbed pine kitchen tables, accompanied by a rag-tag assortment of seating (usually with a scattering of chairs and pews reclaimed from deconsecrated churches) and sanded floorboards or quarry tiles, all decorated with a studied eccentricity. Habitat, as a major high-street store, has gone; it went into receivership in

2011 (figure 10.1).[1] The brand continues, but its high-street presence is now a thing of the past. In many respects, the shop's role in Britain had already been taken over in the 1990s by IKEA. IKEA's global success is very much in line with the tastes that made Habitat a household name in the 1970s and 1980s. Its mixture of cheap household goods, a rough adherence to Scandinavian modernism, simple modern and classic furniture (with a range of prices: something for everyone), lively fabrics and kitchenware that moves from peasant-style to hi-tech, was the shape of Habitat in the 1970s. IKEA today is a version of mid-1970s Habitat on a massive global scale.[2] By the 1990s Habitat had already shrunk in scale (due in part to the competition from IKEA) and gone back to focus on more up-market design with prices to match.

But while there are clear continuities of taste and feelings across the last sixty or seventy years, there have also been significant changes. The 1980s and 1990s saw changes in the way affluence was distributed as the gap between the wealthiest and what most people were earning grew considerably. Journalism became less interested in the new middle classes and started to identify smaller groups to write about. The 1980s gave us Sloane Rangers, Yuppies, and even YAPs (Young Aspiring Professionals).[3] At the same time the safety net of the welfare state was falling into disrepair, unemployment grew, and the new work conditions of zero-hour contracts and generalised piece work became more usual. Sociologists eventually found a name for a new class: the precariat. The figure of Margaret Thatcher hangs over the 1980s and 1990s and it is hard to imagine her embracing any of the tastes I've been describing. She looked as if she had been dressed in the 1940s and had her social

10.1 Habitat closing down in Bristol, 2011

conscience forged in the 1840s. Time seemed to be playing tricks: it was as if we were all trapped in a new version of Dickens's *Hard Times*, though this time decked out in Laura Ashley prints. Taste, though, isn't a zero-sum game, and consumerism revels in that fact. Styles proliferate, variety thrives.

In this book I haven't tried to give an overview of British tastes since the mid-1950s; instead, I've focused on a limited spectrum of tastes to argue that taste has had an active social role in Britain in the last seventy years. It hasn't merely sat there on the side-lines, reflecting the class culture of Britain, it has had a hand in shaping it too. The new middle classes wouldn't have come into being as a social and cultural force in the quite the way that they did without quarry tiles, duvets, well-scrubbed kitchen tables, and sanded floorboards. This book has concentrated on the 1960s and 1970s and looked at how taste brought about new feelings of class and classlessness, as well as a culture of 'boutique' cosmopolitanism. This was a world of taste made up of objects and behaviours that were rarely adopted wholesale but incrementally spread out to shape aspects of everyday life for many, and sometimes, most people.

My proposition about taste has been fairly simple. Taste fashions the world around us – those bits that we can control at any rate – to produce atmospheres and ambience. It shapes how we feel in the world. But often the tone of taste and its particular feelings are the first things that get lost when we try and write about taste as social history: it is much easier to cast it all in the soft glow of nostalgia or to focus on the daftness of chopper bicycles, space hoppers, and stacked shoes. Capturing the lightness of taste, sometimes its frivolousness and incidental quality, without making it insignificant and unimportant in the process has been the aim of this book. The scale of consumer society in the last seventy years has altered how we feel we exist in the world. There is an existential dimension to consumerism. Perhaps that sounds too weighty, too filled with feelings of angst. One of the ways of understanding consumer society might be to think about it in terms of what Malcolm Bradbury (writing in 1962 under the name of Max Parrish) described as 'consumer existentialism', when 'the consumer society gradually comes to the point where everything people once took for granted has to be consciously chosen'.[4] Consumer existentialism might name the feelings you have when faced with too much choice – feelings that can range from excitement to a sort of anguished indecision.

To capture consumer existentialism, philosophy and sociology might be of less use than something much lighter in tone. There is a reason that I've often relied on comic novels and magazine journalism in this book. There is something about the tone and register of that sort of work which captures the feel of taste. You can do things with humour that you can't do in the harsh glare of serious consideration; you can get a feel for the seemingly inconsequential, for the flotsam and jetsam of everyday life. Humour is more at ease with the thinness of this world, more comfortable in the presence of the airiness of consumer existentialism. It is also less prone to moral judgement, less happy to cast thinness, superficiality, lightness, and frivolity as the bad guys in a world that should be thick, deep, and serious.

Sue Townsend's purposefully silly *Adrian Mole* books provide a way of seeing taste as part of social change across the last forty years and offers a fitting way to round off this book.

The world according to Adrian Mole

Sue Townsend died in 2014 at the age of 68. By the time of her death, she had published eight *Adrian Mole* books, and was working on a ninth. The first book *The Secret Diary of Adrian Mole: Aged 13¾*, published in 1982, made her a household name and established the fictional character Adrian Mole as a central part of British culture (especially when the first two books were televised in 1985 and 1987). The diaries, set primarily in and around Leicester, follow Adrian from his adolescent infatuation with Pandora Braithwaite, through a long string of misadventures and poor decisions to his treatment for prostate cancer in his early forties in the final volume. In many respects Adrian remains an adolescent: his thirteen-year-old obsession with the length of his penis just gets replaced with other fixations. Across the books Adrian maintains his mostly unreciprocated love for Pandora, his unswerving self-belief that he is an undiscovered literary genius, and his total lack of material, romantic, and literary success.

Various elements of the *Adrian Mole* books make them particularly useful for talking about taste in Britain from the 1970s to the present. First, the writing and publishing of the books stretches from the summer of 1975 when Townsend first 'heard' the voice of Adrian Mole ('that adolescent, self-pitying voice. Mole's voice. I just heard it. He descended with his family in the space of an afternoon'[5]) up to 2009 when the final volume was published. They benefit from being a sustained look at taste and everyday life across almost four decades. Second, they are told from the perspective of a deluded, self-aggrandising, naïve and deeply unreliable narrator: Adrian Mole. This gives the books their satirical flavour: Adrian might be obsessed with the subtle niceties of class distinction (between the upper working class and the lower middle class) but we as readers can see such distinctions as both real and ridiculous (played out in the choice of cigarettes and newspapers). Third, the books are drenched in consumerism. Brands are always mentioned, shopping lists are fully itemised, retailers are named. Clothes are never just clothes, they come from Next or George at Asda or Christian Dior. Fourth, Townsend has an astute and critical sense of social history. The political realm (the change from the Conservative Party to the Labour Party, for instance) is woven into everyday life. Sometimes this is just background noise but it also takes on a physical reality in under-funded NHS hospitals, and in the lives of individual British soldiers serving in Iraq (Adrian's son Glenn, and his best friend), pursuing a war they can't see the point of.

The book series circles around two families – the Moles and the Braithwaites – both seen through Adrian's eyes. Pandora's father, Ivan Braithwaite, is described as 'upper-lower-middle class',[6] while Adrian's father, George Mole, exists in the borderland of 'upper working/lower middle'.[7] Both fathers start the series employed in jobs that are on the cusp of becoming outdated: George sells 'electrical storage heaters' (a form of central heating that used cheap electricity but often heated your home when you least required it or expected it); Ivan is an accountant for the co-operative dairy which delivers milk to your door but which can't compete with the cost and convenience of supermarket milk. Both men are made redundant and try their hand at various other forms of employment but with little success. The women fare slightly better, with the indomitable Pauline Mole becoming a security guard at one point and Tania Braithwaite working as a lecturer at De Montfort University, Leicester. The two families intermingle when Pauline Mole marries Ivan Braithwaite, and George moves in with Tania Braithwaite. The unpredictability of employment, housing, love, and health upturn expectations and aspirations. Class is obsessively discussed, both as something inherited and something acquired, and is shown to be a performance that is constantly changing and often ridiculous.

Adrian is a snob, but his snobbery stems from his class instability and his desire to be an intellectual. The Moles are forever failing to become middle class, but they are no longer working class either. George Mole wants to be middle class but is not too keen on middle-class tastes. At one point Adrian has a brief dalliance with Marxism (he is reading 'Fred Engels') and notes in his diary: 'My father said, "I have worked and slaved and fought to join the middle classes, Adrian, and now I'm here I don't want my son admiring proles and revolutionaries". He is deluding himself if he thinks he has joined the middle classes' notes Adrian, 'he still puts HP sauce on his toast'.[8] When George is living with Tania Braithwaite (who is securely middle class) her shopping list consists of 'Coriander (fresh), Sun-dried tomatoes, Pesto, Goat's cheese & feta, Taramasalata, Pitta bread, Fromage frais, Natural yoghurt (Greek)'.[9] This is clearly not to George's taste and he sends Adrian to the shops 'to get him forty Rothman's, a white sliced loaf and a pack of pork dripping'.[10] Similarly, Pauline's claims to the status of being middle class are constantly undercut by her ostentations: 'My mother drew heavily on her St Moritz menthol fag with the gold-rimmed filter and said, "Ivan, I'm no longer working class. I read the *Guardian* and buy coffee beans now, or hadn't you noticed?"'[11] It is the gold-rimmed cigarette that gives her away.

These are class tastes painted in very broad brushstrokes. They are meant to be stereotypical and ludicrous. More subtle points are made in the realm of housing and furnishing. Here the difference between the Moles and the Braithwaites are to do with scale. The Braithwaites' house – the Lawns – is, for Adrian, a haven of good taste. When he first introduces us to it, he is a thirteen-year-old delivering newspapers: the house 'has got rolled-up wooden blinds at all the windows, and the rooms look like jungles because of all the green plants. I looked through the letterbox and saw the big ginger cat eating something on the kitchen table. They have the *Guardian*, *Punch*, *Private Eye*, and *New Society*'.[12] No doubt the kitchen table was made of 'well-scrubbed pine'. Later, he lets us in on the history of the house:

> The Lawns won an architectural award when it was built in the late 1970s. It was designed for entertaining: the downstairs rooms flowed into each other but were on several levels. The décor had undergone many changes since I first visited the house in 1982. Then it was full of books, potted plants and Indian rugs; now it was a creamy, decluttered, multi-levelled 'space'.[13]

And, of course, the Lawns is stuffed to the rafters with Habitat furnishings. In the books, Habitat is both a sign of a certain kind of good taste as well as being everywhere. For instance, Adrian tells us that Ivan Braithwaite has a Habitat dressing grown and that Pandora's bed comes from Habitat: 'I couldn't sleep so I got up very early and went for a walk past Pandora's house. I thought about her lying in her Habitat bed wearing her Laura Ashley nightgown and I don't mind admitting that tears sprang to my eyes'.[14] But if Habitat is a presence in the lives of the Braithwaites, it is also an essential ingredient for the Moles, but at a reduced scale. When Pauline first leaves George to go and live in Sheffield with her neighbour Alan Lucas, she chooses Habitat to decorate her new life: 'Me and mum went shopping today. We bought a Habitat lampshade for her bedroom'.[15] As Adrian explains to his American pen pal in the 1980s 'Habitat' is a 'store selling cheap, fashionable furniture'.[16]

By the end of the 1990s, IKEA features in the litany of tastes, but even then, the cheaper items of Habitat are mixed with IKEA to create, for Adrian, a sort of minimal 'living kit' that he takes with him to move back into his childhood bedroom at the age of 29. This kit includes: '1 high-tog value fibre-filled duvet [...], 1 MFI folding desk, in black ash [...], 1 *faux* Indian rug, 2 Habitat director's chairs [...], Ikea cutlery set, Ikea dinner service, Ikea cork noticeboard, Floor cushion (burgundy)'.[17] With its smattering of Habitat furniture and *faux* Indian rug it is an approximation of the taste more luxuriously demonstrated at the Lawns.

A full-blown Habitat lifestyle in the early twenty-first century, when the shop had regained a reputation as a high-end boutique furnishing store, was expensive. It didn't just require a taste for Mediterranean food, stripped floorboards, and Japanese paper lampshades, it required money and real estate. In 2002 Adrian, aged 34, buys a loft-style apartment in a converted industrial warehouse in Leicester, ominously called 'Rat Wharf'. In attempting to live the lifestyle that he thinks should accompany the apartment he gets caught in a spiral of debt, buying furniture with store cards, paying mortgage instalments with credit cards, and having to deal with eyewatering interest rates. But as he says: 'What is the point of living in a loft if you can't pad around the wooden floors in your white towelling bathrobe, sit on a white sofa while waiting for the coffee to brew in your cafetière, then take the pot to the galvanised table on the balcony and eat a croissant from your hexagonal-shaped black plate?'[18] The apartment of course gets repossessed.

The world that Adrian Mole inhabits is one framed by consumer existentialism, and it isn't just Adrian who succumbs; everyone seems, to some extent at least, in its thrall. Apart, that is, from some of the older characters. The Adrian Mole books usually include someone far outside the world of commodity culture, untouched by its appeals. In the early books it is the irascible communist pensioner, Bert. When Adrian suggests that he could read out some of the *Sunday Times* colour supplement to him, Bert's reply is adamant: 'Do you think I'm interested in bleedin' Italian furniture, or "A day in the life" of a soddin' piano player?'[19] In the final two volumes a similar role is taken by the alcoholic antiquarian,

Bernard. Approving of some colourful Christmas decorations 'Bernard said, "I like a bit of vulgarity myself. I despise the minimalistic, arty-farty, tight-arsed, bare-floorboard, Habitat foolery"'.[20]

Taste, in the *Adrian Mole* series, is treated as an ever-present aspect of consumer society, but political opinions are never straightforwardly linked to it. For instance, Michael Flowers, owner of the health food shop 'Country Organics', becomes a staunch supporter of the anti-immigration and anti-Europe party UKIP (United Kingdom Independence Party). Taste is given a firmer political and historical dimension in the shape of the unfulfilled promises that accompany a lifestyle of easy-living and controlled casualness. Fashions come and go – like Adrian's attraction to black-ash furniture – but the taste for 'good taste' and the promises that it contains remains. The world of middle-class ease and 'the good life' that accompanies it comes at a cost that many people living on the edges of the new middle classes (and experiencing class confusion) can ill afford. Without general economic affluence – well-paid and secure manual and clerical labour, for instance – the striving for middle-class lifestyles leads to debt, physical illness, and depression. Both Adrian's and Pandora's fathers are hospitalised due to work-related illnesses. The books are, in part, a blistering critique of the culture of Thatcherism Mark I (overseen by Margaret Thatcher and then John Major) as well as Thatcherism Mark II (continued but given a pop-culture feel by Tony Blair). The period from 1970 to 2021 saw a staggering rise in house prices, making home ownership (the golden key for joining the new middle classes) an unaffordable dream for most of today's young people.[21] The only fully successful character in the series is Pandora Braithwaite, Labour MP for Ashby-de-la-Zouch and named the 'shiniest star in Blair's sky' and one of 'Blair's Babes'.[22] On one level the taste differences between the Moles and Braithwaites matter, but on another level, they don't really matter at all. Both families share a taste for duvets while suffering from the turbulent changing fortunes of an unplanned economy.

Duvets and the end of Empire

One of the arguments in this book is that the UK has undergone a 'soft revolution' over the last seventy years. It has changed how many of us live our everyday lives – altered what we eat, how we furnish our rooms, how we imagine the 'good life'. It has been responsible for altering perceptions of class and class feelings.[23] It has altered, too, what it means to feel 'British' or English, Welsh, Scottish, or Northern Irish. This might seem to place an extraordinary burden on such seemingly incidental elements as duvets, quiches, paper lampshades, and mayonnaise. My argument sounds silly when each item is taken in isolation but when seen as part of a set of tastes things start to look different. This, at any rate, is the view of the *Daily Telegraph*.

In January 2013 the *Telegraph*'s website ran an article by their columnist, Harry Wallop, on the omnipresence of duvets in British homes. The newspaper had run a poll and found that 83.9 per cent of respondents slept under duvets rather than sheets and blankets. The article notes that 1987 was the year when various department stores started selling more duvets than blankets and sheets. This was when duvets were no longer a new fashion item but were on their way to becoming the standard form of bedding in Britain.[24] The article was headed by the question 'Is the decline in blankets linked to the fall in Britain's standing in the world?' A lot hung on the term 'linked' in that question. The tone of the article seems to suggest that duvets are a symptom of something larger, and that the something larger appears to be the loss of the British Empire. The article quotes someone who had launched a campaign against duvets, claiming, with presumably some levity, that it was 'an invention of the misguided Continentals and should be sent back where it belongs along with the ridiculous metric system, chilled lager, and Brussels pâté'.[25] There is more than a whiff of pro-Brexit jingoism here, a sentiment that Paul Gilroy terms postcolonial melancholia – a morbid fixation on an Imperial past, where that past is wiped clean of contradiction and complexity. But, of course, it's just a laugh, isn't it?

When Terence Conran was asked by the photographer Georgia Glynn Smith 'what is the best product you have ever sold?' he replied: 'The duvet, as it was symbolic of social change'.[26] Conran's goes on to claim that duvets 'undoubtedly changed the sex life of Europe'.[27] A more realistic assessment might suggest that the duvet was part of a sexual revolution where the more substantial agents of change were chemical (the female contraceptive pill, for instance) and legal (the decriminalisation of homosexuality, for instance). Yet this book is about giving space to more minor agents of change and drawing out their social significance. We can see something of the social and sexual promise of the duvet from the way it was photographed when it was first included in the Habitat catalogue (figure 10.2). The image shows us what we imagine is a loved-up couple, sprawled on a mattress lying on bare floorboards. Of course, it would be hard to imagine in 1973 a same-sex couple in this scene, or an older couple lying across each other like this, nor a black or mixed-race couple. Conran's memory of why Habitat promoted duvets was tied up with sexual energy as well as feelings of liberation: 'People do credit me with bringing the duvet to Britain. I had been in Sweden in the 1950s and was given a duvet to sleep under. I probably had a girl with me and I thought this was all part of the mood of the time – liberated sex and easy living. It was wonderful that when you came to make your bed, it was just a couple of shakes'.[28]

In 1978, when a market research team asked consumers what they thought and felt about continental quilts (as duvets were often called at that point), their responses combined practical concerns with accounts of feelings, atmospheres. The more practical responses are aimed at recognising the convenience of duvets: 'To me they are a luxury AND it saves time – no cleaning of blankets, no storage problems, no summer and winter bedding', claims one respondent, while another states that 'continental quilts suit our way of life; I don't enjoy unnecessary housework'.[29] Those more attuned to the ambience of duvets suggested that 'you feel refreshed in the morning, like getting up to a sunny day when you have

10.2 Habitat catalogue, 1973, p. 26, 'the 10 second bed'

been camping',[30] while a common refrain was a sense of freedom: 'It took me awhile to get used to it but I couldn't go back to blankets and feeling all tied down, I like the freedom'.[31] One much heralded claim for duvets was that it altered the chore of bedmaking, not simply by reducing the time that it took, but by changing who did it. (Though who changed the bedding and washed it probably remained the same.)

The duvet embodied aspects of a soft revolution that was linked to more informal lifestyles, and ones that were, potentially, more equal. The sense of duvets being connected to Scandinavian social democracy is not, I don't think, incidental. In the career of Terence Conran, you get a sense that the purpose behind Habitat included modes of feeling that can be linked back to the emergence of the welfare state. Conran studied design at the Bauhaus-influenced Central School of Arts and Crafts in London between 1948 and 1950. The sense that taste might be collective, democratic even, that it might imbue a nation with a social attitude and feeling is a crucial element of his thinking. You can hear it in the 1973 interview cited in chapter 2 where Conran claims that Habitat is producing 'solid-citizen furniture'. What would a 'solid-citizen' piece of furniture look like? How would it function? And what were 'solid-citizen' values? My guess is that in this context 'solid-citizen' named a society less uptight, more open to European lifestyles, less class-conscious, more informal, and less weighed down by tradition, by a sense of Britishness and all the Imperial baggage that goes with it.

Habitat might have wanted to provide access to the good life for all, but it also needed to constantly increase turnover and profits for shareholders. While commercial culture might deliver social democratic benefits, the costs are high, and those costs are neither democratic nor beneficial to all. On the one hand the push towards economies of scale was required to make goods affordable within a commercial context. On the other hand, commodity culture is geared towards the rhythms of fashion, of producing a surplus of styles that quickly become outdated. The ethos of commercialisation encourages planned obsolescence and a desire for more and more stuff (hardly conducive to good citizenship). The conflict was played out socially too. If the taste for controlled casualness looks outward towards a new cosmopolitan world of other lifestyles (however 'boutique' that contact is), then it also looks inward, prioritising the private home as the main location of taste. It is no wonder, then, that the period of Habitat not only corresponds to an astronomic rise in house prices but also in a decimation of more public spaces for socialising: 'a third of British pubs have now closed since the 1970s'.[32] As one Habitat customer puts it in a catalogue from 1999: 'Home is the most important place in our lives, and so it's equally important that the stuff that surrounds us should feel right. We need our everyday things to have integrity, things that inspire emotion and promote an enormous sense of well-being. Habitat is all about the immanent sense of luxury'.[33] And yet, however privatised it was, it would be hard to imagine the Habitat ethos (however contradictory it is) sitting easily with the duvet-hating sentiment that demands a return to warm beer and Imperial measurements, and probably an end to any and all immigration, if not a more malevolent commitment to repatriation of those that can't trace their genealogy in Britain back to the time of King Harold.

Two Johns

In 1997, in the run up to the general election, John Prescott, at that point Deputy Leader of the Labour Party, claimed that 'we are all middle class now', partly as a mocking assessment of John Major's premiership.[34] It was presumably in part also a riff on an interview he had conducted on BBC radio the previous April when Prescott 'observed that, though his [Prescott's] social origins are working class, he is middle class now because he is a Member of Parliament'.[35] People were quick to disagree with his own self-assessment, including his dad: 'He is the son of a railwayman and grandson of a miner. How can he be anything other than working class? John worked as a steward on ships serving drinks to well-to-do passengers. If that's not working class I cannot think what is. When I see him I shall ask him what he thinks he's playing at'.[36] Perhaps, like Adrian Mole's dad, John still puts HP sauce on his toast.

The claim that the class system is finished and that 'we are all middle class now' is a well-known political aspiration that crosses Conservatives and New Labour, and echoes across the period charted in this book.[37] John Major's desire for 'a society of opportunity, an open society, a society in which what people fulfil will depend upon their talent, their application and their good fortune'[38] didn't result in classlessness, and 'Major and his family have not become emblems of classlessness, but figures of twerpish, lower-middle-class fun: connoisseurs of Butlins and garden gnomes, fans of curry dinners and Little Chefs'.[39] In a country with exclusive private schools and a hierarchical university system, as well as parents who can't afford to pay for their children's school dinners, it is simply political bad-faith not to recognise the material realities of class. As warehouse worker, Chris Mason, commented 'Class? I don't take much notice, cause we're skint'.[40]

Towards the end of the *Adrian Mole* books, George and Pauline Mole move into the aptly named Prescott Estate: 'It's a new housing complex, purpose-built for tenants aspiring to join the new middle class'.[41] They end up defaulting on their mortgage. Class is not the same in twenty-first-century Britain as it was in the first half of the twentieth, and these changes took place across the 1960s, 1970s, and 1980s. In a series of documentaries conducted by Ray Gosling in 1991, he shows that while an older generation wore their class on their sleeve, so to say, in the form of clothing, manners, accent, and employment, their children and grandchildren all had quite similar accents and ways of dressing and a comparable sense of their place in the world. But what Gosling also finds is a vast underclass of those living from hand to mouth, some homeless, some as pensioners and benefit claimants, all barely getting by. He also finds extraordinary wealth. His final words have the odd ambience of someone still coming to terms with his own social mobility from working-class Nottingham to the life of a jobbing broadcaster:

> The old British class system, I had some affection for its subtleties and eccentricities, but I'd not mourn its passing. Too many people in my generation suffered by having their lives pinned like butterflies, fixed for them by class distinction. So, I said, cheers to Mrs Thatcher for pushing a few more privileged off their perches. But all is not well. For with the passing of the old system I can see now we've lost respect for the qualities that can't be measured in pounds and pence, education and learning, the sense of duty that the better off ought to show, the responsibility for the losers among us. These qualities were built into the old system and are now being lost in a Darwinian struggle for money and status.
>
> I wish that we could be classless but to pretend we are is to close our eyes to all the new divisions and inequalities that are crystalizing around us.[42]

In Gosling's eyes the subtle class differences between George Mole (upper working/lower middle) and Ivan Braithwaite (upper-lower-middle), which are so obsessively rehearsed in consumer society, are in danger of blinding us to the compulsive and dangerous hoarding of resources and opportunity amongst the very wealthy and the systematic removal of a decent standard of living for those for whom the good life is only ever something to watch on TV.

The term 'new middle classes' was sometimes named the 'New Working Class', while still pointing to the same broad set of circumstances.[43] What might have happened if John Prescott had said 'we are all working class now' in 1997 instead of 'we are all middle class'? No doubt a similar furore would have resulted. It might, though, have been a little nearer to the social world that was being produced, and it might have provided a platform for building a new political consensus, a new political consciousness. For the phrase 'new middle class' to have currency a degree of affluence and stability is required. People need to feel as though they are going 'up in the world'. But if we take seriously Stuart Hall's 1958 argument about 'classlessness', then what we have been witnessing in the blurring of class divisions in the area around working-class and lower middle-class culture is better named as an 'upward proletarianisation', which was simultaneously rewarding secure employment in some industries and levelling down the lower rungs of professional employment (in education, social work, health services, local government, etc.).

The taste for 'controlled casualness' could be seen as a symptom of a new vastly expanded property-owning *working class* – made up of dentists and electrical engineers, nurses and taxi drivers, teachers and lecturers, factory workers and builders, flight attendants and pilots. But we would also need to add a massive qualification to this too. This would be a property-owning working class whose class identity was largely *obscured* by taste. Here taste, as something perceived as status striving, didn't lead to class consciousness and collective identity, but just the opposite. The fine nuances of taste (between say a Habitat lampshade and a Habitat bed in Adrian Mole's world) concealed similar levels of alienation, similar experiences of dependency on employer power. Taste always has the ability to draw people together, to establish communities of shared values and shared desires. But it can create division as well. In the golden age of affluence, it was this dual nature of taste that was so visible: on the one hand a shared world of TVs and duvets, convenience foods and flat pack furniture; on the other a consumer culture dedicated to 'exquisite' distinctions that sought to endlessly differentiate levels of achievement and sensitivity. If you emphasise the former you might catch a glimpse of a new class landscape emerging, a new property-owning working class; if you emphasise the latter, you see the endless reassertion of nineteenth-century class categories.

*****

Like many people, I've become increasingly aware of the environmental catastrophe looming on the horizon. While I was writing this book, I was acutely aware of it. What was I doing writing about taste when I should be talking about waste? And weren't the tastes that I was describing often particularly wasteful? Habitat's desire to bring the speed of the fashion industry to furniture, immediately inflicted built-in obsolescence on the world of furnishings. And wasn't consumer society simply about making more and more people want more and more things, and wasn't that something that needed condemning rather than describing? Talk about fiddling while Rome burns! Of course, there were other elements which from the perspective of today seemed to be worth championing: the recycling and upcycling, the wooden spoons and second-hand tables, and the peasant food were tastes that could lead to more sustainable ways of living.

But there was something else at the heart of this book that wasn't simply tied to increased consumption. What was so central for my understanding of taste was the way that it was attached to promises and feelings: the promise of a different way of living, of new feelings – for informality and casual enjoyment. Promises and feelings seem to me to be the heart of taste, its social role. And it seems clear that in facing the climate emergency we will also need to foster a taste for degrowth, for having less.[44] Consuming less, using less energy, making less stuff will require new tastes, and this means that new feelings and promises will emerge. What kinds of promises and feeling are going to be attached to the taste for degrowth? Call me a cynic but I just don't see degrowth being embraced if the only feelings that accompany it is one of moral virtue. Bring on the hair shirts! If that is the only feeling that's on offer, then the future looks bleak. But what if getting a taste for degrowth meant developing new and pleasurable feelings, what if it meant a promise for a future that looked better! Looked more enjoyable. That is the challenge that we face, and as far as that goes, this book is a tiny lesson in what one sort of revolution looked like and how it succeeded. That soft revolution used taste to enlarge consumption but also to change our world in relation to manners, class, and experience. We will need another revolution and another set of tastes to go with it. And perhaps this time taste won't be an agent that obscures new class realities and instead will be an agent that reveals them. In developing tastes and feelings for less consumption and more sustainable living perhaps we will be able to recognise that we are actually part of the same class of employees, we are the 99 per cent, and that it will be us who will be left to deal with climate breakdown while the 1 per cent head off into space.

Notes

Introduction

1 At the time of writing (January 2022), the educational background of the cabinet at Westminster was made up of 60 per cent who were privately educated and 47 per cent who attended either Oxford or Cambridge University, www.suttontrust.com/our-research/sutton-trust-cabinet-analysis-2021/, accessed 16 December 2021.

2 See, for instance, Arthur Marwick's *A History of the Modern British Isles 1914–1999*, Oxford: Blackwell, 2000. Marwick's chapter for this period is simply titled 'Affluent Britain, 1955–1974'.

3 Within a capitalist economy the slowing down of growth is often experienced as a recession.

4 Stuart Hall interviewed by Kieran Connell, in Kieran Connell and Matthew Hilton eds, *Cultural Studies 50 Years On*, London: Rowman and Littlefield International, 2016, p. 289.

5 Richard Hoggart, *The Uses of Literacy*, Handsworth: Pelican Books, 1958, p. 9.

6 Tom Harrisson, 'Notes on Class Consciousness and Class Unconsciousness', *Sociological Review*, vol. 34, nos. 3–4, 1942, p. 156.

7 The findings of this survey form the basis of Mike Savage, Niall Cunningham, Fiona Devine, Sam Friedman, Daniel Laurison, Lisa McKenzie, Andrew Miles, Helene Snee, and Paul Wakeling's, *Social Class in the 21st Century*, Harmondsworth: Pelican, 2015.

8 Mass-Observation Archive. This is the testimony of a nurse (L1444), whose husband worked his way up in sales within a breakfast cereal company, responding to a request for information on 'objects about the house' (Summer Directive 1988).

Chapter 1

1 If this kind of discussion isn't your bag and you want to get to the meat of the book, then you might want to skip this chapter or return to it later.

2 David Hume, 'Of the Standard of Taste' [1757], in Charles W. Eliott (ed.), *English Essays from Sir Philip Sidney to Macaulay*, New York: P. F. Collier & Son, 1910, p. 215.

3 Ibid., p. 215.

4 Charles Madge and Tom Harrisson eds, *First Year's Work 1937–38 by Mass-Observation*, London: Lindsay Drummond, 1938, pp. 13–14. The gender of these responses wasn't noted. This hostility to non-smokers wasn't a majority response, but it included a substantial minority.

5 Both magazines were published by Joseph Addison and Richard Steele. *The Tatler* was published between 1709 and 1711, *The Spectator* between 1711 and 1712.

6 From a letter published in no. 175 of *The Spectator* reproduced in Erin Mackie, ed. *The Commerce of Everyday Life: Selections from* The Tatler *and* The Spectator, Boston: Bedford/St. Martin's, 1998, p. 375.

7 Jonathan Raban, *Soft City*, London: Fontana, 1975, p. 66.

8 Robert Millar, *The Affluent Sheep*, London: Longmans, 1963, p. 9.
9 Dorothy Meade, *Bedrooms: Practical Bedrooms for Today*, London: A Design Centre Publication, 1967, p. 30.
10 Ibid., p. 30.
11 Advert, *Good Housekeeping*, January 1968, p. 12.
12 'Few objects today are offered *alone* [...] they are always arranged to mark out directive paths, to orientate the purchasing impulse towards *networks* of objects in order to captivate that impulse and bring it, in keeping with its own logic, to the highest degree of commitment, to the limits of its economic potential', Jean Baudrillard, *The Consumer Society: Myths and Structures*, London: Sage, 1998, p. 27 [first published in France in 1970].
13 In trying to mitigate the catastrophic consequences of global warming and climate change, the task will be to promote a form of reduced consumption by breaking this chain of association. We will need to develop tastes for less, and tastes that can be satisfied. This will mean, I think, reimagining the role of taste and the role of all those industries promoting tastes. We will need an advertising industry as exciting and as creative as we have had but geared to much, much slower rates of consumption.
14 Frank Trentmann, *Empire of Things: How We Became a World of Consumers, from the Fifteenth Century to the Twenty First*, London: Allen Lane, 2016, p. 203.
15 Jenny Diski, *The Sixties*, London: Profile, 2010, p. 12.
16 Ibid., p. 26.
17 Ibid., p. 22.
18 Grayson Perry, *The Vanity of Small Differences*, London: Hayward Publishing, 2013, p. 11. Perry's book is based around a series of tapestries which offer a contemporary retelling of Hogarth's *Rake's Progress*, but played out as a story of 'upward' social mobility in South East England, and the changing tastes (and their accoutrements) that mark the 'ascent' (and subsequent downfall) of the protagonist.
19 Thorstein Veblen, *Theory of the Leisure Class*, Oxford: Oxford University Press, 2007 [first published in 1899].
20 Pierre Bourdieu, *Distinction: A Social Critique of the Judgement of Taste*, translated by Richard Nice, London: Routledge, 1986, p. 56.
21 Tony Bennett, Michael Emmison, and John Frow, *Accounting for Tastes: Australian Everyday Cultures*, Cambridge: Cambridge University Press, 1999, p. 8.

Chapter 2

1 Elizabeth Good, 'What the smart chicks are buying', *Sunday Times*, 10 May 1964, p. 43.
2 Nicholas Ind, *Terence Conran: The Authorised Biography*, London: Sidgwick & Jackson 1995, p. 139.
3 Anne Donaldson, 'Back to Nature in Home Equipment', Habitat press clipping, source not given and unpaginated, V&A Archive.
4 Anne Barrie, 'Terence Conran: young man leading a furniture revolution', *House Beautiful*, December 1964, pp. 57–8.
5 Our Woman's Editor, 'New Habitat for home connoisseurs', *Financial Times*, 16 May 1964, p. 12.
6 Good, 'What the smart chicks are buying', p. 43.
7 Conran quoted in Good, 'What the smart chicks are buying', p. 43. Tuffin and Foale were *the* young fashion designers at the time, part of the generation following on the heels of Mary Quant.
8 Donaldson, 'Back to Nature in Home Equipment', unpaginated.
9 Ind, *Terence Conran*, pp. 139–41.
10 Fiona MacCarthy, *A History of British Design, 1830–1970*, London: Allen and Unwin, 1972, pp. 103–4.
11 Good, 'What the smart chicks are buying', p. 43.
12 Habitat press release, 11 May 1964, V&A archive, AAD/1995/12/16/143.
13 Habitat press release, 11 May 1964, V&A archive, AAD/1995/12/16/145.
14 Ibid.

15 Libby, in Ind, *Terence Conran*, p. 144.
16 Fiona MacCarthy, 'In Habitat', *Guardian*, 5 October 1966, p. 8.
17 Barry Curtis, 'A New Domestic Landscape: British Interior Design, 1960–73', in D. A. Mellor and L. Gervereau eds, *The Sixties: Britain and France, 1960–1973, The Utopian Years* (London: Philip Wilson, 1997), p. 190. Before Habitat had opened Conran and his design team had been actively involved in developing a 'boutique aesthetic' by designing the interior of Mary Quant's *Bazaar* store in London's Knightsbridge in 1957.
18 Habitat press release, 11 May 1964, V&A archive, AAD/1995/12/16/143.
19 Habitat press release, 11 May 1964, V&A archive, AAD/1995/12/16/145.
20 Ibid.
21 Good, 'What the smart chicks are buying', p. 43. On the opening night all the female staff wore Mary Quant dresses and had haircuts from Vidal Sassoon.
22 Conran quoted in Ind, *Terence Conran*, p. 177.
23 Richard Carr, 'The Marks and Sparks of instant furniture?', *Guardian*, 3 December 1970, p. 11.
24 Anon., 'Shopping around', *Observer*, 16 October 1966, p. 29.
25 Because Habitat insisted on casualness and non-intrusive customer service, it suffered from extensive shoplifting, as did similar shops such as Biba (see chapter 3).
26 Habitat press release, 10 October 1966, V&A archive, AAD/1995/12/16/147.
27 Carr, 'The Marks and Sparks of instant furniture?', p. 11.
28 Ibid., p. 11.
29 *Sunday Times*, 21 September 1969.
30 Habitat press release, 21 August 1970, V&A archive, AAD/1995/12/16/145.
31 Ibid.
32 'Counterpoint', *The Times*, 16 February 1973, p. 20.
33 Stephen Bayley, 'A Look Back at the Bauhaus', Habitat 1981/2 catalogue, p. 15.
34 Habitat press release, February 1972, V&A archive, AAD/1995/12/16/143–176.
35 From the soundtrack to *Insight: Terence Conran* (1981).
36 Anne Barrie, 'Terence Conran: young man leading a furniture revolution', *House Beautiful*, December 1964, pp. 56–9.
37 Conran quoted in Ind, *Terence Conran*, p. 37.
38 'Counterpoint', *The Times*, 16 February, 1973, p. 20.
39 Margaret Duckett, 'Conran's own Habitat', *Telegraph Colour Magazine*, 2 February 1968, p. 29.
40 MacCarthy, *A History of British Design*, p. 104.
41 Lucia van der Post, 'What's new', *Sunday Telegraph*, 10 September 1967, p. 9.
42 For more on *New Society* see chapter 6.
43 Angela Carter, 'What the Hell – It's Home!' in *Shaking a Leg: Collected Journalism and Writings*, London: Vintage, 2013, p. 207 [first published in *New Society*, 13 May 1976].
44 Ibid., p. 205.
45 Peter Lloyd Jones, 'The pop art of living', *The Listener*, 11 August 1977, p. 171.
46 Julia Wade, 'The Wooden Spoon Award', *Guardian*, 30 November 1978, p. 11.
47 *Honey*, January 1968. Unpaginated, V&A Archive.
48 Heather Standring, 'Boxing clever', *Observer*, 13 March 1966, p. 28.

Chapter 3

1 Juliet Gardiner, *Joining the Dots: A Woman in her Time*, London: William Collins, 2017, p. 110.
2 Ibid., p. 110.
3 Ibid., p. 111.
4 Ibid., p. 111.
5 Ibid., p. 112.

6 Terence Conran, *My Life in Design*, London: Conran Octopus, 2016, p. 54.
7 Margaret Duckett, 'Conran's own Habitat', *Telegraph Colour Magazine*, 2 February 1968, pp. 26–9.
8 For instance, it was followed by *The Kitchen Book* in 1977, and led to the emergence of Conran Octopus Publishing.
9 Habitat 1975 catalogue, p. 108.
10 The book included items that could be purchased from Habitat and elsewhere alongside older 'found' furnishings. In many ways it could be read as Conran's response to criticism that Habitat offered 'instant good taste' in an ersatz form.
11 Terence Conran, *The House Book* (London: Mitchell Beazley, 1974), p. 10.
12 Ibid., p. 9.
13 Ibid., p. 21.
14 Ibid., p. 11.
15 Ibid., p. 218.
16 Ibid., p. 187.
17 Ibid., p. 187.
18 Ibid., p. 22.
19 '1957: BBC fools the nation', http://news.bbc.co.uk/onthisday/hi/dates/stories/april/1/newsid_2819000/2819261.stm, accessed 12 June 2021.
20 Keith Floyd, *Out of the Frying Pan*, London: Harper Collins, 2001, p. 39.
21 See Nicholas Ind, *Terence Conran: The Authorised Biography*, London: Sidgwick & Jackson 1995, pp. 111–12.
22 Elizabeth David, *An Omelette and a Glass of Wine*, London: Grub Street, 2009, pp. 39–40 [first published in *The Spectator*, 3 August 1962].
23 Alysa Levene, 'The Meanings of Margarine in England: Class, Consumption and Material Culture from 1918 to 1953', *Contemporary British History*, vol. 28, no. 2, pp. 145–65.
24 David, *An Omelette and a Glass of Wine*, p. 27.
25 Len Deighton, *Len Deighton's Action Cook Book*, London: Harper Perennial, 2009 [first published by Cape in 1965], p. 259.
26 'Using the brain – Len Deighton's Cook-strip shows how', *Observer*, 22 July 1962, p. 25.
27 For the history of Indian Restaurants in Britain see my 'The Taj Mahal in the High Street: The Indian Restaurant as Diasporic Popular Culture in Britain', *Food, Culture and Society*, vol. 12, no. 2, 2009, pp. 173–90. The word 'Indian' when used in the phrase 'Indian restaurants' refers back to the colonial period of 'British India'; most so-called Indian restaurants have Bangladeshi heritage with menus based around Bengali foods but also including what became a standardised repertoire of sub-continental cuisine.
28 Peter Boizot (co-written with Matthew Reville), *Mr Pizza and All That Jazz*, London: Large Things, 2016, p. 106.
29 Boizot, *Mr Pizza and All That Jazz*, p. 107.
30 Keith Floyd, *Out of the Frying Pan*, p. 90.
31 Ibid., p. 90.
32 Barbara Hulanicki, *From A to Biba: The Autobiography of Barbara Hulanicki*, London: V&A Publishing, 2009, p. 81 [first published in 1983].
33 Felicity Green, 'Four girls prove that beauty and business ideas can go together', *Daily Mirror*, 7 May 1964, p. 17. 'Twenty-five bob' (25 shillings) translates to about £1.15 in decimal currency.
34 Advert, 'Biba's Bonus', *Daily Mirror*, 5 October 1964, p. 8.
35 Georgina Howell, 'The boutique belt', *Observer*, 4 July 1965, p. 24.
36 Jonathan Aitken, 'Rag trade revolution', *Sunday Telegraph*, 9 April 1967, p. 6.
37 Ibid., p. 6.
38 Ibid., p. 6.
39 Marnie Fogg, *Boutique: A '60s Cultural Phenomenon*, London: Mitchell Beazley, 2003, p. 77.
40 Aitken, 'Rag trade revolution', p. 6.

41 Stella Shamoon, 'How Biba went her own way to success', *Daily Telegraph*, 31 October 1970, p. 16.
42 Sue Arnold, 'Bye-bye Biba', *Observer*, 5 October 1975, p. 1.
43 Fogg, *Boutique*, p. 81.
44 Renate Köhler, 'Where does Biba go from here?', *Daily Mail*, 2 July 1975, p. 10.
45 Cited in Robin Stummer, 'Len Deighton's *Observer* cookstrips, Michael Caine and the 1960s', *Observer*, 14 December 2014, www.theguardian.com/books/2014/dec/14/len-deighton-observer-cookstrips-michael-caine-1960s, accessed 13 November 2021.
46 Len Deighton, *The IPCRESS File/Funeral in Berlin*, London: Cresset Press, 1992, p. 181.
47 Ibid., p. 19.
48 Dixon Scott, 'Presenting the Mirror boat – a revolutionary idea that makes sailing cheap for everybody', *Daily Mirror*, 20 February 1963, p. 12.
49 Ibid., p. 13. For more on the Mirror Dinghy see Andrew Jackson, 'Labour as Leisure – The Mirror Dinghy and DIY Sailors', *Journal of Design History*, vol. 19, no. 1, pp. 57–67.
50 John Smith, 'What a winner!' *Daily Mirror*, 13 April 1963, p. 9.
51 Anon, '1,200 Pick a winner', *Daily Mirror*, 9 March 1964, p. 5.
52 Paul Hughes, 'The red sails of freedom!' *Daily Mirror*, 23 November 1963, p. 12.

Chapter 4

1 Angela Carter, 'What the Hell – It's Home!' in *Shaking a Leg: Collected Journalism and Writings*, London: Vintage, 2013, p. 206 [first published in *New Society*, 13 May 1976].
2 For the economics of the Sunday supplements, see Richard Farmer, 'Supplemental Income: British Newspaper Colour Supplements in the 1960s', *Media History*, vol. 25, no. 3, pp. 371–86. Farmer notes that 'the high rates that each of the quality Sundays was able to charge for "selling its readers' incomes to advertisers" allowed them to survive on relatively small circulations. In 1973, the *Sunday Times*, *Observer*, and *Sunday Telegraph* accounted for only 14 per cent of national Sunday circulation, yet earned 20 per cent more advertising revenue than all the popular Sundays combined' (p. 375).
3 Tom Stacey, 'The Changing Mood of Britain', *Sunday Times Colour Section*, 4 February 1964, p. 9.
4 'English' is the magazine's description. In the discourse of nationality and race in the postwar period the word 'English' often stood in for whiteness in a way that 'British' didn't. As race consciousness developed, composite identities such as British Asian, Anglo-Indian and Black British were deployed, but not English Asian, etc. In descriptions of people throughout the postwar period newspapers like *The Times* would routinely describe a racially mixed group of people as consisting of Blacks, Indians, and English.
5 Mark Boxer, quoted in Martin Slavin, 'Colour Supplement Living', *Ten: 8 (Quarterly Photographic Magazine)*, no. 23, 1986, p. 3.
6 Even where lifestyle publications are aimed at both sexes – for instance running magazines – the advertising and features are often specifically gendered.
7 See, for instance, Brenda Payne, 'Sexual incompatibility: the discord that leads to disillusionment', *Good Housekeeping*, March 1968, pp. 38–9, 88 and 91, and Monica Furlong, 'The sin that makes a mockery of marriage', *Good Housekeeping*, November 1967, pp. 45–7, 152.
8 Good Housekeeping's *Setting Up Home*, London: Ebury Press, 1963, p. 138.
9 Ibid., p. 29. 'Radiant heat' was heat that radiated in an intense but restricted area (gas fires, coal fires, etc.) as opposed to 'ambient' central heating.
10 'Central heating: the luxury you can afford', *Good Housekeeping*, October 1967, p. 123.
11 'Good Housekeeping Institute warms the cold spots', *Good Housekeeping*, November 1967, p. 85.
12 Colston Turbo-jets advert, *Homes and Gardens*, February 1968, p. 15.
13 'Good Housekeeping Institute does the dishes', *Good Housekeeping*, January 1968, p. 57.
14 Kenwood advert, *Good Housekeeping*, January 1968, p. 65.
15 Shirley Green, 'Furnishing with flair', *Good Housekeeping*, January 1968, p. 25.

16 Ibid., p. 28.
17 Anon., 'Make mine country style', *Good Housekeeping*, March 1968, p. 47.
18 Ibid., p. 45.
19 Ibid., p. 45.
20 See David Gibbs, ed. *Nova 1965–1975*, compiled by David Hillman and Harry Peeccinotti, London: Pavilion Books, 1993, pp. 6–7.
21 This lasted until December 1965, after which they dispensed with a subtitle: see Ibid., p. 7.
22 'Statement of Editorial Intent', *Nova Dummy Issue* (George Newnes/IPC, unpublished, 1964) cited in Alice Beard, 'Nova Magazine 1965–1975: A History', unpublished PhD Thesis, Goldsmiths, 2013, p. 93.
23 Janet Fitch, 'Designs on your house', *Nova*, May 1973, pp. 76–9.
24 Gibbs, ed. *Nova 1965–1975*, p. 39.
25 *Nova*, March 1965, p. 74 cited in Beard, 'Nova Magazine 1965–1975: A History', p. 108.
26 Carolyn Faulder, 'After the wedding – making sense of the marriage', *Nova*, May 1973, p. 50.
27 Faulder, 'After the wedding', p. 51.
28 Caroline Younger, 'The rapping of Holloway', *Spare Rib*, July 1972, p. 9, and Mary Finnigan, 'This is Holloway, a house of correction for women. It no longer claims to correct anyone. Pull it down', *Nova*, pp. 66–71.
29 *Nova* reader June Thornton, interviewed by Alice Beard in Beard, 'Nova Magazine 1965–1975: A History', p. 108.
30 Quoted in Ibid., p. 116.
31 Peter Martin, 'Brixton: the ghetto that Britain built', *Nova*, November 1971, p. 48, reproduced in Gibbs, ed. *Nova 1965–1975*, p. 129.
32 It should be clear that this doesn't mean that people of colour weren't consuming lifestyle magazines, or that they weren't reading newspaper colour supplements.

Chapter 5

1 Fiona MacCarthy, 'Geared up', *Guardian*, 16 January 1965, p. 6.
2 Fiona MacCarthy, 'In Habitat', *Guardian*, 5 October 1966, p. 8.
3 Ibid., p. 8.
4 Michael Thompson, *Rubbish Theory: The Creation and Destruction of Value*, London: Pluto, 2017, p. 49 [first published in 1979].
5 Ibid., p. 50.
6 Ibid., p. 50.
7 Ibid., p. 57.
8 Margaret Duckett, 'Conran's own Habitat', *Telegraph Colour Magazine*, 2 February 1968, pp. 26–9.
9 See Jonathan Raban, *For Love & Money: Writing, Reading, Travelling, 1969–1987*, London: Collins Harvill, 1987, for biographical information and for the details of his earnings.
10 Jonathan Raban, *Soft City*, London: Fontana, 1975, p. 87 [first published in 1974 by Hamish Hamilton].
11 Nicholas Tomalin, 'Conspicuous thrift' [1963] in, *Nicholas Tomalin Reporting*, London: André Deutsch, 1975, pp. 245–53.
12 Raban, *Soft City*, p. 190.
13 Ibid., p. 86.
14 Joe Moran, 'Early Cultures of Gentrification in London, 1955–1980', *Journal of Urban History*, vol. 34, no. 1, 2007, pp. 113–14.
15 Jeremy Bugler 'The invaders of Islington', *New Society*, 15 August, 1968, cited in Moran, 'Early Cultures of Gentrification', p. 114.
16 BBC TV, *All Mod Cons* (Wall to Wall production), first aired 21 July 1997.
17 Raban, *Soft City*, p. 193.

18 Ibid., p. 85.
19 Ibid., p. 88.
20 Ibid., p. 85.
21 Neal Ascherson, *Games with Shadows*, London: Radius, 1988, p. 21. The book is primarily a collection of Ascherson's *Observer* articles. This quotation is from an article published in 1986.
22 Raban, *Soft City*, p. 89.
23 Neil Smith, 'Gentrification and Uneven Development', *Economic Geography*, vol. 58, no. 2, 1982, p. 139.
24 Ruth Glass, 'Aspects of Change', in the Centre for Urban Studies, ed. *London: Aspects of Change*, London: MacGibbon & Kee, 1964, p. xiv.
25 Ibid., p. xiv.
26 Ibid., pp. xviii–xix.
27 Ibid., p. xx. Ray Gosling offers a first-hand account of how an area of Nottingham where he was living in the late 1960s was seen as an area of 'urban blight'. The reality was of a much more heterogenous and thriving community of mutual aid, eccentricity, and impoverished bohemia. See Ray Gosling, *Personal Copy: A Memoir of the Sixties*, London: Faber and Faber, 1980. Areas in London that were left to decay in the 1960s and 1970s might include areas of Brixton and neighbourhoods such as Notting Dale (next to Notting Hill). Both areas were sites of alternative communities in the 1970s.
28 Glass, 'Aspects of Change', p. xvii–xviii.
29 Ruth Glass, *Newcomers: The West Indians in London*, London: Centre for Urban Studies, 1960.
30 Glass, 'Aspects of Change', pp. xxi–xxii.
31 Michael Young and Peter Willmott, *The Symmetrical Family: A Study of Work and Leisure in the London Region*, Harmondsworth: Penguin Books, 1975, p. 2.
32 Glass, 'Aspects of Change', p. xxii.
33 Mark Abrams, 'The home-centred society', *The Listener*, 26 November 1959, p. 914.
34 Ibid., p. 914.
35 Ibid., p. 915.
36 Ibid., p. 915.
37 Michael Heseltine, Environment Minister statement, January 1980, cited in Stephen Merrett, with Fred Gray, *Owner Occupation in Britain*, London: Routledge & Kegan Paul, 1982, p. 269.
38 Merrett with Gray, *Owner Occupation in Britain*, p. 269.
39 Ibid., p. 240.
40 Jon Lawrence, 'Class, "Affluence" and the Study of Everyday Life in Britain, c. 1930–64', *Cultural and Social History: The Journal of the Social History Society*, vol. 10, no. 2, pp. 273–4.
41 Merrett with Gray, *Owner Occupation in Britain*, p. 249.
42 Alan Bennett, 'The stripped-pine wilderness', *The Listener*, 28 November 1968, pp. 735–6. The writer, Bennett, was satirising himself as someone who lived in this 'stripped-pine wilderness'. For an account of the Bennett milieu in the early 1980s see Nina Stibbe, *Love, Nina: Despatches from Family Life*, Harmondsworth: Penguin, 2014. This is set nearly twenty years after this area of London had been gentrified.
43 To give you an idea of how late central heating came to Britain, an advert for some new Taylor Woodrow homes in 1976, notes that 'A garage is included with each type, and in some cases the specification includes central heating', *Daily Mail Ideal Home Exhibition 1976: Official Catalogue & Guide*, London, Olympia, p. 77.
44 *Daily Mail Ideal Home Exhibition 1976: Official Catalogue & Guide*, London, Olympia, p. 38.

Chapter 6

1 Terence Morris, 'Alan Neville Little (1934–1986)', *The British Journal of Sociology*, vol. 38, no. 1, 1987, unpaginated front piece.

2 Perry Anderson, for example, wrote in 1968, that 'the non-emergence of any classical sociology in England, and its consequences, the withered half-life of the subject to this day, are momentous historical events', in 'Components of the National Culture', *New Left Review*, vol. 1, no. 50, 1968, p. 7.
3 See, for instance, Lawrence Black, '*Which?*craft in Post-War Britain: The Consumers' Association and the Politics of Affluence', *Albion*, vol. 36, no. 1, 2004, pp. 52–82.
4 Harold Perkin, *New Universities in the United Kingdom: Case Studies on Innovation in Higher Education*, Paris: Organisation for Economic Cooperation and Development, 1969, p. 15. The OECD was founded in 1961 and today includes 38 countries (see www.oecd.org/about/, accessed 9 September 2022). Perkin's report was prepared as a case study that might inform policy decisions about higher education/tertiary education across OECD countries.
5 Perkin, *New Universities in the United Kingdom*, p. 16. The ten universities are: Keele (1950), Sussex (1961), York (1963), East Anglia (1963), Essex (1964), Lancaster (1964), Kent (1965), Warwick (1965), Stirling (1967) and the University of Ulster at Coleraine in Norther Ireland (1968).
6 Perkin, *New Universities in the United Kingdom*, p. 28.
7 Ibid., p. 25.
8 Michael Beloff, *The Plateglass Universities*, Rutherford: Fairleigh Dickinson University Press, 1970, p. 71 [first published in 1968].
9 David Riesman, 'Notes on New Universities: British and American', *Higher Education Quarterly*, vol. 20, no. 2, 1966, pp. 129–30.
10 Beloff, *The Plateglass Universities*, p. 30.
11 Ann Eatwell 'Early University Dining Culture' in Fred Gray, ed. *Making the Future: A History of the University of Sussex*, Falmer: University of Sussex, 2011, p. 139.
12 William Whyte, *Redbrick: A Social and Architectural History of Britain's Civic Universities*, Oxford: Oxford University Press, 2016, p. 259.
13 Alan Powers, 'John Morton obituary', *Guardian*, 10 May 2017, www.theguardian.com/artanddesign/2017/may/10/john-morton-obituary, accessed 4 June 2021.
14 The novels are collected as: Colin MacInnes, *The London Novels*, London: Allison and Busby, 1985.
15 Colin MacInnes, *England, Half English*, London: MacGibbon & Kee, 1961.
16 Griselda Rowntree, 'New facts on teenage marriage', *New Society*, 4 October 1962, pp. 12–15.
17 Barbara Wootton, *Testament for Social Science: An Essay in the Application of Scientific Method to Human Problems*, New York: W. W. Norton, 1950.
18 Barbara Wootton, 'Socrates, science and social problems', *New Society*, 4 October 1962, pp. 16–17.
19 Ibid., p. 17.
20 Asa Briggs, 'University social studies: the Sussex idea', *New Society*, 18 October 1962, p. 20.
21 John Goldthorpe and David Lockwood, 'Not so bourgeois after all', *New Society*, 18 October 1962, p. 19.
22 C. C. Harris, 'Who are the people in between?', *New Society*, 29 November 1962, p. 19.
23 Ibid., p. 20.
24 Ibid., p. 20.
25 For instance, George Melly, 'Pop world and words', *New Society*, 18 October 1962, p. 32.
26 Cited in Anthony Sampson, *Anatomy of Britain Today*, London: Hodder and Stoughton, 1965, p. 235.
27 The full curriculum for the University is provided as an appendix in David Daiches, ed. *The Idea of a New University: An Experiment in Sussex*, London: André Deutsch, 1964.
28 Stephen Aris, 'The anatomy of Mrs. 1970', *New Society*, 21 March 1963, pp. 19–20.
29 Malcolm Bradbury, *The History Man*, Arena Books, London, 1984, p. 3 [first published in 1975].
30 Ibid., p. 38.
31 Ibid., p. 13.
32 Ibid., p. 42.
33 Phillip Simpson, '"Presentness Precise": Notes on "The History Man"', *Screen*, vol. 23, no. 1, 1982, p. 21.

34 Bradbury, *The History Man*, p. 44.
35 Ibid., pp. 43–4.
36 Ibid., p. 11.
37 Ibid., p. 53.
38 Ibid., pp. 62, 107.
39 Elizabeth Berridge, 'Recent Fiction', *The Daily Telegraph*, 6 November 1975, p. 13.
40 Mary Sullivan, 'Dynamo of a don', *The Sunday Telegraph*, 2 November 1975, p. 14.
41 Malcolm Bradbury, *All Dressed Up and Nowhere to Go*, Basingstoke: Picador, 1982, pp. xv–xvi.
42 Malcolm Bradbury, *The History Man*, p. 38.
43 Ibid., p. 91.
44 David Lewis, 'A Conversation with Posy Simmonds', *Children's Literature in Education*, vol. 38, no. 4, 2007, pp. 265–6.
45 Jennifer Curry, 'Who scrubs whose floors?', *Guardian*, 20 November 1979, p. 10.
46 Anon, 'Posy scoops the bunch', *Guardian*, 25 September 1978, p. 11.
47 Posy Simmonds, *Mrs Weber's Omnibus*, London: Jonathan Cape, 2012, unpaginated.
48 Brenda Polan, 'The road to Tresoddit', *Guardian*, 19 September 1984, p. 12.
49 For readers with a passing interest in the social sciences the name Weber would have connected immediately to the figure of Max Weber, the German sociologist, who along with Marx and Emile Durkheim were seen as providing the foundations of the discipline of sociology.
50 Tim Radford, 'A swift kick in the shins for the "science" of sociology', *Guardian*, 3 September 1981, p. 4 is illustrated with an image of George Weber that is captioned: 'the image of the sociologist: Posy's George Weber'.
51 The novelist and critic David Lodge suggests that the Posy Simmonds strip is one of the only places where you can find a mainstream representation of structuralism in British culture: 'Posy Simmons' [*sic*] genial jeering at George Weber, the Polytechnic lecturer, in her witty *Guardian* cartoon strip, is about all the national press has done to recover the most significant intellectual movement of our time', David Lodge, 'Structural defects', *Observer*, 23 March 1980, p. 11.

Chapter 7

1 J. B. Priestley, *The Image Men*, London: Mandarin Paperbacks, 1996, p. 12 [first published in two volumes in 1968].
2 Ibid., p. 75.
3 Ibid., p. 143.
4 Ibid., p. 110.
5 Ibid., p. 181.
6 Dennis Chapman, *The Home and Social Status*, London: Routledge & Kegan Paul, 1955, p. 23.
7 George Orwell, *The Complete Novels*, Harmondsworth: Penguin, 1983, p. 349.
8 Tom Harrisson, Humphrey Jennings, and Charles Madge, 'Anthropology at Home', *The New Statesman and Nation*, 30 January 1937, p. 155.
9 Malcolm Bradbury, *Liar's Landscape: Collected Writing from a Storyteller's Life*, edited by Dominic Bradbury, London: Picador, 2006, p. 145.
10 Priestley, *The Image Men*, p. 110.
11 Chapman, *The Home and Social Status*, p. 22.
12 Ibid., pp. 22–3. Of course, one simple explanation for this is that the working classes spend their money (which is more limited) elsewhere, rather than being indifferent to the lures of consumerism.
13 Vance Packard, *The Status Seekers*, Harmondsworth: Penguin, 1961 [published in the USA in 1959; first published in the UK in 1960].
14 Eve Perrick, 'Your status is showing', *Daily Mail*, 19 June 1959, p. 4.

15 A representative sample would include: Perrick, 'Your status is showing'; Anon., 'But some are more equal than others', *The Times*, 14 January, 1960, p. 15; Patrick O'Donovan, 'Playing the status game', *Observer*, 1 November 1959, p. 8; Alex Faulkner, 'America's new age of snobbery', *Daily Telegraph*, 9 January 1960, p. 8.
16 Peter Willmott, 'The Status Seekers', *New Left Review*, vol. 1, no. 3, 1960, p. 71.
17 Peter Willmott and Michael Young, *Family and Class in a London Suburb*, London: New English Library, 1967 [first published in 1960 by Routledge & Kegan Paul].
18 Willmott, 'The Status Seekers', p. 70.
19 Ibid., pp. 70–1.
20 Robert Millar, *The Affluent Sheep*, London: Longmans, 1963 and Robert Millar, *The New Classes: The New Patterns of British Life*, London: Longmans, 1966.
21 Chapman, *The Home and Social Status*, p. 23.
22 Robert Millar, *The New Classes: The New Patterns of British Life*, London: Longmans, 1966, p. 202.
23 Shirley Green, 'Flowers underfoot', *Good Housekeeping*, October 1967, p. 55.
24 Geoffrey Gorer, 'Putting us in our places', *Observer*, 3 January 1960, p. 9.
25 Frank Marcus, 'The way some live now', *The Sunday Telegraph*, July 24, 1977, p. 14.
26 Ibid., p. 14.
27 Mike Leigh, *Abigail's Party & Goose-Pimples*, Harmondsworth: Penguin, 1983, pp. 62–3.
28 See Miranda Sawyer, 'A temple to Athena', *Observer*, 15 November 2009, www.theguardian.com/artanddesign/2009/nov/15/athena-posters-miranda-sawyer, accessed 7 November 2021.
29 Interflex advert, *Homes and Gardens*, February 1968, p. 116.
30 Sheridan Morley, 'Mike Leigh: anything but anarchy', *The Times*, 15 July 1977, p. 13.
31 Marcus, 'The way some live now', p. 14.
32 Shaun Usher, 'I'm ashamed to say that I laughed', *Daily Mail*, 2 November 1977, p. 28.
33 Sean Day-Lewis, 'Improvisation snipes at class veneers', *Daily Telegraph*, 2 November 1977, p. 15.
34 Dennis Potter, 'Review of *Abigail's Party*', *Sunday Times*, 6 November 1977, p. 35.
35 Gorer, 'Putting us in our places', p. 9.
36 There is not space here to discuss all the television representations of taste, class, and status on British television in the 1960s, 1970s, 1980s, and 1990s – that would fill several volumes. Such a work would need to make space for at least the following: *Keeping Up Appearances* (1990–95), *To the Manor Born* (1979–2007), *Butterflies* (1978–83), *The Fall and Rise of Reginald Perrin* (1976–79). More recent sitcoms that paint the 'lower middle classes' in a more human light would include *Two Doors Down* (2013 onwards) and *Mum* (2016–19).
37 This assessment is from the man who first taught her to cook – Lionel Evans in Alison Bowyer, *Delia Smith: The Biography*, London: Andre Deutsch, 2002, p. 5. Of course, regionless, here, is a London-centric identification. To someone from the midlands, or the north of England, it would have been an identifiable 'southern English' and middle-class accent.
38 Ibid., p. 4.
39 Ibid., p. 96.
40 Keith Floyd, *Out of the Frying Pan*, London: Harper Collins, 2001, pp. 195–6.

Chapter 8

1 Mass-Observation Autumn 1983 Directive, September, available online at: www.massobs.org.uk/mass-observation-project-directives, accessed 7 September 2022.
2 Mass-Observation Archive, Autumn 1983 Directive, # 586, capitalisation as in the original.
3 As in Thorstein Veblen's *The Theory of the Leisure Class*, New York: Dover, 1994 [first published in New York in 1899].
4 Karl Marx and Frederick Engels, *Manifesto of the Communist Party*, second edition, New York: National Executive of the Socialist Labor Party, 1898, p. 13 [first published in German and French in 1848].

5 Angus Calder and Dorothy Sheridan, eds, *Speak for Yourself: A Mass-Observation Anthology 1937–1949*, Oxford: Oxford University Press, 1985, p. 159.
6 Ibid., p. 159.
7 Ibid., p. 160.
8 George Orwell, *Road to Wigan Pier*, New York: Harcourt, Brace and Company, 1958, p. 153 [first published in 1937].
9 Jonathan Raban, *Coasting*, London: Picador, 1987, p. 84.
10 Ann Oakley, *Father and Daughter: Patriarchy, Gender and Social Science*, Bristol: Policy Press, 2014, pp. 1–2.
11 Frank Mort, 'Social and Symbolic Fathers and Sons in Postwar Britain', *Journal of British Studies*, vol. 38, no. 3, 1999, p. 365.
12 Commercial colleges, despite the name, were part of the same state education provision as education, art and design, and technical colleges in the 1950s and 1960s, but were aimed primarily at providing training in clerical professions outside those areas. If you were working in local government, for instance, and wanted a qualification in administration or housing you would probably take an evening class at a commercial college.
13 Mort, 'Social and Symbolic Fathers and Sons in Postwar Britain', p. 365.
14 Ibid., p. 376. Capitalisation as in original.
15 Editorial, *The Times*, 7 May 1965, p. 15.
16 Siegfried Kracauer, *The Salaried Masses: Duty and Distraction in Weimar Germany*, translated by Quintin Hoare, London: Verso, 1998 [first published in Germany in 1930].
17 Peter Willmott and Michael Young, *Family and Class in a London Suburb*, London: New English Library 1967, pp. 100–1 [first published by Routledge & Kegan Paul in 1960].
18 Ibid., p. 101.
19 Ibid., p. 23.
20 Ibid., p. 103.
21 There is a vast literature of class studies in this period. Perhaps the most famous studies are those by David Lockwood and John Goldthorpe, for instance: David Lockwood, *The Blackcoated Worker: A Study in Class Consciousness*, London: George Allen & Unwin, 1958; and John H. Goldthorpe, David Lockwood, Frank Bechhofer, and Jennifer Platt, *The Affluent Worker in the Class Structure*, Cambridge: Cambridge University Press, 1969 (which was their final instalment of the 'affluent worker' studies that they undertook across the 1960s). Recent historians of sociology have revisited these studies and many others. Of particular interest are Mike Savage, *Identities and Social Change in Britain since 1940: The Politics of Method*, Oxford: Oxford University Press, 2010, and Jon Lawrence, *Me Me Me? The Search for Community in Post-war England*, Oxford: Oxford University Press, 2019.
22 Willmott and Young, *Family and Class in a London Suburb*, p. 104.
23 This is from the original affluent worker studies interviews cited in Savage, *Identities and Social Change in Britain since 1940*, p. 220–1.
24 Stuart Hall, 'A Sense of Classlessness', *Universities & Left Review*, no. 5, 1958, p. 30. The reference to 'exquisite' distinctions comes from the epigraph that heads the essay. It is from the American sociologist William H. Whyte's book *The Organization Man* from 1956: 'the more that distinctions are broken down, the more exquisite they become'. An example of what Whyte means might be if everyone is wearing jeans, then the differences of labels, styles, ways of wearing them, and so on, become more and more nuanced, and 'exquisite'.
25 Hall, 'A Sense of Classlessness', p. 28.
26 Ibid., p. 28.
27 Ibid., p. 31.
28 Ibid., p. 28.
29 Ralph Samuel, 'Class and Classlessness', *Universities & Left Review*, no. 6, 1959, p. 48.

30 E. P. Thompson, 'Commitment in Politics', *Universities & Left Review*, no. 6, 1959, pp. 50–1. The reference to John Braine's 1957 novel, *Room at the Top*, was a reference to the social climbing undertaken by the protagonist.
31 Thompson, 'Commitment in Politics', p. 53.
32 E. P. Thompson, *The Making of the English Working Class*, Harmondsworth: Penguin, 2013, p. 939.
33 Thompson, 'Commitment in Politics', p. 54.
34 Stuart Hall, 'The Big Swipe', *Universities & Left Review*, no. 7, 1959, p. 51.
35 Thompson, 'Commitment in Politics', p. 55.
36 In the words of Peter Bailey, 'putting the boot in on the lower middle class has long been the intellectual's blood sport, an exorcism, so we are told, of the guilty secret so many of us share as closet petit bourgeois denying our own class origins' – Peter Bailey, 'White Collars, Gray Lives? The Lower Middle Class Revisited', *Journal of British Studies*, vol. 38, no. 3, Masculinity and the Lower Middle Class (1999), p. 274.
37 Malcolm Bradbury, *All Dressed Up and Nowhere to Go*, Basingstoke: Picador, 1982, p. 77. This book is a reprint of two humorous volumes – *Phogey! How to Have Class in a Classless Society* (1960) and *All Dressed Up and Nowhere To Go, or the Poor Man's Guide to the Affluent Society* (1962).
38 Michael Young, *The Rise of the Meritocracy 1870–2033: An Essay on Education and Equality*, Harmondsworth: Penguin Books, 1975 [first published by Thames & Hudson in 1958].
39 Robert Millar, *The New Classes: The New Patterns of British Life*, London: Longmans, 1966.
40 Ibid., p. 180.
41 Ibid., p. 177.
42 Ibid., p. 176.
43 Millar, *The New Classes*, p. 177.
44 A Special Correspondent, 'Who buys wine?' *The Times*, 5 December 1963, supplement, p. iii.
45 Raphael Samuel, 'The SDP and the new middle classes', *New Society*, 22 April 1982, reprinted in *Island Stories: Unravelling Britain (Theatres of Memory, Volume II)*, London: Verso, 1998, p. 259.
46 Samuel, 'The SDP and the New Middle Classes', p. 258.
47 Ibid., p. 258.
48 Ibid., p. 264.
49 Fyodor Dostoyevsky, *Crime and Punishment*, Harmondsworth: Penguin, 2003 [first published in Russian in 1866].

Chapter 9

1 Ian Sanjay Patel, *We're Here Because You Were There: Immigration and the End of Empire*, London: Verso, 2021, p. 4.
2 Ali Meghji, *Black Middle-Class Britannia: Identities, Repertoires, Cultural Consumption*, Manchester: Manchester University Press, 2019, p. 33. Italics in the original.
3 Ibid., p. 126.
4 Vaughan Robinson, 'The New Indian Middle Class in Britain', *Ethnic and Racial Studies*, vol. 11, no. 4, 1988, p. 458.
5 Meghji, *Black Middle-Class Britannia*, p. 137. While 'Black' is sometimes used as synonymous with 'non-white', as a political identity that would include, for instance, British Asians, Meghji is using the term to refer 'to those from the African and Caribbean diasporas', p. 19.
6 Stanley Fish, 'Boutique Multiculturalism, or Why Liberals are Incapable of Thinking about Hate Speech', *Critical Inquiry*, vol. 23, no. 2, 1997, p. 378.
7 Mike Leigh, *Abigail's Party & Goose-Pimples*, Harmondsworth: Penguin, 1983, p. 54.
8 For a useful history of the way racial categories were produced see Nell Irvin Painter, *The History of White People*, New York: W. W. Norton, 2011.

9 Given that the *Daily Telegraph* in their review of the play saw the character of Laurence as evidently Jewish and that Mike Leigh was brought up in Jewish family and had been part of the Labour Zionist youth movement, these comments take on more complexity in terms of English ethnicities.
10 Patel, *We're Here Because You Were There*, p. 56 and p. 5. The West Indies Federation was a transitional stage of decolonisation, as the 'British Caribbean' was politically reconstituted before becoming sovereign states. The Federation included Antigua and Barbuda, Barbados, Dominica, Grenada, Jamaica, Saint Kitts and Nevis, Saint Lucia, Saint Vincent and the Grenadines, and Trinidad and Tobago. British Guiana (Guyana) and British Honduras (Belize) held 'observer status' within the Federation. Anguilla, Montserrat, the Cayman Islands, and Turks and Caicos Islands became 'British Overseas Territories'. For more see Patel, *We're Here Because You Were There* and Adom Getachew, *Worldmaking after Empire: The Rise and Fall of Self-Determination*, Princeton: Princeton University Press, 2019.
11 The British Broadcasting Corporation, *Going to Britain?* BBC Caribbean Service, 1959, p. 53. In the 1950s it was predominantly Caribbean men who were coming to Britain. Women from the Caribbean suffered a similar downward mobility.
12 Ibid., p. 52.
13 Ibid., p. 59.
14 Ibid., p. 59.
15 Stuart Hall, *The Young Englanders*, London: National Committee for Commonwealth Immigrants, 1967, p. 10. Hall is describing the lives of the sons and daughters of those who came to Britain in the 1950s and 1960s from the Caribbean. Their 'tiptoeing' is not just the echo of this injunction not to appear and not to be ambitious, it was also a response to the multiple hostilities they faced and still face in a white dominant culture.
16 On the structural racism of professional work environments such as law, the civil service, and education see Sharon J. Daye, *Middle-Class Blacks in Britain: A Racial Fraction of a Class Group or a Class Fraction of a Racial Group?* Houndmills: Macmillan Press, 1994.
17 Hanif Kureishi, *The Buddha of Suburbia*, London: Faber & Faber, 1990, p. 23.
18 Ibid., p. 7.
19 Ibid., p. 27.
20 Ibid., p. 51.
21 Ziauddin Sardar, *Balti Britain: A Provocative Journey through Asian Britain*, London: Granta, 2008, p. 93.
22 Ibid., p. 97.
23 Ibid., p. 91.
24 Richard Hooper, ed. *Colour in Britain*, London: British Broadcasting Corporation, 1965, p. 11.
25 Ken Pryce, *Endless Pressure: A Study of West Indian Lifestyles in Bristol*, Bristol: Bristol Classical Press, 1986, p. 107 [first published in 1979].
26 Ibid., p. 223.
27 Ibid., p. 223.
28 Ibid., p. 279.
29 'Barbara Blake on Parties', *Magnet*, 27 April 1965, cited in Clair Wills, *Lovers and Strangers: An Immigrant History of Post-War Britain*, Harmondsworth: Penguin, 2018, p. 322. *Magnet* was a short-lived West Indian newspaper.
30 Ekow Eshun, *Black Gold of the Sun: Searching for Home in England and Africa*, London: Hamish Hamilton, 2005, pp. 3–4.
31 Sardar, *Balti Britain*, p. 117.
32 Michael McMillan, 'The West Indian Front Room: Reflections on a Diasporic Phenomenon', *Small Axe*, no. 28, 2009, p. 137.
33 The installation grew as it moved from The High Wycombe Local History and Chair Museum to the Zion Arts Centre/Black Arts Alliance, Manchester, to The Albany, Deptford, London, and to the Geffrye in London. A version of the room is now on permanent display as 'A Front Room in 1970' as one of the period rooms in the Museum of the Home, London. The Geffrye Museum was renamed

The Museum of the Home in 2019, in part to clarify the themes it covered and in part to distance itself from the name Geffrye, whose money paid for the almshouses that house the Museum's collection. In July 2020 the museum issued a statement acknowledging that Sir Robert Geffrye had made 'part of his money from his involvement in the exploitative East India Company and Royal African Company and his investment in the forced labour and trading of enslaved people', but that 'there is no connection between Sir Robert Geffrye and the Museum's collections and programmes', www.museumofthehome.org.uk/media/0q1n1dh4/statement-by-the-board-of-trustees-of-the-museum-of-the-home-29-july-2020.pdf, accessed 12 October 2021.

34 Michael McMillan, *The Front Room: Migrant Aesthetics in the Home*, London: Black Dog, 2009, p. 60.

35 Stuart Hall, 'The "West Indian" Front Room', in Michael McMillan, *The Front Room: Migrant Aesthetics in the Home*, London: Black Dog, 2009, p. 19.

36 McMillan, *The Front Room*, p. 105.

37 Hall, 'The "West Indian" Front Room', pp. 19–20.

38 Grace Dent, *Comfort Eating (with Krishnan Guru-Murthy)*, season 1, episode 9, *Guardian podcast*, 10 August 2021.

39 Steve Pope in McMillan, *The Front Room*, p. 102.

40 McMillan, *The Front Room*, p. 102.

41 Cyril Husbands in Ibid., p. 106.

42 Pryce, *Endless Pressure*, p. 241.

43 Michael Edmands, 'All the right choices: Patrick Berry founded England's first black radio station. Michael Edmands spoke to him', *Guardian*, 14 April 2001, p. 24.

44 Lionel Morrison, *A Century of Black Journalism in Britain: A Kaleidoscopic view of Race and the Media (1893–2003)*, London: Truebay, 2007, p. 37.

45 Editorial, *West Indian World*, 11 June 1971, p. 1.

46 Neil Kenlock interviewed in Hazelann Williams, 'Reliving the British Black Panther Movement', *The Voice*, 9 January 2012, https://archive.voice-online.co.uk/article/reliving-british-black-panther-movement, accessed 14 September 2021.

47 John Ryle, 'Rasta in the Promised Land', *Root*, vol. 3, no. 2, 1982, pp. 12–15; various authors, 'Nigeria Today', *Root*, vol. 2, no. 8, 1981, pp. 32–49; Kim Gordon, 'Arson Attacks on Black Homes', *Root*, vol. 2, no. 8, 1981, pp. 22–3.

48 Brian Parks, 'Buying the Right House', *Root*, vol. 2, no. 8, 1981, p. 103.

49 'House and Home: Best Buys', *Root*, vol. 2. no. 8, 1981, p. 101.

50 'Conservatories', a 4-page promotional section sponsored by the Halifax bank, *Root*, May 1987, p. 47.

51 Early North American studies of a Black middle class go back to the 1950s, for instance E. Franklin Frazier, *Black Bourgeoisie*, New York: Free Press, 1957. See also Bart Landry, *The New Black Middle Class*, Berkeley: University of California, 1987 and Annie S. Barnes, *The Black Middle Class Family*, Bristol (Indiana): Wyndham Hall Press, 1985.

52 Deborah Phillips and Philip Sarre, 'Black Middle-Class Formation in Contemporary Britain', in Tim Butler and Mike Savage, eds, *Social Change and the Middle Classes*, London: University College London Press, 1995, p. 76.

53 Ibid., p. 76.

Chapter 10

1 At the time of writing, Habitat exists on a much smaller scale as a set of showroom shops (in London, Brighton, and Leeds and as an online retailer. It is part of the Sainsbury's Group and has concession displays in various retailers that are part of the group. The Paris-based Habitat also continues to trade under this name but is a different company.

2 Habitat, at its most successful, had branches in Canada, the USA, Japan, France, and Belgium, as well as across the UK. Today IKEA has 456 stores: 67 in North America, 274 in Europe, 14 in the Middle East, 87 in Asia, 3 in Africa, and 11 in Oceania (from the IKEA website on 3 August 2021).
3 Pearson Phillips, *YAPs: The Complete Guide to Young Aspiring Professionals*, London: Arrow Books, 1984.
4 Malcolm Bradbury, *All Dressed Up and Nowhere to Go*, Basingstoke: Picador, 1982, p. 121.
5 Sue Townsend, *The Secret Diary of Adrian Mole: Aged 13¾*, Harmondsworth: Penguin, 2012, p. 270 [first published in 1982].
6 Sue Townsend, *The Lost Diaries of Adrian Mole 1999–2001* [volume 6], Harmondsworth: Penguin, 2009, p. 142 [first published in 2008].
7 Sue Townsend, *Adrian Mole: The Wilderness Years* [volume 4], Harmondsworth: Penguin 2003, p. 115 [first published in 1993].
8 Sue Townsend, *The Growing Pains of Adrian Mole* [volume 2], Harmondsworth: Penguin, 2002, p. 35 [first published in 1984].
9 Sue Townsend, *Adrian Mole: The Cappuccino Years* [volume 5], Harmondsworth: Penguin, 2000, p. 182.
10 Ibid., p. 183.
11 Townsend, *The Lost Diaries of Adrian Mole 1999–2001*, p. 110.
12 Townsend, *The Secret Diary of Adrian Mole: Aged 13¾*, p. 42.
13 Sue Townsend, *Adrian Mole and the Weapons of Mass Destruction* [volume 7], Harmondsworth: Penguin, 2005, p. 187.
14 Townsend, *The Growing Pains of Adrian Mole*, p. 36.
15 Townsend, *The Secret Diary of Adrian Mole: Aged 13¾*, p. 84.
16 Sue Townsend, *The True Confessions of Adrian Albert Mole* [volume 3], Harmondsworth: Penguin, 2003, p. 15 [first published in 1989].
17 Townsend, *Adrian Mole: The Cappuccino Years*, p. 170.
18 Townsend, *Adrian Mole and the Weapons of Mass Destruction*, p. 77.
19 Townsend, *The Growing Pains of Adrian Mole*, p. 207.
20 Sue Townsend, *Adrian Mole: The Prostrate Years* [volume 8], Harmondsworth: Penguin, 2010, p. 274 [first published in 2009].
21 According to Amy Borrett in the *New Statesman* (20 May 2021, updated 4 September 2021), 'the average house price is 65 times higher than in 1970 but average wages are only 36 times higher', www.newstatesman.com/politics/2021/05/how-uk-house-prices-have-soared-ahead-average-wages, accessed 20 September 2021.
22 Townsend, *Adrian Mole: The Cappuccino Years*, p. 86.
23 Changes in class perception and class feeling is not the same as claiming that class structures have changed. For an argument about the lack of change in class structures and the 'myth of social mobility' in the postwar period, see Selina Todd, *Snakes & Ladders: The Great British Social Mobility Myth*, London: Chatto & Windus, 2021.
24 Between the first *Adrian Mole* volume (1982) and the second one (1984) Sue Townsend shifts from referring to them as continental quilts to duvets.
25 Harry Wallop, 'Duvets or blankets? Bedding debate splits the nation', *The Telegraph*, 24 January 2013, www.telegraph.co.uk/lifestyle/9823911/Duvets-or-blankets-Bedding-debate-splits-the-nation.html, accessed 23 November 2016.
26 Terence Conran, *Terence Conran: A Sort of Autobiography*, London: Harper Collins, 2001, p. 75.
27 Ibid.
28 Conran, quoted in Kate Watson-Smyth, 'The secret history of the duvet', *The Independent*, 27 August 2010, p. 39.
29 Cooper Research and Marketing Ltd, *The Continental Quilt Story: Qualitative Research among Users and Non-users*, unpublished report, London 1978, p. 4. Accessed online through the Archive of Market and Social Research: https://amsr.contentdm.oclc.org/digital/collection/CRAM/id/30463/rec/10, accessed 21 September 2021.

30 Ibid., p. 6.
31 Ibid., p. 8.
32 Sean Poulter, 'Last orders for the traditional boozer?' *Mail Online*, 14 September 2017, www.dailymail.co.uk/news/article-4881002/One-British-pubs-closed-1970s.html, accessed 21 September 2021.
33 'Alex, Secretary', *Habitat: 1999–2000 Annual Catalogue*, p. 96.
34 See BBC 'Profile: John Prescott', http://news.bbc.co.uk/1/hi/uk_politics/6636565.stm, accessed 28 August 2021. On John Major's claims about a classless society see Alwyn W. Turner, *A Classless Society: Britain in the 1990s*, London: Aurum Press, 2013.
35 John Gray, 'Testing market for the middle classes', *Guardian*, 17 April 1996, p. 17.
36 Andrew Pierce, 'Middle class? John is still working class, says Mr Prescott senior', *The Times*, 13 April 1996, p. 1.
37 See, for instance, W. G. Runciman, 'Social inequality in twentieth-century England: towards a classless society? *The Listener*, 15 July 1965, pp. 75–8.
38 John Major talking to journalists, 28 November 1990, https://johnmajorarchive.org.uk/1990/11/28/doorstep-interview-28-november-1990/, accessed 28 August 2021.
39 Catherine Bennett, 'Classless society that never was', *Guardian*, 16 October 1996, p. 19.
40 Penny Wark, 'People like us', *The Times*, 19 March 2008, p. 6 (supplement).
41 Townsend, *The Lost Diaries of Adrian Mole 1999–2001*, p. 47.
42 Ray Gosling, *Class by Class*, Chanel 4 television, 1991. Gosling is a fascinating character: an anti-gentrification housing activist in Nottingham; an early gay-rights campaigner; an early contributor to *New Society*; and a compelling documentary maker. Examples of his work are available on YouTube. For an account of his life in the 1960s see Ray Gosling, *Personal Copy: A Memoir of the Sixties*, London: Faber, 1980.
43 See, for instance, the collection by Richard Hyman and Robert Price, eds, *The New Working Class? White-Collar Workers and Their Organizations: A Reader*, London: Macmillan, 1983. For an early sociological study that fed into the 'affluent worker' studies, see David Lockwood, *The Blackcoated Worker: A Study in Class Consciousness*, London: George Allen & Unwin, 1958. For a French version of this debate see Serge Mallet, *The New Working Class*, translated by Andrée and Bob Shepherd, Nottingham: Spokesman Books, 1975, as he traces the opportunities for workers after the events of May 1968.
44 See, for instance, Kate Soper, *Post-Growth Living: For an Alternative Hedonism*, London: Verso, 2021.

Index

Abrams, Mark 115–6
affluent workers 134, 171
Aitken, Jonathan 74
Algarve 66, 86–7
Aram, Zeev 96
Aris, Stephen 135
Ashley, Laura 53, 199, 202
Asian British 87, 118, 183, 189, 192–5
Axminster 151–2

Bailey, David 84
Barratt housing 119, 121, 155, 158–9
Barrie, Anne 30
Barthes, Roland 143
Bauhaus 21, 44, 63, 130, 205
bedding, *see* duvet
Behr, Ann 74
Beloff, Michael 126
Biba 27–8, 72–6, 83, 98, 112, 137–9, 191
Blair, Tony 179, 203
Bolton 7, 18, 40, 60, 112
Bond, James 84
Boney M 194
boutique cosmopolitanism 183–5, 199
Boxer, Marc 87
Bradbury, Malcolm 12, 136–40, 176, 199
  History Man, The 136–40
Brexit 204
Briggs, Asa 134
Bristol 56, 66–7, 71, 118, 188, 198
British Colonial Citizen 182
British Empire 85, 182, 204
Britten, Benjamin 86
Brixton 100, 113
Bugler, Jeremy 108
butcher's block 32, 36, 59

Caine, Michael 77–9
carpets 3, 8, 12, 26, 32, 89, 107, 151, 166, 168, 174, 190
Carter, Angela 53–4, 57, 60, 83,
central heating 24, 26, 89–90, 103, 118–9, 135, 168
chalet 119–20, 168–9
Chapman, Dennis 148, 150
Chesterfield sofa 32–3, 63
class 4, 7–8, 29, 112, 166–181, 206–8
  administrator class 78, 177–8
  new middle class 9, 29, 54, 56, 66, 74, 79, 101, 109, 112, 118–9, 121, 135, 144, 150, 155, 158–61, 163, 168, 176, 179, 183, 185, 188, 190, 198–9, 203, 207
  technician class 176–7
  upward proletarianisation 173–4, 208
  working class 4, 6–9, 39, 51, 53–4, 77–8, 87, 104, 107–8, 110–15, 118, 124, 134–36, 148, 158–60, 165–7, 170–3, 174–8, 182, 185–6, 190, 200–1, 206–8
classlessness 7, 10, 112, 172–3, 199, 207–8
clerical work 74, 169–70, 186, 203
CND (Campaign for Nuclear Disarmament) 23, 71, 141, 176
CoID (Council of Industrial Design) 23–4
commercial college 168
Commonwealth Immigrants Act (1962) 182
Conran, Caroline 34, 43, 65
Conran, Terence 10, 12, 30, 34, 52, 58–9, 67, 94–5, 130, 132, 191, 204–5
  House Book, The 58–66, 91, 95, 104, 138, 197
Conservative party 173, 200
consumer existentialism 199, 202
continental quilts, *see* duvets

controlled casualness 65, 84, 104, 106–7, 119, 124–5, 130, 138–9, 144–5, 151, 157, 161, 165, 169, 178, 183, 190, 193–4, 203, 206, 208
Corbusier, Le 130
cosmopolitanism 10, 11, 35, 78, 165, 183–5, 190, 199
Cradock, Fanny 162–3
Crossman, Richard 103–4
Curtis, Barry 37

Daily Mail Ideal Home Exhibition 108, 119
Daily Mirror 73, 79–81, 161
Daily Telegraph 84, 139, 157, 203
Danish 24, 119, 140, 176
David, Elizabeth 67–8, 83, 96
democratisation 3, 51
Deighton, Len 68–9, 77–9, 83
dishwasher 26, 90
Diski, Jenny 27–8
Donaldson, Anne 30
Donovan, Terence 32
Dostoyevsky, Fyodor 27, 180–1
Duckett, Margaret 104
duvets 6, 11, 12, 23–25, 28, 46–48, 60, 119, 124, 183, 199, 202–6, 208

East African Asian 183
Ebony 101, 193
eclecticism 11, 34, 57–8, 63–6, 72, 83, 104, 106, 185
Eshun, Ekow 190

farmhouse 61–3, 78, 102, 140
Fitz-Simon, Stephen 73–4
Floyd, Keith 12, 67, 71, 161, 164–5

Gardiner, Juliet 56–8, 60, 66, 109
Generation Game, The 27
gentrification 85, 103–4, 108–15, 119, 143, 179
Ghana 190
Gilliatt, Mary 91
Gilroy, Paul 204
Glass, Ruth 111, 113, 115
Glendinning, Max 96
Glynn Smith, Juliet 43
Going to Britain? 186
Good Housekeeping 24–5, 88, 90–95, 152
  Good Housekeeping Institute 90, 92
Gorer, Geoffrey 151, 160
Gosling, Ray 207
G-Plan 33
Gray, Fred 117
Green, Felicity 73
Gregory, Oliver 30
Guardian, The 39, 54, 102, 124, 137, 141, 201
Guru-Murthy, Krishnan 192

Habitat 3, 30–55, 56–66, 71–3, 83, 102–4, 106, 108, 111–2, 118, 124, 125, 131, 137–9, 149, 151, 165–6, 168, 178, 191, 194–5, 197–8, 202–6, 208
Hall, Stuart 6, 173–6, 187, 191
Harriott, Ainsley 161
Harris, C. C. 134
Harrisson, Tom 8
hats 18, 76
Heseltine, Michael 116
Hockney, David 63
Hoggart, Richard 7, 54, 160
Homes and Gardens 24, 90, 156
Hulanicki, Barbara 72–4
Hume, David 15–18, 21–3, 28

IKEA 3, 17, 36, 40–1, 44, 47, 65, 193, 198, 202
Indian 35, 69–70, 87, 183–5, 187, 192, 197, 201–2
informality 5, 15, 33–4, 37, 52–4, 58, 63, 65–6, 106, 119, 125, 129–30, 132, 144–5, 169, 179–80, 191, 192–3, 209
Islington 103–4, 111

Jamaica 188, 193
Japan 16, 35, 40, 184
Japanese paper lampshades 8, 95, 202
junk shops 24, 36, 52, 59, 63, 110, 174

Kafka, Franz 129
kitchens 2, 31, 34–5, 40, 52, 60–66, 87, 91, 95, 102, 107, 119, 165, 175, 197
kitchen table 8, 12, 56, 60–3, 107, 124, 138–9, 179, 197, 199, 201
Kureishi, Hanif 187
  Buddha of Suburbia, The 187

Labour party 6, 124, 172, 176, 178–9, 200, 206
Lawson, Nigella 161
Leigh, Mike 12, 152, 156, 157, 160
  Abigail's Party 152–8, 160, 174, 184, 185
Lévi-Strauss, Claude 142

Libby, Maurice 37
Liberal Democrats 179
Little, Alan 84, 123
Lloyd Jones, Peter 53–4
Lockwood, David 172
Lupton Morton 41, 44, 131

MacCarthy, Fiona 35, 37, 52, 102–3
McMillan, Michael 190–2
Magistretti 35, 39, 46, 56, 151
Magnet 189
Major, John 203, 207
Marks and Spencer 39, 41, 140
Mass-Observation 7–8, 134, 147–8
mayonnaise 12, 68–9, 77, 86, 87, 124, 181, 203
Mediterranean 5, 62, 67, 69, 71, 79, 83, 106, 124, 143, 161, 183–4, 185, 190, 197, 202
Meghji, Ali 182, 189
Millar, Robert 22, 150, 177
Affluent Sheep, The 22
New Classes, The 150, 177
Mini 79
Mirror dingy 79–82
Moran, Joe 108
Muirhead, David 186

New Left Review 150
New Society 9, 53, 124, 132–5, 136, 146, 178, 201
Nkosi, Lewis 87
Notting Hill 104–6, 113
Nova 95–100

Oliver, Jamie 161
Orwell, George 147, 167, 168, 170
A Clergyman's Daughter 147
Keep the Aspidistra Flying 147

Packard, Vance 150
Status Seekers, The 150
Pakistan 187, 190
paper lampshades, *see* Japanese paper lampshades
pasta 2, 6, 11, 12, 23, 26, 33, 67, 77, 145
Pearson, Stephen 154–5
peasant culture 35–6, 58, 102, 109–10, 178, 184, 208
pepper mills 35, 43, 61, 72, 102
Percy Bilton 119
Perkin, Harold 125–7
personalisation 174
pesto 145, 201
PizzaExpress 3, 69–72, 75, 83, 165
plateglass university 125–9, 134, 136
Pollock, Philip 34
polytechnics 141, 143
pop music 27, 135, 153
Prescott, John 206–7
Prestige 10, 174
Priestley, J. B. 12, 146, 147, 148
proletarian respectables 188, 190, 193
Provençal herbs 39, 53, 58, 118
Pryce, Ken 188–90

Quant, Mary 39, 84, 139
quiche 12, 67–8, 104, 109, 119, 124, 166, 179, 180, 203

Raban, Jonathan 21–2, 53, 106–11, 123, 167, 168
Rachman, Peter 104
race 82, 87, 98, 113, 118, 183, 185, 187–8, 194–5, 204
racism 87, 95, 118, 183, 187–8, 196
recipes 17, 67–9, 77–8, 161, 165, 180
redbrick university 126
retro 24, 72, 110
Riesman, David 127
Root 193–5
rustic 36, 52, 53, 59, 66, 72, 102, 104, 121

salad cream 68, 124, 143, 181
Samuel, Raphael (Ralph) 174, 178–9
Sardar, Ziauddin 187–8, 190
Scandinavian 26, 28, 35, 66, 119, 180, 183–4, 198, 205
SDP (Social Democratic Party) 178–9
Selvon, Samuel 186
shelving 37, 155–7, 187
Simmonds, Posy 12, 124, 141–5
Ski yogurts, *see* yogurts
Sloane Rangers 198
Smith, Delia 12, 161–5
Smith, Neil 111
smoking 19, 134
sociology 9, 28, 123–7, 132, 136–7, 140, 143, 146–8, 150–1, 160, 176, 194–5, 199
solid-citizen furniture 51–2, 205
Span Housing 56–7, 109, 119
Spare Rib 98
Spence, Basil 129, 130, 132
Stacey, Tom 84

status, status striving 10–11, 23, 28, 53, 61, 86, 112, 123, 146–165, 171, 173–9, 201, 207, 208
St Vincent 191
Sunday Times, The 1, 2, 30, 32, 34, 83–5, 87, 123, 132, 202

Taylor, Pagan 34–7, 58
Taylor Woodrow 119
teachers 2, 7, 56, 118, 171, 173, 175, 189, 193, 208
teapot 35–7
Thatcher, Margaret 198, 203, 207
Thompson, E. P. 174, 180
Townsend, Sue 200–3
Tulloch, Carol 193

UKIP 203
University of Essex 129
University of Sussex 126, 127, 129, 134–5, 166
University of Warwick 127

Veblen, Thorstein 29, 148
Victorian 58, 63, 103, 107, 111–2, 142, 147, 191–3

Wallop, Harry 203
wallpaper 2, 5, 20, 76, 107, 149, 190
Watermouth 136, 141
West Indian 104, 108, 118, 132, 182–196
Whatever Happened to the Likely Lads? 121, 158–60
Which? 124
white working class 185
Willmott, Peter 150, 170–1, 173
Windrush 182
wine 54, 58, 61, 69, 78, 87, 90, 104, 111, 115, 143, 151, 164, 168, 170, 178, 179, 180, 194
Wootton, Barbara 132, 134

yogurt 8, 12, 23, 128, 149, 174, 181
Young, Michael 114, 124, 150, 170, 176
  Rise of the Meritocracy, 1870–2033, The 176
Yuppies 198